In *The Impossible Takes* [...] Elizabeth Rogers show [...] combat alcohol and drug abuse. Both authors share their own chilling yet fascinating testimonies of how God delivered them from life-threatening alcohol and drug problems. You'll also receive effective counsel from Father Joseph Martin, who is a chalk-talk expert for Alcoholics Anonymous. You'll be equipped to answer many of the questions about chemical addiction, including:

- *Why do some drinkers overdo it, while others don't?*
- *When does a drug abuser become hopeless? Is there help for someone who has been told by his doctor, pastor, boss, and psychiatrist that he's too far gone?*
- *Can a highly educated person be a real alcoholic?*
- *Is alcoholism a disease?*
- *How can I get someone to stop drinking and* stay *stopped?*
- *Is caffeine addiction really harmful to one's health?*

As you learn the causes of the use and abuse of alcohol, caffeine, nicotine, and other drugs, you'll gain insights into how to approach addiction with compassion, perseverance, and hope.

THE IMPOSSIBLE TAKES A LITTLE LONGER

will show you how to let God use you as an instrument for helping someone live without alcohol and other drugs.

By Harold Hill With Irene Burk Harrell
How to Live Like a King's Kid
How to Be a Winner
How to Live in High Victory
Bible Answers for King's Kids
How to Flip Your Flab—Forever
A, B, C's for King's Kids
How to Live the Bible Like a King's Kid
God's in Charge Here
The Money Book for King's Kids

**By Harold Hill With Irene Burk Harrell and
        Mary Elizabeth Rogers**
From Goo to You by Way of the Zoo

By Harold Hill and Mary Elizabeth Rogers
The Impossible Takes a Little Longer

THE IMPOSSIBLE TAKES A LITTLE LONGER

HAROLD HILL and MARY ELIZABETH ROGERS

The triumphant story of victory over alcohol.

Power Books

Fleming H. Revell Company
Old Tappan, New Jersey

Scripture quotations identified NKJV are from The New King James Version of the Bible. Copyright © 1979, 1980, 1982, Thomas Nelson, Inc., Publishers.

Excerpt from "The Night They Burned Shanghai" used by permission of Robert D. Abrahams.

Material from *No Laughing Matter* by Father Joseph Martin is used by permission.

In this book, the fellowship of Alcoholics Anonymous and its suggested recovery program are mentioned. The authors do not claim A.A. membership. Their opinions are based on their own experiences, and do not necessarily represent those of Alcoholics Anonymous, which is not allied with any sect, denomination, politics, organization, or institution.

Library of Congress Cataloging in Publication Data

Hill, Harold, date.
    The impossible takes a little longer.

    "Power books."
    Bibliography: p.
    1. Hill, Harold, date. 2. Rogers, Mary
Elizabeth. 3. Alcoholics—United States—Bibliography.
4. Alcoholism. 5. Drug abuse. I. Rogers, Mary
Elizabeth. II. Title.
HV5293.H53A35   1985   362.2'92'0922 [B]   85-1728
ISBN 0-8007-5192-2

We dedicate this book to the untold scores of recovering alcoholics and others who helped us to get free from the bondage of alcohol and other drugs, and to Jesus Christ, our personal God, whose loving concern caused it to happen.

Contents

Part I
His (From a Man's Point of View)
by *Harold Hill*

Part II
Hers (From a Woman's Point of View)
by *Mary Elizabeth Rogers*

0
Read This First

Is someone you care about having trouble with alcohol or other drugs? Have all attempts to help ended in failure?

Are you wondering why your endless prayers of "How long, oh, Lord?" have gone unanswered, or why God doesn't hurry up and *do* something?

Rejoice—He already *has!* That's what this book is all about.

Why do we feel qualified to write such a book?

We're glad you brought that up. It's really an important point.

You've probably seen loads of other books on this subject. There are oodles of them around. Maybe they've added to your confusion. No wonder—many were written by authors who never drank or drugged. They've never battled the problems personally. Like bachelors who pose as experts on raising young 'uns. If you've never changed diapers, it's just a bunch of theory.

We, the coauthors of this book, have lengthy backgrounds of excessive drinking. We've also used and abused other addictive drugs. We've been down the road. We understand.

But here's the good part: We've put together a total of forty-six years of continuous abstinence from alcohol.

Aren't you impressed? We are. In fact, we're amazed.

You will read of the simple and effective answers we and others have found. Then you can begin applying these principles to help someone you care about. They, too, can get free from the syndrome of the twentieth century—drug dependence.

Our purpose is to present workable answers. We have left the matter of statistics to others. Your local news media add daily to the list of fatalities. Many can be avoided as you learn how to help those who still suffer.

The Bible says, "For lack of knowledge my people perish" (see Hosea 4:6), and we are doing something about it.

This book is divided into two parts.

Part I we call His. In it you will read the experiences of Hill and others of his gender who used and abused alcohol and other drugs.

Part II, called Hers, is the record of Rogers and members of the lady sector, who tell you how it was with them.

In addition to alcohol, you will learn about other killer drugs, prescription as well as the "over the counter" and "street" varieties.

Is this just one more book about the use and abuse of alcohol and other drugs?

No indeed. This one is different.

In what way?

Read on and you'll find out.

First, let's see if it's really for you. Here's how to do it.

If you're looking for answers to any of the following questions, it definitely is.

1. Do you have a loved one, friend, relative, or business associate who "drinks too much" and you'd like to help them?

2. Have you wondered how to get someone to stop drinking and *stay stopped?*

3. Is everyone who drinks too much a real alcoholic?

4. How do you tell a real alcoholic from the other kind?

5. Why do they keep on drinking when they know what it's doing to them?

6. Wouldn't joining a church be the best answer?

7. Isn't there some way you can be of help?

Our answer to that last question is a loud *Yes, there is.* How? That's what this book is all about.

You can begin today to help someone cope with the number one problem of this century: the use and abuse of alcohol and other drugs.

God's admonition "For lack of knowledge my people perish" applies. By doing something about it, you are being an obedient King's Kid. God will bless you for trying to help others.

Someone has said that a problem well stated is half solved. Nowhere is this more true than when dealing with alcoholics. Probably your past failures in trying to be helpful were due to lack of understanding. That's generally the case.

This book will equip you to handle these and other questions:

Why do some drinkers overdo it while others don't?

Can someone who "drinks too much" be taught to drink normally?

When does a drug abuser become hopeless? Is there help for someone who has been told by his doctor, pastor, boss, and psychiatrist that he's too far gone?

Can an alcoholic be cured and return to social drinking?

Isn't alcoholism a sign of sin or immorality?

Is alcoholism hereditary?

How can a real alcoholic "stay stopped" for life?

Some say alcoholism is a disease while other insist it's sin. Who is right?

Doesn't the Bible say that no drunkard shall enter the Kingdom of heaven?

Isn't excessive drinking generally due to stressful working conditions, deep-seated emotional problems, inverted enzymes, or mother-in-law syndrome?

How does a controlled drinker differ from an alcoholic?

Can a highly educated person be a real alcoholic?

Why does he keep "falling off the wagon" after months of sobriety?

These and scores of other questions are answered in *The Impossible Takes a Little Longer.* You will gain understanding of great value in dealing with that most frustrating of all problems—the drinking alcoholic.

At this point maybe you're asking, "Just why do you guys think you have better answers than my dedicated pastor and skilled physician? They've both given up on my loved one who drinks too much."

We're not claiming more "smarts" than anyone else. Our qualifications are these:

A. We were problem drinkers for a combined total of forty-four years.

B. We have been continuously without a drink of alcohol or any mood-changing drugs for longer than that.

So this book is definitely different. It was written by "experts." We write from personal experience, not from theory. We have lived it. That makes the difference.

You will also read about others whose stories differ from ours in detail but are similar in pattern. That way you'll gain further insight into the strange behavior of those of us who are allergic to alcohol and other drugs.

Are we claiming answers superior to those offered by our state and federally funded programs? Not at all. We appreciate their efforts in trying to help those who still suffer. In fact, we quote numerous passages from their studies.

We are reporters. We tell you about various methods used to combat alcohol and drug addiction. Some have found an "added dimension" which speeds recovery.

What is that dimension?

One that has worked since time began: a personal relationship with a loving, caring God, whose help is readily available to all who seek Him.

That's the God who made *us* winners over alcohol and other drugs.

Religion? No way. Many of us tried all that stuff and kept on drinking and drugging.

What happened?

One night in desperation we hit upon the "secret." Amazing things began happening.

What are they? That's what you're about to discover.

So don't stop here. Keep on reading, and God bless you as you, too, seek Him for answers to whatever ails you.

We suggest laying aside all preconceived notions, religious ideas, and church doctrines. If our experiences differ from your opinions, remember, we are not attempting to prove anything. We have no intention of converting you to our way of thinking.

We are reporting on things which have worked for us and thousands of others.

In the words of Herbert Spencer:

"There is a principle which is a bar against all information, which is proof against all arguments and which cannot fail to keep a man in everlasting ignorance. That principle is contempt prior to investigation."

God bless you real big as you read and share with others what He has done in the lives of those whose stories we share in *The Impossible Takes a Little Longer.*

Harold Hill
and
Mary Elizabeth Rogers

P.S. If alcohol could talk, how would it answer the question "Who are you?"

Who am I? Please allow me to introduce myself.

I, sir, am alcohol. I have the power to control the lives of my victims. I determine the destinies of the nations they live in.

I am more powerful than the combined armies of the world.

I have destroyed more men and women than all the wars ever fought.

I am more deadly than bullets. I have wrecked more homes than the mightiest of guns or the most powerful atomic bombs.

I am the world's cleverest thief, stealing untold billions each year.

I spare no one. My victims are the rich and poor alike. Young and old, strong and weak, widows and orphans all know me well.

I cast my shadow over every field of labor.

I lurk in unseen places and do my most lethal work in silence.

You are warned about my unfair tactics. Like others you heed not. You insist, "But I'm different." So did they.

I am ruthless and relentless. I am everywhere, in the home, the office, on the street, and where you work. The sea and the air lanes are not immune to my murderous tactics.

I specialize in sickness, degradation, death, and destruction, yet none would banish me.

I crush, maim, and murder. I take all and give in return heartache and death.

I am your worst enemy.

I am ethanol alcohol . . . the deadliest of all drugs.

May I offer you a drink? Oh, come now, one or two never hurt anyone, did it? You don't want to be different, do you? Come on, drink up Old Man . . . old man . . . o l d . . . m a n.

ANONYMOUS

THE IMPOSSIBLE TAKES A LITTLE LONGER

Part I

HIS

(From a Man's Point of View)

by

Harold Hill

1
Flying Blind

Somewhere in Missouri, November 1942

The snow-covered earth far below met my startled gaze, as I regained consciousness, gripping the controls of an airplane I didn't know how to fly.

"*Uh-h-h-h,* where am I?" I moaned, peering through the windshield just ahead. Sick, shaking badly, and half-frozen, I tried to make sense out of the scene around me. A victim of alcohol amnesia, I had no idea where I was or how I had gotten there.

Not only had I been "high" on alcohol. I was high in the sky, eighteen thousand feet up, with gas gauges nearing ZERO and darkness fast approaching.

"Hill, you've really blown it this time. How're you going to get out of *this* mess?" I spoke out loud.

Flying was not new to me. I had been traveling that way since the early days of commercial aviation. I had often taken over the controls of our company plane, while the pilot took a breather.

This was different. There was no pilot to turn to. Alone and panic-striken, I was holding my head on with one hand and trying to keep the plane in the air with the other.

As if that were not enough misery, a new brand of fear gripped my gizzard. My unbelieving eyeballs goggled at this scary bit of news on the instrument panel before me:

PROPERTY OF THE U.S. AIR FORCE

"Air Force! Good grief! I wonder what the penalty is for stealing a government airplane? I'd better land this crate and find a good lawyer."

As my foggy mind cleared, I began to daydream about things in general and alcohol in particular. *Was Sir Percy right? Was I really an alcoholic?*

Some of you are wondering how all this could have happened without my being aware of it. I was in an alcoholic "blackout," a total memory lapse, caused by drinking too much booze. That's where the victim appears to be functioning normally but is oblivious to what's happening. Afterward, there is no memory of it. Decisions are drug motivated. The results are unpredictable.

For those who drink too much, blackouts are commonplace. To others they are baffling and mysterious.

In that condition I had driven to the airport, gassed up the plane, and filed a flight plan with the FAA. Then I had taken off on a busy runway and flown for several hours—in a state of complete unawareness.

No, I was not unconscious. I was functioning mechanically, but the memory of all events in that time frame is blacked out. I have no recall of what happened after the party the previous evening.

"I don't believe a word of that," someone is squawking. We don't blame you. Only those of us who have abused alcohol can understand how such things are possible.

Awakening the "morning after" with no memory of the night before sounds weird and unreal. It is. Drinkers are sitting ducks for any accusations thrown at them. Having no memory, they are defenseless.

I dimly recalled last night's celebration. A meddling old biddy had sidled up to me with a sermon.

"Mr. Hill, aren't you drinking a little too much? You've had seven drinks already."

Meddlers and busybodies. They're everywhere, trying to spoil my fun, I fumed to myself. To her I said, "Thanks a lot, ma'am. When I need your advice, I'll notify you by fast courier turtle."

After that *bon mot* came the memory blank, ending in my present mess from which only a miracle could save me.

"Aren't you exaggerating just a little bit?" Not at all.

When mild-mannered Malcolm drinks too much, slugs his wife, hassles his children, and assures the judge, "Your Honor, I wouldn't hurt a fly!" he is telling the truth. Influenced by drugs, Malcolm turns into a monster.

Blackout Barney pleads for mercy at his hit-and-run trial, "But, Judge, I don't remember a thing about it."

Although no one believes him, he is telling the truth. With no memory of the accidents, Malcolm and Barney are dupes of the same drug which was about to wipe me out, I figured. My then-situation was no isolated event. Such exciting episodes started in my early twenties. As my tolerance for alcohol progressed, so did they.

I recalled those words of warning four years before, when my boss had suggested I might become an alcoholic.

"Ridiculous! I've never had trouble with alcohol in my life. Well . . . hardly ever."

Suffering from memory blackout, we alcoholics, without knowing what we got into, deny ever having problems with booze. We just don't remember.

How could I be an alcoholic? I had just received a fabulous promotion. I was headed for the top in my profession. I had the world by the tail. An alcoholic is a *poor soul,* lying in the gutter. He's nattily attired in a World War I trench coat, one tennis shoe, and no socks. A festooning of vermin, vomit, and empty vino bottles completes the image.

No way was I like that. Immaculately dressed in my London-tailored tweeds, smoking an expensive Dunhill pipe, and driving a fine car, I was far from one of "those" people.

Besides, I had recently invented the ground energizer, a device used on all airfields for starting airplane engines.

In addition, I was the CEO (Chief Executive Officer), responsible for my employer's multimillion dollar operations both in the United States and Canada. Just two days ago I had clinched a huge contract for more millions. That's what triggered last night's festivities.

An alcoholic? How absurd. Maybe I did drink a little too much now and then—but doesn't everyone? How could anyone classify me with those derelicts lying in the filth of Waterfront, USA? It was unthinkable.

"You mind your business and I'll mind mine," was my standard response to those who suggested that I drank too much.

Does all that *denial* sound familiar?

Denial is the standard hideout of the person who "drinks too much now and then," trapped by a progressive disease called *alcoholism.*

Often called the Disease of Denial, its victims resort to this irrational behavior, rather than admit defeat.

Self-deception is another symptom. Even in my scary predicament, I continued to rationalize. *If I'd quit at the sixth drink like that old meddler suggested, I would have been okay.*

My fantasizing was interrupted by the sudden coughing and sputtering of the big Pratt and Whitney engine up ahead.

Out of gas with no Esso station in sight!

"That's all I need," I groaned, eyeballing the farmland below. Perhaps I could maneuver a belly landing without totaling the plane and myself. Then panic struck.

I'm not ready to die. I'm too young, too successful. I have too much to live for. What have I done to deserve this?

As the engine continued to backfire and lose rpms, fear gripped my gizzard.

"You've always wondered about life after death, Hill. Now you're about to find out. Maybe knowing God isn't such a bad idea after all."

According to family legend, my grandmother, Emma Wadleigh Hill, was the first licensed woman Baptist preacher in New Hampshire. We all felt she held the keys to the Kingdom. But her religion was as grim and gray as a wintry day in Manchester, where I was born. Whatever was fun was sin. If you smiled on Sunday, you got belted. It turned my dad off early in life. Mention of religion or church sent him into a rage. So I grew up a religious "nothing." My Christian mother's early death ended all Christian contact for me until many years later.

But now, in the face of certain death, even Grandma's God seemed a good idea.

Mustn't panic, Hill.

I had heard that panic causes "tunnel vision," a loss of eye coordination, resulting in almost certain death. Each eye sees its own objective. It has killed many experienced pilots. I must remain calm at all costs.

But how do you cool it when your insides are a mess of quivering jelly, palms are sweaty, knees rubbery, brow drippy, and eyeballs rolling on the floor?

Holding my aching head with one hand, I fought to hold the plane level, as it continued to lose speed and altitude.

Pray? I didn't know how! My life had been spent in the world of science and engineering. Running corporations was my bag. What did I know about talking to God? Prayer was for women and preachers. I was a self-made man and proud of my maker.

But desperation overcame stupidity, and my foxhole faith squeaked out these words: "Please, God, get me out of this mess, and I'll never do it again."

Continuing to lose engine rpms and, with the gas gauge on EMPTY, the controls got mushy and nonresponsive. I was about to become one more statistical notch in the gun of John Barleycorn; just another victim of America's Number 1 Killer Drug: *alcohol.*

Violent tremors racked my body. Sudden withdrawal from the drug alcohol, together with high-altitude-oxygen shortage, had depleted my system. Then came the old familiar withdrawal symptoms—stomach cramps, chest pains, splitting headache, hyperventilation, nausea, and dry heaves.

I gritted my teeth. *I've got to hang in there. Maybe the snow is not too deep for a belly landing. It's my only chance!*

I glanced below. A fresh wave of panic washed over me: **T R E E- T O P S !**

That was the last straw. It was too much for my drugged brain. Things began to get dim and spooky.

2

Introduction

Why on earth is the Introduction in chapter 2? For a very good reason. So *you will read it!*

Hardly anyone reads a book Introduction. At least we often don't, and so we end up missing a lot of good stuff.

"But I want to find out how Hill got out of that mess alive," you're complaining.

Just be patient. You will. We purposely left him slogging along among the treetops. In the meantime here's a clue. Things haven't gotten any better in the last thirty seconds.

So use your willpower and don't peek.

At this point, we want you to know what this book is all about, and why you should bother to read it.

Possibly the life of someone close to you is being threatened by alcohol or other drugs. Would you like to help?

You can, if you know how.

And that's our purpose, to tell you what's available in the way of help, through firsthand reports and personal experiences. Then you, in turn, can help to solve this growing problem.

We, the authors, Harold Hill and Liz Rogers, were for many years users and abusers of alcohol and other drugs. We were slaves to them. They ran our lives. They demanded our attention. They robbed us of the power of choice. We drank against our wills. We could not not drink. Then God set us free. By His grace we no longer drink or drug. We haven't in many years. We are delighted to share these answers with you. You can then pass them along to those who are still fighting the losing battle of alcohol and other drugs.

Why do we feel qualified to write?

Because we have been without a drink or a "fix" for a combined total of forty-six continuous years.

You will learn how it all happened, and how you may be able to help others to find relief from drug dependency, alcohol addiction, and chemical bondage.

God says in numerous Bible passages, "For lack of knowledge my people perish." We are doing something about it.

In addition to our own experiences, you will read about the answers others have found.

Laura from Kentucky (not her real name) was run over by a truck. Her face was mutilated by an enraged husband. Now happily remarried, she is living a victorious, sober life, enjoying her first grandchild.

Father Martin is a Catholic priest from Maryland. He travels the world dramatizing the disease concept of alcoholism with his famous Chalk Talk. He explains in detail how to diagnose and treat alcoholism, the Number 1 killer disease of our time.

Mary Lynn's marijuana and medication just about blew her mind and marriage. Reared in an alcoholic home and driven by a desire to please the unpleasable, she sought escape in the oblivion of drugs and in the supposed security of a strong mate upon whom she could transfer all responsibility.

Through these and many other real-life reports, you will learn much about the use and abuse of alcohol so that you can help others to deal with them.

And who are we, the authors? Glad you brought that up!

(Don't you hate having to scrounge through a book to find out about the characters who wrote it? We do.) So here goes!

Harold Hill, corporation president, electrical engineer, scientist, inventor, and successful businessman.

Liz Rogers, Phi Kappa Phi, mathematician, Dallas socialite, and former Sweetheart of Sigma Chi.

So much for Hill and Rogers for now. We'll get better acquainted as you go along.

You will learn the difference between Social Drinkers (SD), Heavy Drinkers (HD), Problem Drinkers (PD), and Alcoholics (AL). You will also learn to distinguish between real Alcoholics and other kinds of drinkers.

"But how do you get them to stop drinking and to stay stopped?" You'll find that out, too.

Francis Bacon said, "Knowledge is Power." (It's in Proverbs too!) That's so true in successfully combating alcohol and other drugs.

Here we present drinkers and drug users in broadly defined categories or behavior patterns. This will help in making your own analysis of each case.

Here are a few broad definitions to get you started.

Drinker: Everyone who drinks alcohol in any quantity, as opposed to everyone else who drinks water and such stuff.

User: Everyone who swallows, sniffs, snorts, puffs, injects, inhales, shoots up, or in any other manner takes into his body any chemical substance classed as a drug, on a regular basis.

Drug: Any chemical substance that, when taken into the body, causes a change of mood or personality.

The *Random House College Dictionary* says that a drug is a "habit-forming medicinal substance, especially a narcotic."

Drugs are also called by names such as: *sedative, painkiller, mood-changer, muscle-relaxer, sleeping pill, tranquilizer, upper, downer,* and so forth.

Addict: A drinker or drug user who claims to be able to "take it or leave it" but never does. He can't. He needs help. You may be the one God has in mind for that assignment.

You will pick up a lot of new information about drinkers and their peculiar quirks. You will also learn how to treat alcoholism as a disease instead of a disgrace. That way, recovery for the victim is often sudden and spectacular.

You will find answers to questions like these, which may have bothered you:

Can a person be an alcoholic who never takes a drink of alcohol?

When does a drinker become a "real" alcoholic?

Can an alcoholic ever return to social drinking?

Is alcoholism hereditary?

How much can a person drink safely before it becomes a problem?

Is alcoholism proof of immorality?
Some claim alcoholism is a sin, not a sickness. Who is right?
Does getting drunk once in a while prove a person is an alcoholic?
Why does A.A. work for some but not for others?
How can you tell the drug-dependent person from the other kind?

So, to sum it all up:
If you are married to, acquainted with, or live inside of someone who *drinks too much,* and you would like to help them do something about it, this book is definitely for you!

As you study each situation, see if you can classify the various levels of addiction. Mail your scores with a self-addressed envelope to the address at the back of the book. In return we will send you your King's Kid Drug Awareness Award.

No, you won't be put on any mailing list or asked for money. This is not a fund-raising gimmick. It's a fun freebie.

Here's a helpful suggestion.

Temporarily forget everything you have believed in the past about alcohol and other drugs. Keep an open mind to receive new ideas. Remember that a problem well stated is a problem half-solved. Armed with sufficient knowledge about these things, the life you save may be your own.

Now back to our harried hero, Flyboy Hill. He's an accident getting ready to happen, trying to land an unfamiliar flying machine, property of the U.S. Air Force.

How do you rate Hill's drinking level?

Make a score card. We suggest using a pencil. You may decide to change your mind as you learn more about the behavior of alcohol abusers in general and Flyboy Hill in particular.

Remember: SD = Social Drinker
            HD = Heavy Drinker
            PD = Problem Drinker
            AL = Alcoholic

As we return to the perils of Harold Hill, let's consider this question:
Do you suppose the drug alcohol had anything to do with his impending doom?

3
Back to Earth

Somewhere in Kansas, November 1942

"Hill, wake up! Come on, boy, you're going to be okay! Let me help you out of this box kite."

As this reassuring voice penetrated my drugged brain, the word *Treetops* wouldn't quit.

Good grief, I'm dead! I thought. *Maybe that's an angel comin' for to carry me home.*

My booze-soaked head slowly cleared. What a relief. Still among the living! I was still strapped into the forward pilot's seat of a dual-control Air Force Advanced Trainer.

I raised my aching head and looked out.

The ground! I was on the ground. No more treetops! To my further amazement, I was parked on the apron of a small, rural airport. Close by was a huge Snow-go machine, surrounded by high snowdrifts.

Hands were tugging at the straps across my chest. "Relax, boy, I'll have you out of this contraption in a jiffy."

A face to match the voice came into focus, and I recognized Bob, my drinking buddy from the previous evening.

"Hi, Bob, what are you doing here? Where are we?"

"You almost buried both of us and this airplane in the middle of Kansas," Bob growled. "What's the matter with you? You told me last night you could fly this thing. Don't you remember?"

"Sure, sure, I remember," I lied. My mind was a blank. I didn't remember a thing about last night.

Bob looked closely at me. "Hill, you're nuts—a real psycho. You need help. You've got a booze problem." He continued, "Last night at the party I told you that I had to deliver this airplane to Saint Louis today."

"Yeah?" I replied, anticipating with dread what I knew was coming.

"And you said to me, 'Fear not, old buddy, I've forgotten more about flying Air Force Trainers than you'll ever know. Enjoy yourself! I'll fly it to Saint Louis for you.' "

"I said *that?*"

"That's what you told me. And I was stupid enough to believe you. When we got into the plane, I settled down in the backseat and went to sleep. You had the plane all to yourself. And you almost killed us both."

He finally got me unbuckled and out of the cockpit.

The time was up for playing games. I got honest for a change.

"Bob, you're right," I admitted, "I don't remember a thing about taking off or flying this crate. The whole scene's a blank."

"You were in a blackout, Hill," he said, as we walked toward the coffee shop, "I know. I've had them myself."

Bob was right. I didn't remember a thing. Alcohol amnesia had blanked out my memory bank.

In a blackout nothing said or done registers. The mind is like a tape recorder trying to replay a blank tape. Appearing to behave normally, the victim may not act drunk. His speech may be reasonable and unslurred, and his steps steady. Only afterward, when there is no memory recall, does the blackout become apparent.

The most frightening physical changes caused by alcohol occur in the brain. Studies show that drinking interferes with learning and memory functions, which may cause the blackouts.

Bob hit the nail on the head. He understood.

"Yeah? Well, what else did I do last night?"

"You appeared normal. I had no idea you were drunk."

He put his arm around me. "Come on, pal. I'll buy you some hot coffee. We both need it."

I looked more closely at Bob. He looked like I felt—awful.

"The last thing I recall was the engine's sputtering and a bunch of treetops coming at me. What happened after that, Bob?"

He hesitated, then in a low voice he asked, "Hill, do you believe in the grace of God?"

The waitress brought two steaming mugs of coffee. I took several swallows and began to warm up.

"I don't know much about those things, Bob," I admitted. "But one thing is certain. I had nothing to do with flying that airplane. Someone had to be looking after me."

"You're right about that, pal," he said. "When I came to, we were brushing the treetops. I was barely able to pull the nose up and switch over to the emergency fuel tank. I said a prayer, circled, and found this little airstrip. It was a miracle."

His words impressed me. I drank my coffee in silence.

"That's more than just a coincidence. I believe God takes care of drunks like you, and idiots like me who risk their lives with drunks like you."

I smiled sheepishly. "Maybe you're right."

"Drink up, pal, and let's get going. We've still got to deliver that airplane, or I'm in big trouble."

We took more gulps of the hot brew.

Then he thoughtfully added, "I meant what I said about your getting professional help. Did it ever occur to you that if you don't watch your drinking you might become an alcoholic?"

Bob's warning echoed in my mind as we went out into the cold Kansas air. Little did he realize that I had heard those same words a few years earlier.

My thoughts went back to a beautiful autumn afternoon in England, in 1938, when that nasty tag ALCOHOLIC had first come my way.

4
Who—ME—
an *Alcoholic?*

Dursley, England, May 1938

"So you're leaving England tomorrow, Hill? Hope you've enjoyed your stay in our little country."

The Big Boss and I were motoring through the lovely Cotswold countryside in his huge Lagonda limousine. It was our last day together. Tomorrow I would be leaving Southampton for New York on a Cunard ocean liner. There I would begin my new assignment as Director of Operations for the entire North American continent.

I was riding on Cloud 9, unaware that Sir Percy had something more serious in mind.

"I've had a great time, Sir, and I appreciate all the nice things you've done for me. Especially the promotion. I'll do my best to live up to your confidence in me."

For several weeks I had been the guest of Sir Percy Lister, my employer and head of one of Britain's great industrial empires. The Lister Company, of which he was managing director, pioneered in the field of lightweight diesel engines. And here I was, the "dumb country kid from Connecticut," on the ground floor of a new industry, skyrocketing to the top—and still in my early thirties.

Being a workaholic had paid off. I had invested every waking moment in making it big. I allowed nothing to stand in my way. Family, friends, health—all had to take second place. My career came first. (You can read all about that in my book *The Money Book for King's Kids*.)

Sir Percy abruptly changed the subject. He was like that. A man of few words, he meant what he said and said what he meant.

"Hill, during your stay with us you've made quite a name for yourself as a beer drinker."

"Well, Sir," I replied, startled by his awareness of my drinking prowess. "Heh, heh, only trying to do my bit for the British brewing industry."

It was 1938, prior to the outbreak of World War II. The countryside was dotted with billboards proclaiming BEER IS BEST.

"I understand you are now an official member of the A.O.F.B. Is that correct?"

How had he heard about that? The Ancient Order of Froth Blowers was an exclusive and venerable drinking society. In a solemn ceremony the previous evening I had been presented with the official emblem, a quart-sized Imperial tankard. I had qualified for Lifetime Overseas Membership! It required downing two tankards of bitter ale at one sitting, without leaving the table. Not even for a potty break. What a thrill to hear the cheers of applause for my prowess as a real "he-man boozer." (For your information, an Imperial quart is one-fifth larger than ours.)

But how had Sir Percy found out about it? Why was my drinking any concern of his? Didn't I have it well under control?

Then came the bombshell. Driving into a parking area, he turned off the engine, looked me straight in the eye, and in his clipped British accent came right to the point.

"Hill, did it ever occur to you that if you continue to drink at your present rate, you might become an alcoholic?"

An *alcoholic!* Cold chills ran through my gizzard. Everything inside me shuddered under the impact of that terrible word.

A deep feeling of guilty resentment flared up within me. That's the defense mechanism of the Problem Drinker, caught with egg on his face . . . I mean, beer on his breath.

Under the circumstances I was in no position to vent my feelings. I had too much at stake. So I bit my tongue to keep from saying what I thought of "nosy bosses who meddle in the private affairs of their employees."

But Sir Percy was deadly serious. He had a huge investment in me, which he intended to protect. His sharp, penetrating gaze held my eyeballs like a magnet, awaiting my reply.

"But, Sir, I'm not *that bad.* I can take it or leave it. I can quit drinking anytime I choose!"

"Quite so, quite so, Hill," he responded, "but please watch yourself more carefully from now on, won't you?"

So indeed I did. I watched the drug alcohol gradually infiltrate my life and affairs until that fateful day thirteen years later when . . . but we'll get to that later.

Willpower? Yes, I had an enormous amount of it. Most problem drinkers do. But willpower lies in the realm of the personality. It is powerless to control a three-part disease, which alcoholism is.

Have you ever heard of willpower curing diarrhea?

Aboard the SS Franconia *in Midocean*

Crossing the Atlantic Ocean on a luxury liner is an ideal place to think things over, and that's what I did. My alcohol-biased reasoning followed the usual pattern.

Me, an alcoholic? That's completely ridiculous. How can a top-level executive, holding down a big job, be a real *alcoholic?*

That's like asking, "Can a *real* cardiac patient, an authentic cancer victim, or a certified TB sufferer hold down good jobs, while dying of their diseases?"

"Of course they can," you quickly agree.

So can an alcoholic.

One of the most baffling aspects of alcoholism is the ability of the victim to function right down to the grave. Only a trained observer can detect the symptoms. The family *knows* something is wrong, but generally calls it lack of willpower.

"Certainly he could straighten up and quit drinking if he would only put his mind to it."

That's exactly what I would do. I'd show Sir Percy and everyone else I could drink like a gentleman. I'd control my drinking. If I ever got into trouble with alcohol, I'd quit.

With this Master Plan to guide me, I set out to win fame and fortune in my new position. I knew what I wanted and how to get it. I'd certainly not let alcohol interfere.

For the next thirteen years I used my willpower, carefully controlled my drinking, and progressed rapidly. I had no idea that a controlled drinker *is* an alcoholic. Normal drinkers never worry about such things. They can walk away when things become tacky in the booze department.

Dursley, England, May 1939

"So there it is, Hill, your new employment contract. You are to move to Milwaukee at once, establish manufacturing operations, and reproduce our British diesels according to U.S. standards."

Without waiting for my reply, Sir Percy Lister continued, "It won't be easy, but you will be well paid. You'll receive a living salary plus a generous bonus on all company profits before taxes."

Wow! What an opportunity for a workaholic to prove himself.

"Thank you for your confidence in me, Sir," I replied. "Of course, I can do it. You can count on me all the way."

"Just one more thing before you leave. Please watch your drinking. You made a complete fool of yourself last evening."

"Sorry about that, Sir, I must have been overtired. I generally hold my liquor better than that."

I had really bombed out at the sailing party in my honor. The butler had to put me to bed.

"I do appreciate that lovely party. Please extend my apologies to the rest of your guests. I am truly sorry."

So back to New York and on to Milwaukee, where, during the next seven years, alcohol would demand increasingly more of my time and attention as my disease progressed.

Milwaukee, Wisconsin, December 7, 1941

Pearl Harbor Day, followed by a seven-day work week, as we turned to wartime production. Our diesel engines were in great demand by the armed services. There were not enough to go around. Production had to be increased. Day and night ran together. Material shortages, government priorities, manpower problems, and enemy espionage left no time for rest or relaxation. More and more I became alcohol dependent.

A few drinks were great for unwinding after a twenty-hour workday. Sleep came easier after several doubles with beer chasers.

After a grueling planning session, no one could complain about a few drinks to settle my nerves.

A few drinks before dinner "whetted the old appetite and aided digestion."

Silently and subtly my alcoholism progressed.

When I moved to Milwaukee in 1939, I could comfortably say *no* to a drink. I could walk away from it. Alcohol had no power over my freedom of choice. I could take it or leave it, although when I drank, it was generally more than I intended.

Seven years later I could no longer take it or leave it. I was compelled to drink *every night.*

I learned later that I had crossed an imaginary but very real line, separating the social drinker from the alcohol abuser.

A simple explanation goes like this: Once a cucumber has become a pickle, it can never again return to being a cucumber. Likewise the alcohol addict can never reverse the process. For an alcoholic, controlled drinking is physically impossible.

Why? No one knows. There are lots of theories but no real solution, except total abstinence.

At that time in my life I was impervious to the suggestions of my family, friends, and fellow workers.

Had I been aware of how alcoholism works, I might have been spared lots of misery and numerous near-death experiences.

Baltimore, Maryland, September 1946

The opportunity of a lifetime had come, a chance to get into my very own business. I'd be my own boss, quit traveling the world, settle down, and enjoy my successes. So after nineteen years I left the Lister organization and moved to Baltimore, Maryland.

I had saved enough money out of my huge bonus checks to finance the business. I was off and running. Nothing could hold me back.

I was an overnight success, because of my superb training and extensive experience; there was no way I could fail. Success was mine, beyond my fondest dreams. With unlimited opportunities for progress, I had the world by the tail.

But I had overlooked a developing flaw in my carefully laid plans. I was relying more and more on alcohol as an all-around soothing syrup for whatever ailed me.

Accustomed to a seven-day workweek pattern established in Milwaukee, I brought it with me to Baltimore.

Also, firmly established in my life-style was an increasing dependence on alcohol. Without it relaxation was impossible. I needed it. I looked forward to the cocktail hour every day. Life without it was incomplete.

A few drinks before dinner was a pleasant way of unwinding. When sleep was slow in coming, a few drinks cured that problem. I could deliver an address much better after a few drinks.

Who could criticize my having a few drinks after a golf game? And certainly a fishing trip was rather dull without plenty of booze to ward off possible snake bite.

Gradually, over the years, alcohol had taken control of my life. Could I admit it? Never.

A definite symptom of alcoholism is the victim's inability to accept the fact he can't drink like other people. They could take one drink and quit. I couldn't.

For thirty years my symptoms had progressed. From my first drink at age fourteen, until my last one at age forty-five, no one, including myself, suspected what was happening.

Nagging, nit-picking, criticism, and threats didn't help. No one understood that I couldn't stop drinking. And no one told me how to do it. They didn't know either.

Baltimore, March 1951

Five years of nonstop work had brought top-level success. I had it all together. The list was impressive:

president of my own corporation

a beautiful four-acre estate in Baltimore County

many worldly honors including an important invention

highly educated in four of our finest universities

an abundance of this world's goods

a safe deposit box stuffed with war bonds and other good stuff like that.

Not bad for a poor country boy, I told myself, surveying my treasures.

But something was wrong. Life had lost its meaning and purpose. At age forty-five, with everything to live for, I was planning to kill myself.

Is this as good as it will ever get? You mean there's nothing better to look forward to?

Those questions began to bug me not long after I had received my "Big P" degree.

What's that?

It's what the world calls top-hole success. *President* of your own company. Doing your own thing. Living it up. Having to answer to no one for anything.

You mean I've got to put up with those idiots at the yacht club, the country club, the bridge club, the chess club, the sailing club, the money club, for the rest of my life? *You've got to be kidding. I want* out.

"Number One Rat ain't where it's at," I philosophized.

Alcohol, a depressant drug, had done a number on me. Fed up with hangovers, lies, evasions, and alibis, I was sick and tired of being sick and tired. I'd end it all. Winning the rat race of life had brought nothing worth living for. It was all phony and make-believe.

Religion had done nothing for me. I had tried a dozen or so of the "biggies" and nothing good happened. God just wasn't getting involved in my case. Or maybe their God *was* dead. They couldn't prove He wasn't.

Many years of working with the laws of science and technology convinced me that an intelligent God had put the universe together. The nonevolutionary theory was obviously a religious idea. But no one ever told me I could know that God personally. My education was sadly lacking. (Read *From Goo to You by Way of the Zoo.*)

Towson, Maryland, March 23, 1951

Death should have been quick and painless. I had carefully planned it that way. My estate was in good order. The family was well provided for. I hoped that what I was getting into was better than what I was leaving. Suicide is pretty iffy at best!

The paradox was I had hated alcohol all my life, ever since it killed Uncle Harry. I hated it still more when it killed Eddie, my brother and best friend.

I had promised myself it would never get me. But it had. It's like that. Cunning, powerful, baffling, insidious, a silent and merciless killer. That's alcoholism. That's what I had tried to conquer for twenty-nine years. That's disaster in the making.

In a tumbler of whiskey I mixed a lethal overdose of a fast-acting heart paralyzer. Gulping it down, I eased back in my leather contour chair. "Here goes nothing," I groaned, and waited to die.

As things began to get dim and far away, sudden panic set in.

"I'm too young, too successful, too intelligent, to die like this. I've changed my mind. I want out."

But it was too late. The fast-acting drug had gone to work. It had taken away my choice. I was dying.

Barely conscious, I was dimly aware of these words oozing from deep inside my gizzard.

"God . . . help . . . me."

Then down came the curtain on the final act of Hill's Bottle Battle.

Did the small glass of wine Smitty forced on me when I was fourteen have anything to do with my present suicide attempt?

How could one little drink thirty years earlier end in disaster?

That's the cunning and baffling aspect of alcoholism. It's always triggered by the first drink. It never quits. Like a time bomb, it ticks away, until the hour of destruction arrives.

The countdown started the moment I drank it and didn't end for thirty years.

It did for me everything a country boy with a poor self-image could desire.

5

Math, Muscatel, and Moonshine

South Norwalk, Connecticut, September 1924

At last the great day had arrived, the one I had dreamed of since boyhood. It was finally here. I was leaving for the college of my choice, to become an electrical engineer.

It began at age ten when I read a book about the physics of electricity. Always curious about what made things work, that book literally turned me on for a career in science and technology.

"Dad, I want to become an electrical engineer," I announced. Electricity was just beginning to replace gas lighting in stores and public buildings. Most homes, including ours, still used oil lamps.

"Son," he replied, "you can become the best engineer in the business. Just work hard and let nothing interfere." Then he continued, "But a college education costs a lot of money which we don't have. So it's up to you to start earning it now."

And I had. That was all behind me. I was ready to go.

My dad's encouragement gave me a great head start. His reassurance overcame my slow-learning handicap and poor self-image.

I could hardly contain myself, as I loaded my bags into our Model T Ford for the trip to: *college*—Wow!

I had been the slowest learner in our two-room Brookside, Connecticut, school where my academic career began. Then I had a vision. I would become an electrical engineer; in fact, *Chief Engineer,* earn one hundred dollars a week; have a home with an acre of lawn, and be the happiest person around.

In those days no one earned that much, so I was really "thinking big." My dad told me to.

There was no holding me back. I began skipping grades, jumping ahead of the smart kids. Gone was my fear of failure. I became a studyholic, with high school behind me at age fourteen.

A genius in disguise? No, indeed. I was in a hurry to put behind me our "poor folks" life-style and prove I could make it big.

The Bible says in Proverbs 29:18, "Where there is no vision the people perish:" (King James Version).

Without a life plan, boredom and frustration steal ambition and initiative. Then self-destruction takes over.

Skipping grades was fine as far as it went, but it left great gaps in my mathematics groundwork. Lack of training in basics proved to be a severe handicap when taking college-entrance exams. I was accepted on condition I make up the deficits during the first semester.

Brooklyn, New York, November 1924

I had saved enough money between high school and college to pay for tuition and other bare essentials. My eating budget of three dollars a week was truly a "no frills" food plan. So I found extra work in the campus engineering department. In exchange for meals, I acted as busboy in the dining hall and played tenor banjo in the dance band. Doing homework for the rich guys, who were there for fun and games, was more lucrative.

In addition to all that, I was doing electrical engineering in two years—a real grind—but I loved every minute of it.

My daily routine began at six A.M. and ended after midnight. Sandwiched in between were special tutoring sessions needed to upgrade my math.

Toward the end of the first semester, under that grueling schedule, my health began to fail. One morning I awoke, too ill to get out of bed.

"What's wrong, Hill?" my roommate asked.

Seeing I was struggling unsuccessfully to answer, he came over and felt my head.

"Hey . . . this kid is sick. Feels like his temp is at least two hundred. I'd better call the infirmary."

For the next three weeks I hovered between this world and the next, battling double pneumonia, pleurisy, anemia, and exhaustion. Then back to the grind. But my health was slow in returning. In the words of my roommate I looked like "death warmed over."

One day as I crossed the campus a voice shouted, "Hill, is that really you?"

Staring in unbelief, I responded, "Why, Ralph, old buddy. I had no idea you were a student here." I hadn't seen him since high school days.

"Yep, I'm enrolled in the School of Architecture. I've got lots to tell you. Why not stop by my digs tonight for a good old gab fest?"

Then looking more closely at me he added, "Hill, have you been sick? You look awful."

"Just recently out of the sick bay with a touch of something or other, and still a little rocky."

"You're in luck, Hill. I have the perfect answer for what ails you. Be sure to come over tonight. Your good friend Doctor Ralph will administer the magic potion, and you'll be as good as new."

"Same old Ralph—haven't a changed a bit. Always quick with an answer."

"I'm serious. See you about eight?"

As we parted, I wondered what Ralph's "magic potion" was all about.

Later that evening Ralph greeted me at his dormitory apartment. "Come on in, Hill, and make yourself at home."

Pointing to the table he said, "Open that jug and pour yourself a large cup of the Elixir of Life. Just what the doctor ordered for quick energy."

"What is it, Ralph?" I asked. It was the first gallon jug of wine I'd ever seen.

"It's a rare vintage of muscatel, fit for a king. Now stop quibbling, and do as I say."

With that he handed me a teacup full of amber fluid, raised his own, and said, "Drink up, old friend. You really need a booster. You look terrible."

He was right about that. Down to one hundred fifty pounds, my six-foot-two frame looked like a string bean. Still wobbly from my recent hospitalization, I was ready to try anything. So I raised my drink and took a big swallow. Then wonder of wonders: As the alcohol coursed through my veins, a beautiful feeling of euphoria I had experienced four years earlier returned with a rush.

"Drink up and have a refill," Ralph urged. "A bird can't fly on one wing."

I didn't need much encouragement. Suddenly I experienced a strange phenomenon known only to alcoholics. The overpowering craving for more alcohol, which willpower cannot control, took over. After that it was downhill all the way.

I remembered back four years, when Smitty had urged on me that first drink of elderberry wine. I was picking up where I had left off, but with one difference. My first exposure to alcohol caused no trouble because the supply had been limited. But that first drink had triggered a built-in craving for more that had never left me. Here's how it happened.

South Norwalk, Connecticut, August 1920

"Come and get it."

The cook was announcing lunch from the farmhouse door. I didn't need a second invitation. I was a part-time farm worker, weeding onions all morning under the broiling sun.

Smitty, the full-time farmhand, was already washing up in the kitchen. That didn't seem to do much for him. He always smelled of cow manure, new-mown hay, and honest sweat.

Shaking the dust and hayseeds from his curly hair, he greeted me. "Hi, kid." He always called me *kid.* The way he said it was so friendly I didn't mind.

"Thirsty, kid?" he asked.

"Sure am," I replied.

"Come with me, and we'll do something about it."

"But it's lunchtime, and I'm as hungry as a bear."

"This won't take long, and you'll feel better in a hurry. Follow me. We'll be back before the spuds are on the table."

He opened the cellar door and led me down the stairs into the cool, musty-smelling cavern below.

The oil lantern Smitty held before him cast spooky shadows on the dusty spider webs festooning the beams overhead. Electric lights? They came much later.

Groping our way past bins of potatoes, apples, and turnips, leftovers from last fall's harvest, Smitty set the lantern down beside a row of wooden kegs.

"Here we are, kid. Now you're in for a treat. You're about to sample a rare brew reserved for only my special friends." With that he removed the wooden plug ("bung," he called it) from the hole in one of the kegs.

Then followed the first experiment in applied physics I had ever seen. Removing a rubber hose from its parking place on a nail overhead, Smitty poked one end into the open bung hole. The other end he put into his mouth.

As I watched in complete fascination, his enormous Adam's apple pumped up and down. His face got redder and his eyes watered. Then taking the hose from his mouth, he held it over a pitcher he had brought along.

Wonder of wonders. A pink liquid flowed *uphill* from the keg, out the end of the hose and into the pitcher.

"What caused the pink juice to flow *uphill*, Smitty? And what is it?"

"That's a syphon, kid, and that pink juice is Smitty's Soothing Syrup for Sensitive Stomachs. It's made from an old Connecticut receipe. You'll never taste better elderberry wine if you live to be a hundred."

Being more interested in things scientific than in alcoholic beverages, I asked, "But Smitty, what makes a syphon work? What about the Law of Gravity?"

"I don't know much about the whys and wherefores, kid. But as long as it works, why worry about it? It's worked for me all my life. I learned it from my dad. He told me it was God's idea in the first place."

Filling two jelly glasses, he handed me the small one and raised the large one to his mouth.

"Drink it, kid."

"What is it, Smitty?" I asked.

I remembered my dad's warning. He hated alcohol. It had brought Grandpa Hill to an "early grave."

"If I ever catch you taking a drink, I'll skin you alive. That goes for wine, whiskey, and beer. It's all devil brew and it'll ruin you if you drink it."

Besides all that, I grew up hating alcohol. It started the day they took Uncle Harry away. That was six years before.

"I hate alcohol," I sobbed, clutching my mother's hand. It had killed Uncle Harry. He had been such fun.

"Won't he ever come back?"

"No, Son. Alcohol finally got him."

We watched the big black wagon with glass sides disappear down our dusty country road.

"Where are they taking him, Mother?"

"To Brookside Cemetery. He's being buried there."

Then my dad squatted beside me.

"Son, don't *ever* take a drink of wine, whiskey, or beer. There's alcohol in all of them. That's what killed Uncle Harry. It will kill you, too, if you drink it."

"No, Dad, I'll never, never touch it."

I meant it. How could anyone drink stuff that kills nice men like Uncle Harry?

So at age eight, I decided never to touch a drop of alcohol—ever.

Little did I realize that determination, willpower, good motives, or logical reasons can never control drug addiction.

No one could have suspected that at Uncle Harry's age I too would barely escape becoming another notch in the gun of John Barleycorn.

So I held back, feeling real uneasy, as if something bad was getting ready to happen.

"Come on, kid. Drink it or we'll be late for dinner."

Back then dinner was the noon meal. Supper happened in the evening. Not wanting to offend my friend Smitty, and under pressure from his persistent urging, I raised the glass to my lips and swallowed that small glass of elderberry wine. Instantly I broke out with unmistakable symptoms of alcohol addiction. As soon as that first drink hit bottom, I reached for another.

I didn't plan it that way. I had no choice. I was reacting to the drug alcohol. My memory of it is so vivid, I clearly recall every detail after seven decades.

When a drinker reaches for another while the first one is still descending, that's proof of alcohol addiction. The disease called *alcoholism* is already at work.

A great sense of well-being flooded my insides, as the alcohol reached my toes, slowly worked its way up through my body and literally "turned me on." All traces of my usual self-consciousness quickly vanished. It was wonderful. I loved everything about it.

Then an overpowering craving consumed me. My insides literally cried out for more. Alcohol addiction, triggered by the first drink, had instantly surfaced. That symptom, so familiar to those of us who drink too much, is unknown to the SD's or Social Drinkers. They can take it or leave it. We can't.

This strange and uncontrollable reaction to the drug alcohol occurs in only 7 or 8 percent of drinkers. It accounts for the ineffectiveness of warnings, admonitions, or threats. Good advice like "use your willpower, be a man, grow up, think of your family, think of your job, don't work. I came equipped with built-in addiction to the drug alcohol. Some have it; some don't.

Familiarity with these early-warning signals of developing alcoholism will help you to help others.

"One's enough, kid. That's high-powered elderberry wine. Anyhow dinner's on the table."

Then another symptom appeared. In place of my usual warm feeling toward Smitty, I suddenly hated him with a deep-down feeling of anger and frustration. The craving for more was overpowering. I needed it but he had cut me off. I was a fourteen-year-old alcoholic, reacting normally toward whatever stands in the way of the next drink.

These symptoms were with me from that first drink until I quit nearly thirty years later. Every time I took a drink, whatever or whoever interfered with my right to the next drink had to go. That's how alcoholics always react. You can spot us every time.

That's the difference between *real alcoholics* and other drinkers. Someone has summed it up like this:

"If you look like a duck, smell like a duck, quack like a duck, waddle like a duck, and swim like a duck, the chances are that you *are* a duck. Denying it won't change a single feather. So relax and enjoy your duckhood, and if you don't take the first drink, you'll never be a drunk duck."

Did that small glass of Smitty's elderberry wine get me drunk? Definitely—four years later. Without realizing it, I was "hooked on alcohol" from Drink 1. My addiction never went away. Four years later it surfaced again, with near-fatal results.

Alcoholism has been called a fatal, progressive disease, and it certainly behaves like one. It began working in me with my first drink, but stayed hidden, until I took the next drink. Then it showed up in a hurry.

Everything was going my way. My grades were good. There were no "stressful conditions" to blame it on. But my alcoholism was still at work. In fact it was so far advanced that when I took that *second* drink, it nearly killed me.

In my opinion I turned "instant alcoholic" at fourteen. At least that's when Symptom Number 1 surfaced. That's when the first drink demands more.

I later learned that a disease called *alcoholism* was at work within my body. I was powerless over the drug alcohol. Within me was no defense mechanism against drinking too much.

The control or "Shutdown" equipment, present in normal drinkers, was strangely missing, as my subsequent behavior proved.

Thus began an evening of drinking which nearly took my life. Here I was, fulfilling my boyhood dream, preparing for a career in engineering. My math credits were all in order, finances were stable, and aside from my physical depletion, I was doing fine in all areas.

For the next hour or so Ralph and I hashed over old times, with frequent refills from the wine jug.

"You're looking almost human," Ralph commented numerous teacups later. Muscatel wine really did seem to be "just what the doctor ordered." Previous feelings of exhaustion had been replaced by an alcohol high which was truly beautiful.

"You're a real friend, Ralph. I should have gotten together with you sooner. This muscatel is doing more for me than all the doctor's prescriptions. Mind if I have another?"

So I continued to pour in the alcohol with no apparent ill effects.

Much later, Ralph observed, "Hill, this has been a great evening. We must do it again real soon. But now I think a good night's sleep is what you need. Let's call it a day, shall we?"

With that I left for my dorm a couple of blocks away.

Stepping from the upper landing onto the circular staircase, I began to lose consciousness. The drug alcohol, taken in such an overdose into my unaccustomed body, went off like a time bomb.

Beginning to pass out, and realizing I was pitching headfirst down that long stairway, I shouted, "Hey, Ralph, *help!*"

Then the curtain came down on Act 1 of Hill's drinking career.

Back to Brooklyn, New York, November 1924

The last thing I remember was leaving Ralph's apartment to walk down a circular staircase to the street below. What happened during the next three days is a total blank.

I recall nothing of falling headfirst down two flights of stairs, of my teeth protruding through my lips, or of my badly mutilated nose. I have no memory of being carried by my roommates, back to our dorm, or of their sewing up my face with black tailor's thread. (Calling a doctor would have been disastrous. Drinking on or off campus was a no-no. At enrollment we were warned, "One drink and you're out.")

Awareness returned three days later, as I came out of an alcohol coma, head bandaged, mouth taped shut, eyes barely open, and deathly sick all over.

"It's alive. Come and see what the cat dragged in. Welcome back to the world of reality, oh, weary traveler."

My roommates, who had taken turns in nursing me back to life, were obviously relieved.

Not being able to respond, I could only point to the wrappings which encased most of my upper ten inches.

"Lie there and do nothing, Hill, until further orders," Jack directed. "You've had a close brush with death. For a while we thought you wouldn't make it."

"Yes, mind us for a few days and you'll be okay," agreed Butch, the football halfback who had carried my remains on his back that fateful night. The first drink of muscatel wine had expanded to three quarts, with nearly fatal results.

Removing the tape from my mouth, he said, "Be careful about moving your lips. They're pretty well mangled from bouncing down those stairs. Its a wonder you've got any face left."

Randy added, "We sewed you up the best we could. Just take it easy. We'll feed you soup for a few days." Then after a pause he continued, "Hill, when did you learn to drink like that? Three quarts of high-powered wine at one sitting. That borders on problem drinking. Do you think you might have alcoholic tendencies?"

Alcoholic? At age eighteen, with everything going my way? How silly—the very idea!

"Of course not," I mumbled through lacerated lips. "I can take it or leave it alone. I'll prove it. I'll never touch another drop until after graduation."

And I didn't.

At that point I had a choice. Much later alcohol robbed me of that choice. That's how the disease alcoholism progresses.

"Don't get excited Hill, we're just trying to be helpful. Maybe you'd better watch your drinking. It might get you in real trouble someday."

Real trouble . . . someday. . . ?

"I really appreciate you guys. Thanks for everything. Now please help me out of bed. I need to make a potty stop real bad."

"You're in no condition for a walk down that long hallway, let me help you," Butch offered.

"No, thanks. I can manage okay," I insisted.

Was that rational thinking? Or was it a drugged decision, resulting from too much alcohol in my bloodstream?

As one of them quipped later, "Hill, after a careful search, we found a trace of blood in your alcohol stream."

Working my way unsteadily to the bathroom, I staggered to the sink and downed a large glass of water, which reactivated the alcohol in my system.

Suddenly passing out, I crashed through the bathroom window and hung suspended on the sill four floors above the pavement.

By the grace of God Butch got to me just in time to pull me back into the bathroom. "Now stay in bed, or we'll strap you down, Hill."

Thus ended my first bout with the drug alcohol, which nearly killed me numerous other times, as my disease progressed.

True to my word, I never drank again until after graduation. As we parted, my lifesaver roommates, in one accord, shouted, "Hill, old buddy, watch out for that first drink. That's the one which causes all the trouble."

I'd never thought of it like that. It's the *first drink* that triggers all alcohol trouble. Without the first one, getting drunk is impossible.

Let's do a flashback to Ralph's apartment and my first exposure to plenty of booze.

Is it normal for a teenager to consume three quarts of high-powered wine by the teacup? I did.

Do normal drinkers develop an overpowering craving for "just one more," when they have already had too much?

Isn't insanity involved when a person comes as close to dying as I had, yet later returns to drinking?

I did, and once again eyeballed death.

It was at a cookout on the beach in Connecticut. Moonshine liquor was flowing freely. The Prohibition Law said, "Thou shalt not drink," which made it the "in" thing to do.

After a couple of hours of cooking and drinking, the heat got to me. Tossing the last of the burgers on the grill, I announced, "I'm going swimming. Who'll join me?"

"Be careful, Hill. The tide's gone out and the water's very shallow."

"Shallow diving happens to be my Olympic specialty, old buddy," I wisecracked. "You're looking at someone who does high swan dives into a damp dish towel."

Alcohol causes fatal drugged decisions. This was one of them.

"Don't be crazy, Hill—you'll break your stupid neck."

That was all the encouragement I needed.

"I'll show you guys who's crazy."

Peeling down to my skivvies, I took a running leap into the water and landed headfirst on a pile of barnacle-covered rocks, just inches below the surface.

Then down came the curtain on Act 2 of Hill's drinking scenario.

Demon Rum had struck again.

Had I recognized the symptoms which appeared with my first drink at age fourteen, years of misery and heartache might have been avoided.

My "one too many" was the *first* one.

Being an alcoholic never causes trouble until alcohol enters the system. Then without help, it's downhill all the way.

It makes no sense for an otherwise-intelligent corporation president to try to kill himself. But that's what alcohol did to me.

It happened Good Friday weekend in 1951.

6

A New Beginning

Towson, Maryland, March 23, 1951

Good Friday.

To some, a symbol of hope and eternal life. To me, just another misery day.

It should have been all over by now. Last night I had overdosed enough for six normal suicides. My memory of it is sketchy. Just before passing out I recall hearing, "God, help me!" ooze from my insides.

I don't recall throwing up the whole mess. God must have appointed an angel to poke its finger down my throat. Just in time.

So here I was again, facing another day of slavery to four drugs, with no hope of ever getting free. ("Four?" you ask. Keep reading!)

Fed up with the dreary monotony of hangovers, blackouts, lies, and failure to control my drinking, this was my second suicide trip.

Last week's attempt had fizzled. Suffocation sounded like a neat way out, but things got so stuffy I had to come up for air. This time should have been different. A fast-acting drug, mixed with booze, should have done the job right. But even that failed to work.

God has a better plan for your life

Those words, not my own, rang through my sick head.

I took a fast inventory of my life. It went like this.

Age forty-five, corporation president, I owned a lovely four-acre estate in beautiful Baltimore County. I had an abundance of this world's goods, was highly educated in four great universities, superbly equipped for successful living, trying to kill myself.

Why? It was a drugged, insane decision, coming from a drugged, sick mind. Alcohol, a depressant narcotic, had battered my emotions and feelings to the breaking point. And where it left off, other drugs took over. I was addicted in four directions.

1. Alcohol   minimum daily dosage, one quart
2. Nicotine   minimum daily dosage, two packs
3. Caffeine   minimum daily dosage, twelve cups
4. Sucrose   minimum daily dosage, several grams.

The bottom line?

I was in continuous withdrawal from the drug alcohol. Knowing that only alcoholics drink in the morning. I shook all day and took my morning drink at five in the afternoon. That proved I was not one of *them*.

The daytime hours were spent in feeding my other addictions!

Two packs a day of cigarettes, plus several cigars and a pipe, did terrible things to my nerves, lungs, and emotions.

A dozen or more cups of "tugboat" coffee didn't help. That's the kind with lots of chicory. It produces inner vibrations and heart spasms that only rugged Maryland watermen and alcoholics can handle.

Sucrose completed the list, battering my frazzled nerves with blood sugar imbalance. The afternoon exhaustion was unreal. Depression, unnamed fears, and a constant feeling of gloom and doom gave me no peace.

Fifty pounds overweight, blood pressure ninety over fifty, memory nearly gone, even a failure at suicide, I was ready for a change.

Good Friday night was no different from all the rest. I was well into my second fifth of Old Pikesville Maryland rye whiskey. (That's the kind they should have quit making for mercy reasons.)

I arrived home in the early morning hours, a religious book under my arm and lots of booze in my innards. Not until much later did I discover where I had been that night. A phone call from the owner of the book provided the clue.

"Where's my book, Hill?"

It was Clem, a neighbor and active church worker. Our paths didn't cross too often. Religion was not my bag. It had let me down too often.

"Do you mean that religious book that says drunkards are all headed for hell?" I asked.

"That's the one. Don't you remember coming to my home Good Friday night for help with your drinking? We recommended church membership, and you promised to think it over?"

I had. But I wasn't ready for another bunch of dead doctrines condemning me to "The Bad Place." That's what my grandma called hell.

No, I don't recall much about that 1951 Good Friday, but before it ended, my life had taken a 180-degree turn. Amazing things began to happen. They haven't stopped and never will, by God's grace.

That's what *The Impossible Takes a Little Longer* is all about. There *is* a way out. We've found it. It's free. It will work for anyone who wants it.

The turnaround happened like this:

Collapsing into my favorite chair, I tried to make sense out of the religious doctrines Clem found so helpful. Finally I gave up. It was all too heavy and confusing.

I tried to read the Sunpaper's account of yesterday's Orioles' game. My memory couldn't carry one sentence to the next. I gave up and sat staring in complete despair at the living-room rug. Suddenly, in the middle of it, appeared a huge, black hole. I saw myself pitching headfirst down that hole. It was so real and vivid I can still see it. In total panic I cried out: "God . . . *help me.*"

And He did.

That's the last time I ever drank alcohol—by God's grace and power.

How very real to me is the Bible promise I discovered much later: "Whosoever shall call on the name of the Lord shall be saved."

Becoming a "whosoever" brings fast help. That's how God operates. It has to do with humility, or self-honesty. It's the principle of giving up to win. The process God used was uniquely His own. He worked through Dick, my next-door neighbor. God delights in using people who have received on-the-job training.

The next night Dick invited me over to meet his friend Don. They told me how it was with them. After many years of alcohol addiction, they had found a way to stay sober, one day at a time.

They were active in a group who had found a way out. Originally a religious organization, it now specialized in fixing alcoholics, so they could live happily without alcohol. They said it also worked with other drugs.

"We haven't taken pledges or made promises. We treat our alcoholism like a three-way disease. Some folks insist it's sin. We don't agree. By applying certain simple principles we no longer drink. And even better, many of us no longer want to."

They told me their Recovery Fellowship principles were not new. They had been around a long time. Jesus taught them in the Sermon on the Mount. They appear in detail in Matthew, chapters 5, 6, and 7.

They said alcoholism could be arrested but not cured. It was like T.B. and some other ailments. It responded well to treatment but never went away. Experience proved that if a recovered alcoholic returned to drinking, things were worse than before.

"But can't God cure all diseases?" I asked. Somewhere I had heard that He could.

"Of course He can—and does. But sometimes His idea of a cure is different from ours. Like the case of Simon the leper.

"Jesus went to the home of Simon the leper for a meeting. The account doesn't say that Simon was a cured leper. It says nothing about his case being healed. It calls him a leper, even though his symptoms must have been arrested. Everyone knows you didn't visit a leper whose disease was acting up. Active cases were isolated from society until the symptoms went away.

"Therefore Simon must have been a leper, whose disease was arrested but not cured.

"That's how we consider our disease. It's arrested but not cured. We can never again drink normally. We have crossed an imaginary line. We're allergic to alcohol and other drugs."

Then they pointed out a principle I had never thought about.

Most people think of a cured alcoholic as one who can drink "normally." But that's not God's idea of a cure. What He offers is a life-style free from the need to drink or drug at all. That's what the folks in Recovery Fellowship had found: a way to live without alcohol or other drugs, and *like* it!

They said it began with admitting I had a problem which I could not handle on my own. I later discovered the Bible verse behind that principle. It is Point 1 of the Sermon on the Mount, in Matthew 5:3:

The man who realizes he is a spiritual pauper, has no resources of his own that amount to anything, and honestly admits he's a no-good slob and needs help, is greatly blessed and God becomes his new manager.

HILL PARAPHRASE

That's the essence of what they shared with me that Good Friday night in 1951. That's the night God chose to bring new hope and eternal life to this alcoholic who, at the end of his rope, asked God for help.

These men told me how it was with them. They openly discussed things I had tried to bury deep inside. Impressed with their honesty and eagerness to help, I asked, "How can I try whatever it is you guys are into?"

"There's a neighborhood meeting here in Towson tomorrow night. It's free. There are no dues or fees."

They didn't say, "Why don't you go and get straightened out, you dirty alcoholic?" They didn't even invite me to go. If I wanted it, there it was. If not, forget it. That was their attitude.

Then Dick said something which triggered a ray of hope deep down inside my quivering gizzard.

"I've been without a drink for four years, because of a personal God."

A sudden burst of hope exploded deep within me. Maybe that was what I needed: a personal God. No one had ever before talked like that. It sounded as though he really knew God.

That simple word of testimony did for me what nothing else could have done.

Without intending to, I heard myself say, "I think I'll try it." Then my sick head stepped in.

Hill, you're not an alcoholic. You're not that bad. You shouldn't have said that. They'll think you're like them.

But it was too late. I had already committed myself.

"Fine, I'll be glad to pick you up about eight."

As I climbed into Dick's car the next evening, an all-gone feeling filled my insides. I knew those people didn't drink. I was developing a huge thirst. The old craving was back, worse than ever. I began to shake real bad.

These thoughts went through my ailing head.

Hill, what have you gotten yourself into? You know you're not an alcoholic. What will the neighbors think? What will your employees think? What will your friends think? How will you turn down booze during the holidays?

I didn't realize they all knew I drank too much "now and then." Many of them had mentioned it. Like most alcoholics, I denied it.

"Me, an alcoholic? I can take it or leave it. I can quit when I want to. I'll let you know when I need help. And anyhow, next time will be different."

And it was, *worse.* That's the only way alcoholism changes. It's downhill all the way.

At the meeting, Dick introduced me to Mike, Eddie, Matt, several Bobs, and numerous others. They all seemed glad to see me.

It was all so strange and wonderful. It was the way I had expected religions to be.

I felt at ease. At last someone understood. They didn't judge; they shared. What a relief. No finger pointing. They said things like:

"If you want what we have, do what we do, and we'll help you to do it."
"Life by the yard is hard, by the inch it's a cinch."
"Don't take the first drink, and you can't get drunk."

Taking a seat in the back of the meeting room, I sat on my hands, trying to hide my shakes. They showed anyhow but no one snickered. They told me:

"Keep coming back, we need you."
"You never have to take a drink as long as you live."
"Alcoholism is a disease, not a disgrace."
"We have a three-way treatment for it. It can be arrested but not cured."
"You can't stay sober for someone else. You have to want it for yourself."
"If you will decide each morning to not drink that day, we'll help you do it."
"Plan ahead; live today."
"Get acquainted with the God of your choice, but make sure you choose a live one." (That really narrows the field, doesn't it?)
"Come to meetings as often as you drank. Pray. Help other alcoholics. Learn to depend on the God of your choice, and you need never drink again as long as you live."
"Stay away from all mood-changing drugs. They block the personality change necessary for recovery from alcoholism."
"The old *you* will drink again. A spiritual rebirth is necessary for complete recovery from alcoholism."

What a strange new set of principles these were—totally foreign to my scientifically trained mind. So I complained to Dick, my sponsor.

"I'm not an alcoholic. I've never wrecked a car, spent a night in jail, lost a job, or visited a loan company. I pay all my bills on time and have cash in the bank. How can I be an alcoholic?"

"Diseases are no respecters of persons. Alcoholism is no exception. It is impersonal, progressive, and fatal. When treated early, big trouble can be avoided. If you have never had large problems with alcohol, you needn't risk having them."

"But suppose I'm here under false pretenses," I chirped. "Could it be I have a very mild case? Maybe I'm a semi-alcoholic. Possibly I can qualify for associate membership?"

Dick's answer saved my career, home, job, and life. He made things so simple and practical that even I couldn't miss. Here's the way he summed it up:

"Maybe you're not a real alcoholic. Maybe you do have a mild case. Probably you could drink for another ten years without too much trouble. *Maybe.* But here's a safer way than experimenting with the iffies of alcohol.

1. "If you're *not* an alcoholic and do what we do, you'll never become one.

2. "If you *are* an alcoholic and do what we do, it'll never get any worse.

3. "If you drink a little too much now and then, that will go away, too. Just don't take one drink, one day at a time, and you can't get drunk."

"But I've never been in the gutter or lost everything like some of these people," I argued. "Aren't all real alcoholics either skid-row bums or close to it?"

The answer was simple and direct.

"Whether you're from jail or from Yale, if you have our disease, without help it can kill. We have an answer that works. If you want it, it's yours free.

"Just give it a fair trial for ninety days by going to ninety meetings. If you don't like what happens, we'll refund your misery at the door."

"But what about all the God talk? Is it another religion which promises a lot but never produces? I've been in too many of those already."

(I didn't know the difference between religion and a way of life which begins with a spiritual rebirth and takes off from there.)

But the promise of a life free from hangovers, shakes, sleepless nights, bad dreams, blackouts, and compulsive drinking was appealing. And besides, it *was* working for them.

I was faced with a life or death decision. Would I admit I needed help and quit fighting booze, or deny it—and die?

The chairman started the meeting by suggesting a silent prayer for still-suffering alcoholics. That was a shocker. Most people cussed them.

He then said, "My name is Joe and I'm an alcoholic. I'm sober by the grace of God."

He explained how their program worked. It was so simple that even my foggy mind could handle it.

"Success with our program," he explained, "depends on taking Step One which deals with self-honesty. It goes like this.

"We simply admit we're powerless over the drug alcohol. We can't handle it in our own strength. Our lives are out of control and in need of new management. From there on the problem is out in the open where it can be dealt with."

That brand of self-honesty blew me away. Whoever heard of anyone standing up in church and confessing:

"My name is Bob Badmouth and I'm a gossip." Or "I'm Florence Fatlip and I'm a glutton."

Imagine hearing someone in the congregation letting it all hang out. "My name is Malcolm Moocher, and I lie, cheat on my wife, and falsify my income-tax returns."

All my religious trips had been with pure and spotless souls, whose proof of holiness depended on what they wore, ate, or didn't get into.

"We don't smoke or drink or chew, and we don't run with the folks who do," was the theme song of one group I tangled with. That's tough for poor, lost sinners who look bad, smell bad, act bad, and *are* bad. I just didn't fit in.

Thank God, His ways are beyond human wisdom or understanding. After twenty-nine years of alcohol addiction, His power instantly set me free. From the moment I walked into that room until now, I have not taken a drink of anything with alcohol in it.

That's "Amazing Grace" in action!

In answer to my questions "Why am I an alcoholic? Where did it come from? Why can't I drink like others?" they said:

"What difference does it make? If we knew all those answers, we still couldn't drink alcohol. Knowing the cause of cancer doesn't make it go away. It's the treatment that counts. If you have a drinking problem, we have an answer, and we're sober to prove it works. If you have problems when you drink, maybe drinking is your problem."

Did I pick up alcoholism from a dirty doorknob or an unsanitary toilet seat?

Did I inherit it from Grandad Noah, the first drunk on record?

Or, as someone suggested, did my mother drop me on my head in front of a brewery horse when I was a tiny tot?

What difference does any of that make? *I can't drink alcohol and remain in control of my life.* It's just that simple. Don't take a drink, and you can't get drunk.

I have never found a flaw in that line of reasoning. It always works for those who want it and are willing to do a few simple things.

"Why doesn't it work for all alcoholics? I know many who tried it and failed."

"Probably for the same reason that many churchgoers avoid salvation and eternal life, by saying *no* to Jesus."

One day a radio preacher bellowed, "Alcoholics are all demon possessed and need deliverance."

"What about that?" I asked Ed, my spiritual adviser in the Recovery Fellowship.

"Maybe that's true," he replied wisely. "If it is, we're in the right place. Recovery Fellowship follows the same process recommended by Jesus for such cases.

"When Jesus and His team came down from their mountaintop retreat, a man with a demon-possessed boy asked why His disciples couldn't handle the problem.

"Jesus answered that this kind of demon comes out only by prayer and fasting."

He pointed out that was exactly what the Fellowship stressed.

"Pray and fast (stay away from the first drink one day at a time), and you'll stay sober."

There it is, the Bible method of staying sober, with or without demons. In case we're infested with the little beasts, our program of fasting and prayer will root them out painlessly and thoroughly.

It took about three years for my spiritual rebirth to take place. It could have happened sooner. My intellect blocked progress in that area. Pride also entered in.

I never doubted that God was responsible for my sobriety, but I wanted some credit for all my other successes and achievements. So I avoided a full and complete surrender—especially after I had learned that the only live God is Jesus, the God who founded our Fellowship.

Then came a crisis crunch which demanded a decision.

A young drunk I had befriended had treated me badly. He ran off with my wife. I resented it deeply. Day and night I brooded on it, until murderous intentions obsessed me.

Ed pointed out that resentments often lead to drinking and that I must pray for those who mistreated me. I did. (I prayed he would drop dead.)

How can you forgive a man who steals your wife? No way, unless a personal God provides the grace—and I didn't have one at the time. (Read *God's in Charge Here* for details.)

So that night, after stalking him for weeks, Elmer, my quarry, emerged from his hiding place under a flat stone.

Pointing my little target pistol at the back of his head, I shouted, "Die, you dirty dog."

7
Life
Under New Management

When Ed arrived home about 1:00 A.M. I was sitting on his front steps. "Come in and tell me about it."

My expression must have told him all was not well with my serenity and peace of mind.

Looking more closely at me Ed, my spiritual adviser, said, "Hal, wouldn't you like to let go and let God run your life?"

I wasn't sure if he had seen the pistol in my pocket. He didn't mention it. He knew things like that were symptoms. My life needed a New Manager.

Emotionally I was on rock bottom. My great moment had arrived, and I had blown it.

After weeks of stalking Elmer, I finally had him lined up in my gun sights. This was it. Vengeance at last. I took careful aim at the back of his head.

"Die, you dirty dog," I shouted, and squeezed the trigger. Nothing happened. My trigger finger froze. It wouldn't move.

Somehow aware that God was in that scene, I put away the gun and headed for Ed's house. He would be able to help. He had a personal God. He called Him *Jesus*. Nothing ever disturbed him.

"Yeah, I guess so. But how do I go about it? I don't have that kind of faith. Anyhow I'm not worthy to meet God in person. There's too much wrong with me. I'm full of hate, murder, vengeance, bitterness, guilt, and anger. My thirst for alcohol has come back worse than ever."

"You have to start by being honest with God about yourself. Otherwise, blaming others will become a way of life and you'll return to drinking. Haven't I heard you say you were a workaholic—that you had totally given yourself to being a business success, at the expense of family relationships? Didn't you tell me you were so morally pure that adultery less than a hundred miles from home was unthinkable? Didn't you ever neglect your family in favor of boozing and lie to them about how all that overtime work was killing you? Just admit it all to God right now and He will give you a new start."

Ed's answer blew away all barriers. He made knowing God sound so simple that even a cluck like me couldn't goof it!

"If you don't have a personal God of your own, borrow mine."

"If you can't believe, make believe."

"Fake it until you make it."

"Go through the motions with God, and He will make Himself real to you."

Could it be that simple? Would God really come and live inside me? With my kind of record could He really forgive all my sins and give me a new beginning?

"That's the God I'm talking about," Ed answered.

"But how do I know all that is true? How can I be sure this is not just another phony trip? I'm fed up with religious gods who never produce."

"Maybe you never tried a live God before. Have you ever asked Jesus Christ to become your personal God? He's the only live One there is. All the rest are dead and buried."

"But others told me the same things about their gods. They were just as sincere as you are, Ed. Their gods simply didn't ever show. How do I know yours is different?

"You can find out right now. I'll pray for you. If something happens, you'll have proof, won't you?"

In a simple prayer, Ed introduced me to his God. The prayer went something like this:

Lord Jesus, meet my friend Hal. He wants to make You the Lord of his life. Please take charge of him and treat him real good. Thank You, Lord. Amen.

I felt myself to see if anything had happened. As far as feelings went, it hadn't. The same anger, hate, bitterness, and murder were there.

"Thanks, Ed, for your interest. Just as I suspected, nothing happened. I really didn't think it would anyhow, so I'm not surprised. I'll be on my way. Nighty-night and all that rot."

I was devastated. My last hope was gone. Ed, my ace in the hole, had no more to offer than the others. They talked a good game. All talk, no action.

I came to Ed's house with two plans in mind:

> Number 1. To meet God personally and see if He could put me together. My insides were in shreds and going downhill fast.
> Number 2. If Number 1 didn't work, I'd reload my shooting iron, blow Elmer away, along with my wife and myself.

Sick in the head? You know it. Sick in the guts as well.

It's humanly impossible for the ego to accept that kind of treatment. Without a personal God, it's an "eye for an eye and a tooth for a tooth."

With my hand on the knob, I started to leave.

"Look, Hal, I just introduced you to the Head Man of the Universe. If you're not satisfied with the introduction, take it up with Him. Don't tell me your troubles. That's His department. Talk it over with Jesus."

"I don't know how to handle all that God talk. The *thees* and *thous* confuse me. That's not my style."

"Be yourself with God and He'll be Himself with you."

With that Ed left the room, leaving me alone with Jesus.

I thought, *What have I got to lose? Murder, anger, fear, bitterness, vengeance, depression, and thirst for alcohol. That's all I've got to lose. And if this thing works, maybe I can be happy like Ed.*

So I got down on my knees on the living-room floor, took a deep breath, and prayed:

> *Lord Jesus Christ, my friend Ed seems to think You're the only real God there is. I personally don't know about that. I've tried so many others but nothing happened. Maybe You're like that also. I'm not really sure about anything, except I need some fast help. If You are really here and can make Yourself real to me right now will You please do it? Thank You very much. Amen.*

And to my utter amazement, He did. He moved right inside me and did a real number on the murder, fear, guilt, and depression. He also took away my thirst for alcohol and it hasn't come back.

That was in March of 1954. I experienced what our Recovery Fellowship calls a *spiritual rebirth.*

Some church folks refer to it as being *born again.*

Others call it *regeneration.*

Second Corinthians 5:17 says it makes us new creatures in Christ Jesus. It certainly did that for me.

Whatever you call it, it was the greatest happening in my life. For the first time ever, I felt clean, forgiven, right with God, and into a new adventure without beginning or end. That's the best way I can describe eternal life.

That's really the backbone of our Recovery program—a personal relationship with a God whose name is Jesus. Nothing else works for me.

There is a spiritual law which says that blessings must be shared with others or they tend to dry up. That's why "carrying the message to alcoholics who still suffer" is a vital part of our program.

The "new birth" experience equips us with the power to share in a new way our experience with God. Empowered by the Holy Spirit, it became as natural as breathing. But *not* as easy. Why?

Jesus tells us in many places in Scripture to expect opposition when we openly use His name.

"If you're on My team you'll never win any popularity contests" (Hill paraphrase).

There are reasons for this. God's enemy Satan cannot stand the name of Jesus. It contains *all* power in heaven and earth. Therefore the enemies of God don't like it. They openly rebel against it. As soon as I began to announce that my Higher Power's first name was Jesus, the fuse was lit.

"I'll fix you so you don't use that name any more," bellowed Sam, a real "sickie," waving a long knife at me.

It was just as the disciples once experienced. They were beaten and told, "Talk about anything else, but don't use that name."

What did they reply?

"We're obeying God, not you characters" (Hill paraphrase).

"Go ahead, loser," I told him. "Put that knife in me, and you'll help me to graduate. What are you waiting for? Are you chicken?"

He was, and is. I'm still here!

In a maximum-security prison meeting, Butch, the bully of the cell block, had bellied up to me.

"You're new around here, ain't you, buddy?"

"That's right. I've just begun attending this meeting. I'm glad to be here to share what God has done in my life."

Ignoring what I had said, then he had pulled from his boot a foot-long knife.

"Listen, buddy, I can cut you up into five-pound slabs and stack you in the corner. No one would know what happened to you."

He was right. There were eighty "hardened criminals," one guard, and three of us from the Fellowship.

"You're right, pal," I replied. "But before you get yourself into a real jam, I want to warn you. I belong to Jesus Christ, and if you chop me up, you will have Him on your hands."

While his beady little eyes blinked and his fat lip quivered, I repeated, "Go ahead, loser; what are you waiting for? Sticking that knife into me will help me graduate. What are you waiting for?"

After he'd been saved a few weeks later, he told me, "Hill, you blew me away that night. I've been the prison bully for years. No one has ever stood up to me like you did and lived to tell it. But your testimony literally tore me up. You made Jesus so real."

The name of Jesus does things like that. It's the working tool of the Holy Spirit in our lives.

That's the Power Hookup offered by Step 11 of our Recovery program. We seek God's will for our lives and the Power to make it operate.

Making Jesus my Higher Power caused other doors to open for carrying the Good News of God's grace.

Schools, churches, colleges, retreats, and Christian groups began inviting me to speak.

In 1969 I reported on the Missing Day incident, when the computers at NASA detected Bible events from Old Testament times. The media publicized it widely. This brought invitations to appear on TV and radio talk shows from coast to coast.

After appearing on Jerry Falwell's great television program, a publisher sent me a contract to do a book on my life. Since I was involved in running several corporations, I tried to weasel out of the assignment when the book was about half-finished.

"Jesus," I whined, "You know how busy I am. I don't have time to finish it. Please give me more time. Thank You. *Amen.*"

I've since learned it's better to use the time you have instead of begging for more!

So He did, in an unexpected way.

A few nights later, I skidded on a few drops of water in my club basement. I landed gently on the tile floor and snapped three bones in my right ankle. That gave me plenty of time—eighteen weeks in plaster casts.

So my first book, *How to Live Like a King's Kid,* got finished without another peep out of me, plus another one about the Bible and science, *From Goo to You by Way of the Zoo.*

When God says, in 1 Samuel 15:22, "Obedience is better than sacrifice," He's not kidding.

I continued attending meetings in plaster casts, which wasn't all that thrilling. I discovered the joys of a stretched-out wire coat hanger for dealing with internal itching.

One night I crutched my way to a meeting in a church basement. Not only was it hot and smoky, I had forgotten my trusty "itch remover." Things inside the cast were going wild.

On top of all that, I was called on to speak.

"My name is Hal Hill and I'm an alcoholic. For three years I attended meetings sober but thirsty. I didn't have a personal Higher Power to do anything about it. Then I met a Higher Power with a first name, and He took away my thirst. I don't break His anonymity. I call him Jesus C."

That's how we do it in our fellowship. Last names are used only by their owners, never by others.

When the meeting ended, I still sat with my aching leg propped up on a cushion. By then the itching inside the cast had gotten worse. The heat was causing swelling. I was in torment.

"I liked what you had to say, Hal. I'm Liz and I'm an alcoholic."

I looked up into the smiling face of a strange female who dared to intrude into my misery. She was grinning like a mule eating briars, or a possum sucking persimmons.

At that point in my life, females were "for the birds." My fractured marriage hadn't gone back together in spite of years of counseling and prayer. Without realizing it, my attitude toward the opposite sex had become cynical, bitter, and hateful. Twenty-five years of enforced celibacy does things like that.

I went to no trouble to cover my feelings.

"Is that right?" I growled. "How long have you known Jesus?"

(I'd know by the way she answered that question if she was for real or just playing religious games. Unless a person really knows Jesus, that question makes their eyeballs swivel.)

Without hestitating, she named a date. Then taking from her purse some pictures she said, "And I was baptized three months ago."

"Big deal," I said under my breath, adding, "do you believe all that Bible stuff?"

"Of course I do. Why?"

"Then pray for my leg. It's killing me."

"I sure will—as soon as I get home."

"Oh, no, you don't," I said, grabbing her. "Pray NOW!" (I knew that would blow her away.)

"Now?" she whispered, glancing around the room.

"NOW!" I yelled.

Women! Bah and humbug. When the going gets tough, they're long gone. No guts. They talked a good game in private, but when persecution arrived, they clammed up about Jesus. I had seen them come and go. No doubt this "Lizzy Baby" was like all the rest. But I'd find out in a hurry. And I did.

Without another word, she placed her hands on my plaster cast and in a loud voice commanded, "Be healed in the name of Jesus."

That nearly blew me out of the saddle, along with a whole roomful of fellow alcoholics.

"Liz, what in ——— are you doing? Are you crazy?" one gimlet-eyed rummy yelled, quickly drawing a curious crowd.

Not batting an eyelash, Liz stood her ground. Hands still on my cast, she gave it right back to him. I admired her courage.

"I'm praying for Hal's leg. Can't you see? Are you blind?"

Later when the cast was removed, the broken ankle was perfect like the other one. The doctor had expected about 85 percent. Jesus answered the prayer Liz placed on it the night we first met.

That's how the King's Kids Korner Ministry got started. It's now worldwide.

Soon the King's Kids books hit the best-seller list, and my travels increased. To help with driving and ministering, the Lord provided a young man who traveled with me until he developed matrimonial intentions.

It was actually then that Liz and I founded the King's Kids Korner. That's where all of our books, tape albums, and other goodies are produced.

We travel the world, sharing our experience, strength, and hope with others, especially those who still suffer from addiction to alcohol and other drugs.

Our fees? None. Jesus provides amply for all our needs.

We are active in Success Seminars, Bible conferences, retreats, Bible-science meetings, and Recovery Fellowship groups. We often share in meetings of Overeaters Anonymous, Narcotics Anonymous, and Alcoholics Anonymous. We often speak at meetings of Full Gospel Business Men's Fellowship, Christian Business Men's Committees, church retreats, and C.F.O. camps (Camps Farthest Out, an international organization).

Yes, we pray for the sick, and Jesus still causes signs and wonders to follow.

Like in the Alabama C.F.O. Camp, when a boy drowned in the pool. All efforts to revive him failed. He was laid out on the poolside, stiff and cold.

Directed to the scene by the Holy Spirit, Liz spoke these words in a loud, firm, authoritative voice: "Death, you can't have that boy . . . Death, you can't have that boy."

Life came back into his body. He sat up and began screaming in terror. He had been given another chance at salvation. Needless to say that got everyone's attention, including his. God still answers prayer!

He's never done anything for you personally?

Do you have a God of your own who can do things like that? Or is yours a dead religious idol, the product of man's intellect? If you don't have a real God of your own, why not borrow ours? He likes to be called by His first name. It's *Jesus* and you can meet Him right where you are.

If you're not too good at making up prayers, borrow one of ours. Just say out loud:

> *Lord Jesus Christ, I'm not too sure You are a living God. I've been told all sorts of things about You. Frankly, You don't have too good an image in some circles. I'm confused. That's why I'm here. I want to settle it all. I'm willing to be shown. Maybe I'm talking to myself. I just don't know. But if You are real and You can make yourself real to me right now, please do it. Thank You very much. Amen.*

Drop us a line at the address in the back of the book, and we will send you some useful freebies to help you in your new spiritual life.

How do we know something good just happened to you?

Because it always does.

God bless you real big and juicy, as you continue, one day at a time, to practice these principles in all your affairs.

8

Alcoholism in a Nutshell

by Father Joe Martin

For Expert Advice, Consult an Expert

That's why we asked Father Joe Martin, our good friend and eminent authority on alcoholism, to write this chapter.

Father Joseph C. Martin was raised, educated, and in 1948 ordained a Catholic priest, in Baltimore, Maryland. There he taught in seminaries until 1970, when he began work as an educator in the field of alcoholism for the State of Maryland. Since 1973 he has lectured widely, not only throughout the USA but in Great Britain, Europe, and the Far East.

In 1972 the United States Navy made a film of his famous "Chalk Talk on Alcohol," which has become a film classic in alcohol treatment centers, school classrooms, and industry. Since then, he has made numerous, widely acclaimed teaching films and tapes on the disease alcoholism and recovery from it.

Chosen by several thousand health professionals for the prestigious Marty Mann Award for Outstanding Achievement in Alcoholism Communications, Father Martin is highly qualified to tell us what alcoholism is all about and how to help the still-suffering victim in your life.

Author of the book *No Laughing Matter* (Harper & Row), he is also cofounder of Ashley, Inc., a nonprofit, tax-exempt alcohol treatment center located in Havre de Grace, Maryland.

Overlooking beautiful Chesapeake Bay, Father Martin's Ashley is the ideal place for sick and suffering alcoholics to find recovery and rehabilitation. In the midst of the breathtakingly beautiful surroundings of this twenty-acre, sixteenth-century former estate of a Maryland senator, getting well can be both pleasant and permanent.

Presently assigned to Saint Joan of Arc Church in Aberdeen, Maryland, as associate pastor, Father Martin is available to assist in solving the drinking problems of those about whom you may be concerned. A phone call to him at 301-273-6600 will bring fast help from one whom we consider Authority Number 1 in his chosen field.

Now, let's listen to Father Martin as he spells out in simple terms what we all need to know about this highly complex disease called alcoholism:

Havre de Grace, Maryland, April 1984
Introduction: The information in this chapter is a condensation of my book *No Laughing Matter,* in which I covered in considerable detail the phenomenon of a disease we call alcoholism.

In Part I of this chapter I would like to explain "alcohol," what it is and what it does, in the simplest of terms.

In Part II I want to talk about the horrible repercussions of this disease on those who live with it or near it.

Finally, I would like to offer a few suggestions as to what we might do to help alcoholics and their families to get well.

Part I: What *Is* Alcohol?

Some years ago I met a man named Walter Green, M.D. Dr. Green was a physician who had lost everything because of his drinking. He got well, arrested his disease, and went back to the top of his profession with this difference: he dedicated his life to the treatment of alcoholics, treating over six thousand of them before he died. Dr. Green was one of the few men I have ever known who had an absolute genius for simplicity. In understandable terms, he explained a few of the facts known about this most devastating of all diseases.

Alcoholism is one of the oldest illnesses known, and certainly one of the most complex. We do not know what causes it. *Alcohol itself is not the cause but only the necessary ingredient.* The cause is whatever is wrong in the body of the person who ingests alcohol. It is certainly one of the most "complete" diseases known, affecting every facet of a human being: body, mind, emotions, and soul. It has been aptly described as a "soul sickness." It is the most destructive, because most people who get it, die of it. No, they are not weak willed or perverse. The reason most alcoholics die is because they are not given a chance at proper treatment. Alcoholics are being successfully treated every day at reputable treatment centers.

Alcoholism is also one of the most baffling diseases, having defeated the best of the professionals. It is the disease about which we know the least and about which most people think they know the most. In the field of alcoholism, more destruction is caused by the half-truth than in any other field of human life.

For example, one of the greatest myths that has killed many alcoholics is the belief that if the alcoholic *finds out why he drinks,* his drinking problem will magically disappear. This is like suggesting that if we know the cause of tooth decay, we'll have no trouble with our teeth.

The only answer to any illness is proper therapy. A man can know *why* he started to drink—and die drunk. However, Doc Green, who inspired these talks, began by explaining the reason why we drink the things we drink, including alcohol.

The first beverages that cross human lips are water and milk, shortly after birth, drunk to slake thirst and maintain health. As the child grows older, he expands his menu to include something sweet, like sodas and hot chocolate. He chooses these sweet drinks because they are pleasant to the taste. They do not fulfill a need. Later he is introduced to coffee, a beverage which he has to "learn" to like. Since it is not necessary nor does it taste good, why does he drink it?

Why Do People Drink Coffee? That's simple: *curiosity.* Coffee is an adult drink, denied to children. When they ask for it, they are told they cannot have it because it is not good for them. Naturally they want some. So when they take their first sip, they take their first step out of childhood.

Another reason for coffee drinking is *custom.* The coffee break has become so customary that it is written into labor-management contracts.

The third reason for drinking coffee is *conviviality.* Others are having coffee; we want some too. We sit around and talk over a cup of coffee.

Why Do People Drink Alcohol? Alcohol is next. Why do people drink alcohol? Forgetting all the so-called psychological reasons, let's look at the actual reasons. They are many but they are simple.

The first reason is that, like coffee drinking, *big people do it.* So, wanting to do what big people do, we might get a little whiskey, cut it with water, add sweetener, put in some ice, call it a cocktail, and drink it. Now we're really grown-up.

The second reason is *custom.* Like coffee, alcohol is drunk customarily for many reasons, usually associated with festive occasions like parties and weddings. The Bible refers to wine as "the gift of God that gladdens the hearts of men" (*see* Psalms 104:15). Cocktail parties, or drinking parties, are given for *conviviality,* for people to get together in fellowship.

By the way, alcohol produces more conviviality than coffee. It has been referred to as a "social lubricant." Indeed, many people are easier to take after they are "oiled."

The fourth reason people drink is for *escape.* There is nothing deeply psychological about this. We are created by God Himself to substitute pleasantness for unpleasantness. When it is cold, we put on a coat. When it rains, we come indoors. When we have a headache, we take an aspirin. So if we want to escape from anxiety, husband, wife, job, or all of it, we take a couple of drinks. Our problems don't go away, but they don't bother us anymore.

The fifth reason people drink alcohol is *to alleviate pain.* In fact, one of the first uses of alcohol was as a painkilling medication. You've all heard the expression "Boy, he was feeling no pain last night." That's why an alcoholic can wake up with his arm in a sling and wonder what happened. He doesn't recall the terrible suffering of the previous night. Nor does he recall the trip to the emergency room. So using alcohol as an analgesic today is not a valid reason. There are far better painkillers available.

The simplest of all reasons why people drink alcohol is for *euphoria.* Basically, that means that alcohol makes you feel good. The word *euphoria* means a "sense of well-being." After a few drinks a person with all sorts of problems feels better and the problems *seem* to recede. A "devil may care" attitude sets in. Now nothing bothers him. A lovely physical tingling of the fingertips and a warming sensation in the belly make everything seem okay.

My good friend, Dr. Green, used to argue by the hour with his medical colleagues about this simple answer to the question, "Why do people drink?" There is no deep, involved explanation. He stated the fact simply, "We drink because it makes us feel good."

What is this magic elixir of life that gives us such a wonderful sense of well-being? Alcohol is a chemical, $C_{10}H_5OH$, composed of carbon, oxygen, and hydrogen. It is *not* a food. Therefore it does not blend with the other foodstuffs found in drinks such as beer. Beer is only 5 percent alcohol. The other 95 percent comes from grain and so forth.

Alcohol is burned up, or digested, by one organ of the body—the liver. And, unless the liver is damaged, it burns at a rather constant rate: three-fourths of an ounce an hour, the equivalent of 1> ounces of 100-proof whiskey. (One-hundred-proof whiskey is only one-half alcohol, and one-half water.) We will refer to this phenomenon of oxidation of alcohol later.

What else is this mysterious stuff that makes us feel so good? Alcohol is also a solvent, an irritant, an antiseptic, and an anesthetic.

As a solvent, alcohol is contained in all cleaning fluids. It is the best solvent on earth. It has been known to remove stains from tables, to dissolve stomachs, paychecks, bankrolls, careers, marriages, families, and lives.

Most after-shave lotions contain alcohol. When you shave and scrape your skin, you'll notice a sting. That's the irritant quality. As an antiseptic, alcohol is used by nurses to purify an area of the body before injecting a needle.

You may recall in the Bible the parable of the poor man who fell among the thieves. A good Samaritan came along and treated his wounds with oil and wine. The wine, containing alcohol, was used as an antiseptic, and the oil was used as a soothing balm.

For centuries alcohol was the only anesthetic that people had. But it is a very poor anesthetic, as we will find out later. Chemically, in its drinkable form, alcohol is a sedative drug and alcoholism is addiction to it.

What Is Addiction? Now let's examine the word *addiction.* What is it? It is a mystery of mysteries. We have only a descriptive definition, which means that we have to look and describe what we see. We see two outstanding characteristics in addicts: *compulsion* and *progression.*

Locked into a compulsive pattern, the alcoholic, like other addicts, drinks against his will. He drinks because he can't *not* drink. In the fellowship of Alcoholics Anonymous there's a saying, "It's the first drink that gets you drunk." It doesn't *make* you drunk, but it sets up the *compulsion* to drink more to get you there. And so, compulsive use is the main characteristic of all addictions.

Second, *progression.* For the rest of the alcoholic's life, as long as he drinks, the disease gets worse, never better. Once he has it, it is always there. There is no cure. If he has been sober for any length of time and then begins to drink again, he will be much worse off than before. The disease is progressive. It simply gets worse from beginning to end. More about that later.

How's Alcohol Like Ether? Let's go back to the statement that alcohol is a sedative drug. Doc Green demonstrated this characteristic of alcohol by the strategy of comparison: If you know something I *don't* know and you wish to communicate it to me, compare it with something I *do* know. A mother tries to explain to her child what a zebra is: "It's like a horse but it has stripes." The child immediately knows. And so, Dr. Green showed that alcohol is a sedative drug by comparing its action with that of another sedative drug: ether. Ether interferes with the oxygen supply to the brain and puts the patient to sleep. Alcohol, like ether, sedates the brain.

Now the brain is an organ composed of parts that control body functions: intellect; emotion; motor activity; semivoluntary functions like the blinking of your eye; purely involuntary functions like those of your intestines and stomach; and then the most protected part of your brain; the vital functions of heartbeat and breathing. During the anesthetizing of a hospital patient, the brain is sedated in the same manner as the houselights in a theater are gradually dimmed.

Let's anesthetize an adult patient with ether. A normal person is one who functions according to the formula: I/E. *Intellect* predominates over *Emotion* . . . in a normal person.

But let's see what happens when we add D for drug to that formula. First of all, upon inhaling the ether, the patient begins to feel a dryness in his throat because it is *only* absorbent of moisture and dries out the mucous membranes of the throat. He experiences a vague sense of suffocation, followed immediately by a wonderful feeling of euphoria. He feels as if he is leaving his body. He's in a state of suspended animation. He's in Valhalla. This is because reason has been deadened. The part of the brain which controls the intellect is going to sleep. The anxiety of the surgery simply disappears. He could care less what the surgeon removes.

The formula has changed to I/E except after D. Add the drug, knock out the intellect, liberate the emotions, and the formula reverses: E/I.

Now our patient enters the excitement stage very quickly. Your reading about it takes longer than it actually happens. However, if we were to stop the process during the excitement stage, remove the patient from the table, and force him to walk over to the other side of the room, he would collapse. His intellect, emotions, and motor activity are severely affected. That is one reason why a sheet is wrapped tightly around him, why he is closely watched, and why he is taken through these stages as quickly as possible. He may or may not be nauseous. Usually the process is too rapid for nausea to occur.

Now his semivoluntary functions are deadened, and he reaches a state of pre-anesthesia, which is a little more than simple unconsciousness. He still can't be cut with a knife until his involuntary functions have been deadened. When that happens, he reaches a "stage of anesthesia," falling into a comatose state, which leaves him with only his vital organs functioning. If they go, so does he.

Coming out of the anesthetized state, he goes through the same process in reverse: from anesthesia to pre-anesthesia to excitement to nausea to normalcy. That is why he is given morphine to alleviate the symptoms and to keep him from harming himself during the excitement stage. Obviously, there will be no euphoria.

Alcohol Progression. We have gone through this little lesson on ether to show you the *identical* parallel of the action of alcohol. If alcohol is processed by the liver at the rate of three-fourths of an ounce an hour, what happens when our normal adult drinks eight or nine of these shots an hour? Well, his liver gets *one* and the rest go into his bloodstream to wait their turn. When his blood brings the alcohol to the brain, the alcohol begins to sedate the brain. His movements are unsteady, his eyes blink slowly, and his tongue becomes thick when he tries to talk. He may stagger, or fall, as his motor functions are deadened.

His emotions are drugged, too, and he may get raucous and loud. If he is normally shy, he may begin to tell jokes, and so forth. His sense of judgment is affected, and he may suggest doing crazy things, like flying to Philadelphia for a cup of coffee at 2:00 A.M.

What happens when the alcohol gets to the brain? It begins to sedate it, and the first part that goes is *reason.* The second part is the *emotions.* The third part that is drugged and sedated is the *motor activity.* While the emotions are predominate, he may or may not get sick. So it's *I* over *E* except after *A. A* for alcohol. Add alcohol, knock out intellect (or judgment), and the emotions come out.

Only they come out *drugged: E/I.* The crazies. This display of drugged emotions is one of the reasons that people think alcohol is a stimulant, but they're wrong. What most people do not know is that we go through an excitement stage in the very process of going to sleep.

Once his automatic functions are deadened, our boy is unconscious. He has *passed out,* not blacked out. But alcohol is a very poor anesthetic because it comes in liquid form and has to be swallowed. Once the drinker has passed out, he cannot swallow any more.

How then does alcohol kill? It rarely kills by overdosing, because one must drink to the point of sedating his *entire* brain and stopping the functions of his vital organs.

Usually alcohol kills indirectly through the occupational hazards of the serious drinker: cirrhosis of the liver, bad gastrointestinal or respiratory problems.

It kills by the ton on the highways. It kills in other accidents, usually around the home, in the bathroom. It kills in the most ignominious way of all, when the alcoholic, with his brain heavily drugged, falling asleep on his back, regurgitates a bit of food and chokes to death on his own vomit.

The paradoxes of alcohol are many. It's a liquid that dries out the throat. It's an irritant that burns all the way down. It's a sedative that seems to stimulate. And it's an anesthetic, but a poor one.

Coming out of it, our boy goes through the same processes in reverse, just like the ether trip, as mentioned before. He goes from pre-anesthesia to the excitement stage, and on up into the hangover symptoms of sickness, vomiting, shaking, and so forth. One thing is for sure: there will be *no euphoria* on the reverse trip. When alcohol oxidizes, it breaks up into poisons, and these toxins make him feel sick.

Just for fun, let's look at two people: one, an alcoholic named Charlie and the other, his nonalcoholic Aunt Mabel. Charlie takes his Aunt Mabel to a New Year's Eve party, makes a beeline for the bar, and proceeds to drink compulsively. He burns his throat, begins to feel good, and goes through the predictable personality changes. For a while, he is the life of the party. Then he turns a little bit nasty. When somebody calls him on his behavior, he cries in his beer and passes out. Now if we get Charlie to bed, he will probably wake up a few hours later, shaking and hung over, and reach for a bottle under the bed to drink three or four ounces, so he doesn't commit suicide when he shaves.

What is Aunt Mabel doing all this time? Well, she is *not drinking*. That's what she's doing. She is disgraced by her nephew's behavior. She doesn't understand his compulsion. *She* has control and she exercises it. In fact, she doesn't drink at all because he does. So they give Mabel a "screwdriver," telling her it's orange juice. Halfway through the drink she has a silly grin on her face and her foot is tapping time to the music. She is in a rather jocose stage of excitement. At the end of her drink Mabel suddenly quits talking, closes her eyes, and falls asleep. The next morning Mabel doesn't even know she's had a drink.

That's the difference between the Charlies and the Mabels of the world.

What is alcoholism? Sometimes it is called Jellinek's Disease, after the man who cataloged its various symptoms. A disease is a malady that manifests itself through a set of symptoms which we call a "syndrome." The very basic characteristics of all alcoholics is that they drink too much. But what is "too much"? "Too much" is the amount of booze that causes problems. When something causes trouble, that "something" *is* the trouble. When one's drinking causes trouble, then the trouble *is* the drinking. I call it alcoholism.

Here are the signs and the symptoms of this disease:

1. The first sign is the one previously mentioned, *excessive drinking*. This doesn't mean that every time the alcoholic drinks he gets

drunk. It simply means that every time he sets out to drink, he usually drinks more than he intends to. I once heard a man say, "When I take a drink, I cannot guarantee my subsequent behavior." That is a *perfect* definition of compulsive drinking, even if the subsequent behavior is drinking more than he intends.

2. An alcoholic is one *whose drinking causes trouble to others.* The people around him discuss his drinking. They are concerned about him. "Where there's smoke, there's fire." People do not discuss non-problems.

3. *An alcoholic has blackouts.* A blackout is a present condition of being unable to recall something done while intoxicated. But during the blacked-out action he was fuzzily aware of what he was doing.

4. *The alcoholic gulps and sneaks drinks.* Normal drinkers *do not do this.* They have no reason to. The alcoholic gulps his drink to get a quick "high," and sneaks his drinks so you won't see him.

5. *The alcoholic loses control.* He sets out to drink a certain amount and then stop. He has not only promised those close to him that he won't disgrace them again, but he has promised *himself,* too. But he goes ahead and rips it anyway. Compulsive behavior forces him to drink more than he intended.

6. *The alcoholic has an alibi system.* He is just as concerned about why he overdrank as you are, but he doesn't know why he did. So, in order to justify his drinking and to make the unreasonable reasonable, he comes up with weird explanations of why he drank. Now an alibi is an unreasonable reason for doing something. He drank because it rained, or because it didn't rain. He drank because his team lost, or because his team won; because he's happy or sad; because his wife nags; because of his job; because it's the dog's birthday; whatever.

7. *An alcoholic needs an eye-opener.* He is desperate for a drink after a period of deprivation. Most eye-openers occur in the morning because the period of deprivation has been the hours that he slept. Notice that I did not call this "the morning drink." This disease does not depend on the clock. Usually after a prolonged period of deprivation, the very cells of his body cry out for the drug without which he cannot function. So he takes another drink.

8. *The alcoholic drinks alone.* He doesn't want anyone to know that he drinks as much as he does, and as often as he does, so he tries to drink where no one can see him.

9. *The alcoholic changes his drinking patterns.* People are talking about him, are concerned about him. *He's* concerned about himself. So, in an attempt to do something about it, he tries switching beverages. But, always, it is from one alcoholic beverage to another alcoholic beverage; never to a nonalcoholic drink. He switches from bourbon to scotch, from scotch to rye, from rye to vodka. Some switch from the hard stuff to the soft stuff, from whiskey to beer. Can someone be a "beer alcoholic"? That's an easy answer: the addiction is to alcohol, not the clothing it wears. The only difference between a "beer alcoholic" and a "whiskey alcoholic," is that the beer alcoholic has to drink more beer in order to get his quota of alcohol.

10. *Antisocial behavior is an outstanding characteristic of the alcoholic.* You've heard it said of him, "He's a wonderful fellow *when he's sober*." His antisocial behavior has repercussions on others, too. He suffers a loss of friends, loss of jobs, loss of families after greatly damaging them, and so forth. Friends can be lost if one doesn't bathe; jobs can be lost if one doesn't show up; and families disintegrate for many reasons. Friends don't want the family around because the family includes the alcoholic. *He* always causes trouble, so don't ask his family.

11. *The alcoholic has job trouble.* Absenteeism and poor production result in the loss of a job, even a career. Families are completely damaged, as the members who live with the alcoholic become as spiritually, mentally, emotionally, and sometimes physically damaged, or more so, as the alcoholic.

12. The alcoholic makes the rounds of doctors and hospitals. Normal drinkers don't usually go to the hospital after a beer with a pizza. The alcoholic drinks so excessively as to do harm to his body, and he begins to go to the doctor for his nerves, his stomach, his head, and so forth. Sometimes he's hospitalized and has to be detoxed over a period of time.

13. The alcoholic enters the stage of benders and binges. Many an alcoholic has been warned, "You have cirrhosis, and if you drink again, you will surely die." And so, with the fear of death hanging over him, plus the horrible fear of withdrawal symptoms, he quits for a while. But, no matter how long the alcoholic stays sober, if he goes back to drinking, it will always be worse with him within a relatively short time. It has been said:

At the punch bowl's brink
Let the thirsty think

What they say in Japan:
"First the man takes a drink,
And the drink takes a drink,
And the drink takes the man."
EDWARD R. SILL

Let's consider the phenomenon of progression. If an alcoholic drinks after a prolonged stretch of sobriety, he does not pick up where he left off; he picks up where he would have been had he been drinking all that time. Over the centuries this fact has been proven by hundreds of thousands of men and women who have tried to drink again after a period of sobriety. It has *never* succeeded.

14. *Tremors.* The inner shakes that would make a man walk through fire for an ounce of alcohol is indicative of a cellular craving for alcohol without which he cannot operate. Now he *must* protect the supply. Keep the line of supply open. Hide the bottle. Pay the bartender. Pay the liquor store first. Hang onto the job above all else to get the money to buy the booze. These are the top priorities in the life of an alcoholic.

15. *He gets unreasonable resentments.* His alibis have long since grown thin. And so, the alcoholic becomes terribly argumentative and irritable at home, whether he's aware of it or not. He has to instigate an argument in order to get angry, flounce out of the house, and get drunk. The family is totally baffled. His poor wife reports, "If I say *yes*, I'm wrong; if I say *no*, I'm wrong." The whole family thinks they're going crazy—and they are.

16. *He has nameless fears and anxieties.* The alcoholic is scared to death and he doesn't know why. He *lives* in fear. He reeks of fear. He hates to hear the phone ring or a knock at the door. He's afraid and he doesn't know what he's afraid of. If he's lucky, he will come to the end of his alibi system. Usually death occurs before this happens. The alcoholic's mind is so topsy-turvy with complete misconceptions of reality about himself and his problem, that he doesn't even see that he has one. He has just about come to the end of his string.

And so, unless someone gets him into treatment, or guides him into A.A., he usually dies before he recognizes what any five-year-old can see: *drinking alcohol is his problem.*

Decision Time. First things first. The alcoholic *must* come to the end of his alibis if he is to live. Until he reaches a "moment of truth," all other problems will remain. Unlike the bullfighter who faces death, the alcoholic must face life. And so he comes to a fork in the road; he can either give in to his addiction and end up in jail, insane, or dead, *or* he can give in to the proper therapy and live. The primary therapy for alcoholism is A.A.—Alcoholics Anonymous, a twelve-step ladder out of the pit of despair.

The moment of decision: "I didn't drink last night because it rained or didn't rain; I don't know what the weather was like. My team neither won nor lost; they didn't play. Her big mouth is gone; she divorced me. The dog is dead. I didn't intend to drink and I got drunk. *I have a drinking problem.*"

Now if we wait until the alcoholic gets to this point all by himself, we're liable to attend his funeral before he does. Now is the perfectly plausible time to approach the alcoholic, to have a confrontation, an intervention, and to force him into treatment.

Another myth is that no one can help an alcoholic *until and unless he wants it.* Not true. An alcoholic can be forced into treatment if one has the authority to do it; however, *he can't be forced to respond to it.* But I submit that we must give the alcoholic something to respond to, so that at least he has something to accept or reject. The old adage says, "You can lead a horse to water but you can't make him drink." I know that. But you can lead a horse to water and make him thirsty.

Most sick people want to be well, especially if you tell them *how.* Most alcoholics, when they learn that they have a disease, when they find out that they are sick, rather than evil, consider it the greatest thing that has ever been done *for them.* A.A. states it simply: "I can't handle it; God can; I think I'll let Him."

Complete Overhaul. Now the alcoholic, sober in A.A., begins a complete overhaul of his personality. He begins to work on himself in order to reconstruct a shattered life. He takes an inventory of himself and openly admits his wrongs in order to resolve guilt. He becomes willing to clean up his life, and then he asks God's help in doing so. He makes up his mind to become willing to adjust himself to his fellowman, and he gets ready to make amends for past wrongs. Then he does it. He continues to take an inventory of his life, so there are no new beginnings of bad things. Through prayer, he deepens his conscious contact with the God who gave him his sobriety.

And then, with his humanity restored through freedom from the bottle, he sets out to help fellow alcoholics, in order that he might remain sober.

Alcoholics Anonymous came into being because a sober alcoholic met with a drinking alcoholic. It is erroneous for people to wait until an alcoholic asks for help before offering it. A.A. did not begin that way. Dr. Bob, the drunk, did not call upon Bill W., the sober alcoholic. It was the other way around.

Part II: Effect on the Family

Families become sick. Whole families become sick. Whole families need to get well, and that is impossible in a home where the ability to love has been damaged.

The alcoholic can't love because he's not free. He is shackled to self by the very chemistry of his disease. His desire to love and to be loved comes out as sentimental, at best, and perverted, at worst. The most sacred affair, the sexual relationship between a husband and wife, is deeply damaged. It doesn't take too many years of being forced to go to bed with a drunk, before sex for the spouse becomes abhorrent. Children learn from parents about sex—not the techniques but attitudes toward it. Children are neither blind, nor deaf, nor stupid. They grow up and bring to their own marriages what they have been taught in their own homes.

The phenomena of infidelity, incest, wife abuse, child abuse, husband abuse, emotional battering, dishonesty, and spiritual damage are meticulously learned in alcoholic households.

How can any woman who learns that her husband has been unfaithful, who has her own love thrown back in her face, who is humiliated and beaten down, remain emotionally stable?

It is impossible for a child to be normal when his drunken parent uses sarcasm and humiliation because he doesn't lead his class. That parent is oblivious when one of his children becomes a recluse; another takes the role of hero; another turns to alcohol or drugs; and rebellion toward all authority sets in. The behavior of a youth who gets in trouble with the law can be traced directly to the alcoholism of a parent or another family member. And, so, the repercussions within the family are most serious. My point is this: since whole families get sick, whole families need help to recover.

Part III: How to Help the Alcoholic

How does one go about getting well from this most horrible of all diseases? Let me share with you, in this last part, a few guidelines for helping the alcoholic. I believe that learning what is involved is at the heart of it all. We sideline observers begin by recognizing our attitudes, realizing that they are negative, and trying someway, somehow to change them.

The attitude is the father of the action. I normally treat people the way I feel about them. If I see someone who is behaving in a totally cruel, obnoxious, or horrible way, I will usually judge him accordingly—through his behavior. We don't have attitudes; they have us. I've often said if you want to prove that, try to change one. All of us have terribly negative and false attitudes toward the alcoholic. But, let's examine some of our attitudes toward a whole lot of aspects of this disease.

Our Attitudes Toward Alcohol and Alcoholism. How about *alcohol* itself? Many people have negative attitudes toward this inanimate liquid, and their behavior follows that attitude. They condemn a substance put on this earth by God. It is no more morally good or bad than dynamite or automobiles or sugar—or beds. It is an inanimate object, and yet there is no other object on earth about which there is such emotion. So horribly people have looked upon it, that they condemn it with such epithets as "devil's brew," "witches' potion," and so forth. They refer to it as "what it did to my father (or my mother, brother, sister, and so forth)." It is the only inanimate object on which we pass moral judgment. In fact, in one point in our country's history, we forbade its use.

Drinking. Some people look upon drinking as evil. If so, then those who feel that way have passed judgment on a great percentage of the population of the earth. Many people, especially in European countries, drink alcoholic beverages with their meals. Is an old German farmer who has worked hard all his life going to hell because he drank a glass of beer with his lunch? Are priests and ministers who use wine in the very worship of God condemned to the fires of hell?

This is the phenomenon of attitude: If you are doing something beneath me, then *you are.*

Now most of us don't *want* to be that way, but we *are built* that way. It is all very well to say, "I judge the sin, but not the sinner; the act, but not the actor; the deed, but not the doer." But the truth is that we judge *people*—you and I do—and we judge them through their behavior. If we think their behavior is immoral, then they are. Many drinkers are condemned by nondrinkers.

What about *drunkenness?* There are two kinds. One is the result of alcoholism, which the victim cannot help. The other is the result of free choice, called alcohol abuse. When I see a drunk, do I even wonder what kind he might be? Or do I simply condemn? The difference between the abuser and the alcoholic is this: the abuser usually gets giggled at and thereby approved, while the alcoholic who shows up drunk at his mother's funeral is condemned.

What is our attitude toward *alcoholism?* Is it really a disease? Are these actually sick people? The American Medical Association defined alcoholism as a disease in 1956—and so it is.

Have the Proper Attitude. Now I have to have the proper attitude toward the alcoholic if I am going to help him. This is so obvious. I can't help someone who knows that I despise him. And every alcoholic, conscious or unconscious, truly knows in the depths of his soul whether you care or whether you condemn. Don't *you* know when people like you? Don't you know when people dislike you? Attitudes are the basis for the success or failure in treating desperately sick people and their families. Therefore, I must learn a little bit about this disease in order to understand it, so that my attitudes might be correct.

Learn the Symptoms. The next guideline is this: *learn to recognize the disease through a knowledge of its symptoms.* It's astounding how we will read up on any disease that we feel a family member might have—*except* alcoholism. We would contact a doctor in ten seconds if we thought our child had multiple sclerosis, but we can live with an alcoholic for years and never bother to read a syllable about it.

How in the world can we get to know about alcoholism? First of all, through the marvelous literature that is available, especially A.A. literature. It's the finest on earth. Their pamphlets are brief; they are free; and they are written by people *who have been there.*

We are invited to seminars, workshops, or public lectures that are sponsored by local councils on alcoholism. Many times we stay away because we don't want to be seen at such affairs because someone might think *we* have the disease.

But the best place of all to learn about alcoholism and its symptoms is where those who have the disease are, from the alcoholics themselves. In A.A. you may attend an "open meeting," so called because they are just that. They are open to families, friends, and the public in general—anyone who is interested in learning. I've often said, "If you want to know anything about anything, ask the man who owns one." And if you want to know about alcoholism, go to where the alcoholics are—to open A.A. meetings.

It's easy to diagnose alcoholism in someone who is dying of it, but how do we spot it in the beginning? Well, there are many indications, but the biggest is *lying about one's drinking.* If you know someone who lies about his drinking, then you know an alcoholic. We come to learn, from those who have it, that it is a compulsion. It is an addiction. And willpower is *not* the answer—proper therapy is. We must become convinced that the alcoholic is drinking because he *can't not drink*.

Therefore, the fourth suggestion is, having straightened out my attitudes; having seen that this really is a disease and that the person who has it is dying; having learned to recognize the disease in a family member, or in a friend, or even in oneself; knowing that the disease is an addiction, and that the alcoholic has little with which to help himself; we try as best we can *to confront the alcoholic with the fact of his illness.* We don't stop there but we suggest *where* he might get help and offer to go with him to get it. *Getting Help.* The best help is proper treatment, and there are treatment centers all over our country in which an alcoholic can learn the nature of what's wrong with him; an education about and an introduction into Alcoholics Anonymous—the primary therapy for it.

Confrontation is best done by someone in authority: a parent to child; employer to employee; spouse to spouse. Many spouses have great power over an alcoholic spouse by saying, "Get well or I'm gone." People wish to hang on to their marriages, their jobs, their families, and if proper authority, strength, and clout are exerted, it may be that the alcoholic might respond and get help.

Next I would suggest that we use all of the resources at our command. There are many treatment centers. The good ones will orient the alcoholic into A.A. He can go straight from the treatment center into his local A.A. meetings.

Help for the Family. Al-Anon is the place family members need to go for help. In Al-Anon they will find others who have gone through or are going through the same thing they have.

MOST PROBLEM DRINKERS CAN BE FORCED INTO TREATMENT BY THE PRESSURES OF THEIR FAMILIES, SWEETHEARTS, OR EMPLOYERS.

We muster all the help we can to get the alcoholic to face the fact of his disease and to get him into treatment. We must realize that it is a family disease and that the family members should get help along with the alcoholic. I believe that people can help people, and I believe that, like all of the so-called self-help groups in which ordinary people share with other ordinary people their own experiences, they can help others get well along with themselves.

Don't Be Discouraged. As a final note, I would most strongly suggest that one never ever become discouraged at an alcoholic's repeated failures or even his death. I believe most strongly that no alcoholic who dies drunk dies in vain. I believe that by dying, they have helped to buy life for alcoholics who do recover here on this earth. Never, never give up hope. Keep praying for them. Pray for them the same way you would pray for those with heart attacks, cancer, or any other disease.

The fact is that many, many people die from alcoholism. You might say, "What a waste." And it *is* a waste. But, nonetheless, it is a disease, it is terminal, and some will die from it. But we must never become discouraged because they died *that way,* rather than in another way. I never look upon an alcoholic who dies drunk except with a prayer.

There is great hope in this world of alcoholism. *Most people who get proper treatment respond to it and get well.* Alcoholism has a much higher rate of recovery than many, many diseases. So, we must *never* lose hope. We must always pray for the alcoholic, hoping that he might respond to the grace of God—offered through the hands of men—and get well.

We cannot live without pain. To live is to hurt. This lovely poem, by Dorothy Nell McDonald, a lady I would dearly love to meet, came to me on a birthday card many years ago, and it was so incredibly beautiful, I memorized it. It holds up a blessed hope for today:

> *I do not wish you joy without a sorrow,*
> *Nor endless day without the healing dark,*
> *Nor brilliant sun without the restful shadow,*
> *Nor tides that never turn against your bark.*
> *I wish you faith and strength and love and wisdom,*
> *Goods, gold enough to help some needy one.*
> *I wish you songs but also blessed silence,*
> *And God's sweet peace when every day is done.*

Father Joseph C. Martin
P.O. Box 240
Havre de Grace, MD 21078
301-273-6600

Thank you, Father Joe, for your valuable contribution to this book. May God continue to bless you, as you keep up your great work of helping alcoholics to get well.

9
Alcohol, Antabuse, and LSD

Baltimore, Maryland, 1953

"Isn't there *some* way I can help Andy to stop drinking, Hal?" Usually a cool, self-sufficient, sophisticated socialite, Andy's wife sounded desperate over the telephone.

"Sure, Sophia. There are lots of ways to help alcohol abusers to control their drinking. The trouble with most programs is that they use other drugs to control alcohol, which is itself a heavy drug. It doesn't work too well that way. You're just trading addictions.

"The only program we know of that stresses total abstinence from all drugs is Alcoholics Anonymous. They tell us that instead of drugs, capsules, or cocktails, they rely on a Power greater than themselves. Their membership of over a million nondrinkers is really impressive, isn't it?"

There was a long silence.

"Andy and I are active church members, Hal. If religion was the answer, he would have been sober long ago. Besides, Andy's best friend tried A.A., and it didn't work. He still drinks."

After a pause she continued, "I'm more interested in something our friend, Dr. Pillpusher suggested, a wonder drug called Antabuse. Surely medical science knows more than *those* A.A. people. But I appreciate your help, Hal. Thanks, anyway."

There it was again, confusing religion with reality. Thinking that a church building or denominational label can cope with alcohol addiction. Pew Piety versus a personal Higher Power.

In one respect she was right. Alcoholics Anonymous doesn't work for everybody—*only for those who want it!*

Like lots of others who depend on their EIB (Educated Idiot Box—read *How to Live Like a King's Kid*), Sophia preferred a godless way of controlling her husband's drinking. I still recall with horror the disastrous results of that decision.

What is Antabuse, and how does it work?

In the early fifties, a so-called wonder drug called Antabuse appeared on the drug scene. This chemical, when combined with alcohol, produced a psychical reaction so violent and ghastly that the drinker would supposedly stay away from alcohol forever out of **sheer terror.**

Here's the Master Plan in essence, as reported by those who survived it:

1. The patient is given a dose of Antabuse.
2. After the Antabuse has begun to do its thing, a generous portion of booze is added. Then this scenario sets in.
3. Patient turns beet-red, eyes bug out, breathing becomes labored, pulse rate skyrockets, panic takes over, and total *yuk* results.
4. At this point, oxygen inhalation may be needed to restore the victim to the land of the living.
5. When all body systems have (hopefully) been restored to GO, the terrified patient is instructed along these lines: "Now, good buddy, if you ever take a drink on top of your pill, you can expect either to die an excruciating death or go insane with brain burnout."

That's what Dr. Pillpusher told Andy after his grueling grog-proofing ordeal.

While sounding like a winner, this plan contains a number of built-in failure factors.

1. It overlooks the irrational, insane thinking and reasoning of the victim of alcoholism.
2. It ignores the overpowering obsession for "just one more," which no one but an alcoholic understands.
3. It relies on fear to keep the alcoholics sober.

If *fear* were effective in keeping drinkers sober, most of us would have quit long ago. Even a few of our hair-raising experiences would have done it. No, it doesn't work that way.

Driven by compulsion, the alcohol addict forgets the desperation and humiliation of even a few hours ago. His insane reasoning tells him, "You can take it or leave it and anyhow, next time will be different."

Now picture the alcoholic "on the pill" and thirsting for his favorite brew. Based on his irrational behavior in the past, do you expect him to "take his pill like a nice little drunk" and stay away from alcohol, just because it might kill him?

That's hardly realistic, is it? That may be Hollywood's version, but in real life, here's what happens.

First, the alcoholic, if at all rational, will quit taking the pill for at least two weeks, until all Antabuse residue leaves his system. Statistics show that this method works better than the obvious alternative.

Next, the not-so-rational method is the one chosen by Andy to his everlasting detriment.

Soon after his deboozing episode, I saw Andy coming out of a liquor store. The telltale, brown-paper sack under his arm matched the guilty look on his face.

"Planning on taking a little toddy for the body?" I inquired.

"As a matter of fact, that is exactly what I'm going to do," he replied defensively. "Why don't you join me? A few drinks will do you good. No one will ever know about it."

"Oh, they'd know, all right, when they saw me laid out in the funeral parlor. And it wouldn't be from guzzling too much iced tea," I assured him. "But you go right ahead and drown your pill with port. If you make it through the night, give me a ring. If I can help, don't hesitate."

"You sound like my doctor. You're both crazy, and I'll prove it. I'm going home, pour two glasses of chilled, red wine for Sophia and myself, and watch 'Masterpiece Theatre.' Henry the Eighth is back."

As he walked away, a cold chill ran through my innards. I had seen others try Andy's plan. It hadn't worked very well.

"Don't do it, Andy!" I called after him, "Antabuse is a new drug. No one knows for sure. . . ."

But he was gone.

No one knows all the side effects of most drugs, including Antabuse. That's the real hazard with them all—the side effects. Sometimes they are stated in fine print on the bottle, sometimes not. They are the unknown factors responsible for many cross-addictive deaths.

About midnight the jangling phone awakened me. It was Sophia. She was frantic.

"Hal, come quickly! Something terrible is happening to Andy. He wants to see you. Please hurry."

"Lord, help Andy," I prayed, as I drove the ten miles to his home. "If he drank that bottle of wine on top of Antabuse, he could be in real trouble."

He had, and he was.

For the next hour, alcoholic convulsions racked his body and mind with deadly regularity. With each spasm, a little more life left his eyeballs. His usual alertness was slowly replaced by the blank, hideous stare of the demented.

Before we arrived at the hospital, Andy's mind had literally melted away.

It had taken only one hour for the combination of alcohol and Antabuse to reduce that highly skilled business executive to the level of a drooling, slobbering idiot. His brain had turned to jelly. **Jelly.**

That's what Dr. Pillpusher told Sophia, after looking inside Andy's head.

For the rest of his life, Andy sat in a wheelchair, staring into space, clad in diapers, incapable of controlling his body functions—one more victim of alcohol and "other drugs."

We repeat, *mixing alcohol and pills often produces a lethal combination.*

Many pill bottles carry this important warning, often overlooked or ignored, with disastrous results:

MAY BE DANGEROUS OR FATAL IF TAKEN WITH ALCOHOL

"Are you authors condemning the use of all drugs by drinkers?" someone is asking.

Please understand that we are in no way attempting to manage, manipulate, control, or condemn anyone in any way. We do hope to influence your thinking by presenting these facts you should know about alcohol and other drugs. That way you may help others to escape Andy's fate.

(P.S. Andy's story is *true*. Only the names were changed.)

It is important to remember that when two or more drugs are mixed, a totally different chemical "monster" is formed, the effects of which are usually unknown. For example, when alcohol and Librium are mixed, as drinkers with prescriptions often do, the drug that is formed is different from either ethanol alcohol or chlordiazepoxide hydrochloride (Librium). Their monster offspring is a killer, resulting in the recent death of a famous newsman.

How about LSD, or "acid," which was at one time given to patients at one of our state hospitals? A firsthand report follows.

But first, a final word about prescription drugs that are freely handed out to problem drinkers to soothe their fractured nerves. They often cause more damage than alcohol by itself. That's why so many patients in treatment centers are double or cross-addicted.

Alcoholics Anonymous, a completely drug-free program, presents no such hazards. It offers instead, a plan built around reliance on a Power greater than themselves for continuous, contented sobriety.

Don't forget! Many meetings of Alcoholics Anonymous are open to the public. Why not pay them a visit? We did, and were favorably impressed.

Now let's take a look at what LSD did to Bob and Frank, two really great guys. At least they were.

Bob and Frank were buddies. They drank together for many years. The day came when Bob's engineering degrees no longer impressed his boss. He was told, "Quit drinking, or you're out! You're a good man when you're sober, but that's not often enough."

Frank liked his foreman's job in a local shipyard. His boss also insisted he "shape up or ship out."

Both tried to quit drinking. They couldn't. So they consulted a psychiatrist who recommended the new "wonder drug," LSD, also known as "acid."

"It's so new we can't guarantee what it will do. If you're willing to be guinea pigs and sign this release, I'll check you into a hospital. Then we'll see what happens."

Bob and Frank were lovable little guys when sober. They got drunk every Saturday night and came home in a blackout. After throwing up on the dog, Bob passed out on the floor and slept it off. Frank pushed the wife and kids around, and collapsed on the living-room sofa. No real problem with booze. Just the early stages of alcohol addiction.

After their hospital trip they looked great and sounded even better. The so-called wonder drug LSD appeared to have beneficial results on its unsuspecting victims. This ghoulish experiment didn't seem bad at all. That came later.

Bob told me, "Hill, you don't know what you're missing, going to all those crazy Rummy Recovery meetings. Why don't you get on LSD? Man, I heard angel music, and I even saw God! He told me, 'Bob, you'll never drink again!' "

Frank's account was way out, too:

"All the saints I ever heard about were in a circle. They told me,

'Frank, now you have the real answer; you won't ever turn to alcohol again.' The heavenly music was so real. They all promised to pray for me. Boy, I'm never going to take another drink. I don't need all that A.A. stuff. See you later."

The night they took Bob to prison his wife wailed, "But it was all so real! God told him he would never drink again!"

And he didn't. But the voices in his head told him, "Bob, go rob the Last National Bank. That money belongs to you as much as it does to them."

I had to ask, "*Which* god told Bob to rob the bank?" Certainly not the God of A.A. He keeps His followers out of trouble.

As far as I know Bob is still serving his long-term sentence for bank robbery, armed assault, resisting arrest, and a few other baddies.

"But God was so real. When He told me to rob that bank, and all those angels agreed with Him; how could I say *no?* It's not the fault of LSD. I goofed somewhere."

Who goofed? The hospital which administered LSD? The doctor who "pushed" it? Or the victims who fell for it? What difference does all that make? At best, drugs are "iffy." At worst . . . ?

For more direct answers ask Bob in his prison cell, or Frank's distraught widow.

What happened to Frank? Thanks for the reminder.

A week after he left the hospital, we took a trip to Florida together. In glowing terms he told me all about the beautiful "life beyond" that LSD permitted him to see.

"Things that the normal vision cannot penetrate," he explained, his face animated with a strange, spooky-looking expression. "Why don't you wise up, Hill, and drop a little acid? Here, try some."

"Not today, thank you, Frank. I'll go with what I've got."

"Then I'll take a little myself."

At that time no one knew about LSD's "flashbacks" and "bum trips," which surfaced later.

Frank also excitedly assured me of his complete deliverance from alcohol. That was apparently true. He never drank again during his short stay on earth. But how can you evaluate "never again," when death interrupts?

One day Frank called me at my office. "Hill, I'm confused."

"What's wrong, old buddy? I thought LSD had all the answers."

"I thought so, too, but now I'm not sure."

"Why the sudden change, Frank?" I asked.

"Voices in my head are telling me to get a gun and shoot myself. Do you think I should?"

"Listen, Frank," I replied, "shooting yourself can become fatal in a hurry. Besides, you can get very bloody that way. Sit tight. I'll be right over!"

"You don't understand, Hill. When God tells me to do something, I have to do it! You don't want me to disobey God, do you?" He hung up.

When I arrived at his home a few minutes later, he was gone.

Later that night his wife told me about it between sobs.

"When I came home, Frank was lying on the floor. A gun was in his hand and a hole in his head. He left this note. Here, read it."

Here's what it said: GOD TOLD ME TO DO IT.

Is LSD the harmless drug some folks claim?

Ask Frank's widow what she thinks.

Both Bob and Frank "looked in on A.A." They agreed it wasn't for them.

"Too much God stuff," they agreed. Until tragedy hit, their wives were inclined to agree. Now they're not too sure.

An A.A. member told us their program lays it out like this:

"Without help it is too much for us. But there is One who has all power. That One is God. May you find Him now."

God's power has worked in our lives for many years longer than we drank, and that totaled over forty. It works for all who sincerely try. Maybe it's the answer for your drinking friends or relatives.

Substituting one drug for another only prolongs the day of reckoning. It also might do bad things to other good guys like Frank and Bob.

We prefer God's way. There are no "iffys" to worry about. And it's so easy to get into. You can do it right now. Just say as we did:

"Lord Jesus, I can't handle this problem any longer on my own. (State the problem.)——————————————. It's got me down. I admit I'm powerless over it. My life is completely unmanageable. I need help. If You can't do it, that makes two of us. I've tried and failed too many times. Right now I turn my life and will over to Your care. Please run it to suit Yourself. Maybe I'm not even sincere in asking You to do it. But You just go ahead and do it anyhow. Thank You, Lord. *Amen.*"

Report back in thirty days, and we'll send some King's Kids goodies to help you along your new Way in Jesus.

God bless you real *big.*

10

The
Great American Drug

Baltimore, Maryland, September 1975

"How about one more before you go, Hill?" It was the host plying me with a third piece of Black Forest cake. For a "gloppyholic" like me, refusing wasn't easy.

"One more won't hurt you," he persisted. My willpower shriveled. Once again the battle of the bulge was lost.

"You'd better take some with you for a quickie bedtime snack."

Losing on both counts, I began the hour's drive home from Bel Air, where we had celebrated Pete's birthday.

Soon the familiar drowsiness, which I had come to expect after eating sweets, came over me like a great, black blanket of depression.

I've done it again. Should have known better than to eat all that sweet stuff. My sugar reaction keeps getting worse. I'll have to learn to say no and mean it.

Like many recovering alcoholics, my system suffers from years of abuse and neglect. Sugar causes the insulin department to act up. Instead of being short on insulin production like a diabetic, we overdo it. This causes a fast burnout of all blood sugar. Exhaustion sets in. Emotions go haywire.

Too many times I had fallen asleep at the wheel after eating sweets. I usually stopped for a nap when a "spell" came on. But this was a short trip, and I decided to tough it out.

A blood analysis had showed I had hypoglycemia. That's not unusual among alcohol abusers. I had been without alcohol for many years but the sugar lows had gotten worse.

Around my middle was a huge roll of excess calories, frowned on by my doctor. He told me in a rather abrupt way, "Hill, if you don't shed it, we'll bury it, and you with it."

As I crawled into bed a feeling of tightness set in around my chest. *I shouldn't have eaten that third piece,* I groaned.

About an hour later, severe chest pains awakened me. An elephant seemed to be standing on my heart. An iron band gripped my chest. Every breath was a struggle.

"Lord," I prayed, "forgive me for mistreating this body temple again. I can't handle the craving for sweets, and You know it. I've failed again. Please make these pains go away."

Things got worse. The pain became unbearable. I fought for every breath, praising the Lord between clenched teeth.

"Lord Jesus," I prayed, "if You don't do something in the next five minutes, I'm finished. Whatever happens is Your business. I'm staying right here in bed."

Was I tempting God? No, just telling Him how I felt. No phony-baloney religious babble. Just honest reporting. Either He moved or I graduated.

Several spasms later all symptoms suddenly went away.

"Thank You, Jesus, for healing me." I immediately fell asleep.

Next morning as I continued to praise Jesus for healing me, He seemed to say, "Go for a checkup."

Years of experience had taught me to obey the "still, small voice of the Lord," so I went.

"Hill, I want you to go to the hospital right *now.*" It was the neighborhood doctor. I was still connected to his EKG machine.

"But I feel just fine. No pains at all."

Ignoring my comments he continued, "A bed will be waiting when you arrive. Now get going."

My week in the Cardiac Intensive Care Unit turned out to be a witnessing trip. My night nurse was newly saved and in need of Christian fellowship. The day nurse was seeking God's power in her life. The in-between nurse was listening. I had a good time, seeing Jesus meet those needs.

"Nothing wrong with you, Hill," the doctor reported the following

Friday. "Not even any ill effects. You're just plain lucky. Now go home and shed some of that blubber—and cut out the sweets."

For a few days I was careful to avoid everything containing sugar. I got a calorie chart and started counting the little beasts. But on Saturday night, at another "eating meeting," the sight of cake and ice cream was too much. Back came the craving, out went the willpower, and down the hatch went the cake. Three large gloppy pieces.

Just one won't hurt me, I rationalized. *Besides, I've been good all week. I deserve a little bonus gloppy.*

Whoever heard of stopping at one piece of vanilla layer cake, heavily festooned with ice cream? (Weight Watchers forgive me!) It's the first bite that triggers craving for more. That's how drugs act.

Then followed a near-fatal replay of the previous weekend.

I had barely gotten into bed when the familiar scenario began. Chest tightness—heavy pains—fighting for each breath. An elephant doing the Jumbo Rhumbo on my chest.

"Lord Jesus," I panicked, "here I am again, in real trouble. You healed me last week. Please do it again. Thank You very much." But He didn't. The pains got worse.

"Lord, I can't handle much more of this. If You don't do something within five minutes, I'll assume You want me to get medical help."

Why didn't Jesus handle it like the last time? I needed to learn an important lesson. It became clear in what followed.

Those five minutes were nearly my last on Planet Earth. What happened after that is vague. I dimly recall the ambulance ride, and the paramedics doing their thing. What a wonderfully efficient team they are. Praise God for them.

The admitting doctor, an old friend, quipped, "Hill, welcome to our modest quarters. Make yourself at home. Tea will be ready shortly."

Praise the Lord for that little touch of humor. I needed it. Things were going downhill fast.

"Doc, I think I'm leaving. Everything is going black."

"Hang in there, Hill, you're going to be okay."

That's all I remember until much later.

Then began an out-of-the-body experience. I had heard about them, but never expected to take part in one.

I was suddenly wide-awake, looking down at my body on the admitting table. I seemed suspended between this world and the next. Looking away,

I saw a distant city, brilliantly glowing like shimmering gold. Between me and it was a shining river.

Behind my right shoulder stood Jesus, waiting to escort me across. What did He look like? I don't know. But I knew if I turned suddenly, I would be eye to eye with Him. I didn't need eyeball proof to experience His loving presence.

I was in a holding pattern between life and *life,* with no real urge in either direction. It seemed that Prayer Power was causing a delaying action. I later learned that members of our Prayer Fellowship stayed on their knees for many hours. They made the difference.

From a great distance I heard Pastor Peter Vroom shouting, "Praise the Lord." He does that all the time, with highly beneficial results. Another voice, that of my daughter, Linda, came on with, "Thank You, Jesus."

Then, after a short blackout, I came back. Those two prayer warriors and the doctor were rejoicing. Jesus had permitted me to return for further Boot Camp Training. I believe that's what this life is all about.

Later Peter told me that when the gauges read STALLED, indicating that Hill's Graduation Day had arrived, they continued to praise God *anyhow.*

You can't argue with results. I'm still here!

What a marvelous experience, knowing that death holds no fear for a King's Kid who belongs to Jesus Christ.

One night during my stay in CICU, another spell came on. After the nurse had done her thing for me, she told me about a problem area of her life. We prayed about it and turned it over to Jesus. Another King's Kid was born into God's family.

Wherever we are is where we belong, on special assignment from God, if we are trusting Him to run our lives.

Romans 8:27 and 28 says so. Take time out to read those verses right now.

One night an alcoholic was brought in. It was his fifth trip to CICU due to alcohol abuse. After he sobered up, I told him how Jesus had taken over my alcohol problem. How He used Recovery Fellowship especially developed in heaven for problem drinkers like us. He got the message. That alone was worth the trip.

Otherwise nothing much happened that week. After a top to bottom checkup, I was released with a clean bill of health. Jesus had done it again, in His own unique way.

"Get rid of that fat or you'll be back," was the doctor's parting shot.

"That's like telling a gloppyholic like me to fly around the moon in shorts," I shot back at him. And it was, until I discovered the "Heaven's Hope for Heavies" weight-control method. Then I shed fifty pounds the "easy way." And it hasn't come back.

You too can slim down without dieting or fasting and stay there as I have for several years.

My book *How to Flip Your Flab Forever* tells all about it. (The prayer on page 51 is the secret.)

But I was still neglecting the source of my trouble, the Great American Drug. Why didn't God answer my prayer for healing? He did, but I stupidly dumped in more of the same poison and got sick all over again. Our body temples were not designed to handle the Great American Drug: *refined white sugar.*

Why doesn't God readjust my system so I *can* handle that deadly naked calorie?

Why would a loving God, who wants only the best for His children, fix our bodies to handle anything that bad? Sugar not only carries with it the demonic power of compulsion. It also robs the body of nutrients gained from real food. Calcium, needed for strong teeth and bones, is sucked up by the drug sugar. Teeth rot, bones become weak and brittle, and emotions turn yo-yo. The body chemistry goes out of balance in many directions. And dental bills get scary.

Why do we call sugar a *drug?* Because it fits the dictionary description. Here's how one dictionary defines *drug:*

Something that soothes, lulls, eases tension, and creates craving.

Sugar does all those things. It also quietly kills the addict. Under its narcotic effect, he insists he can quit but never does.

That's why sugar has been called the Great American Drug, the Number 1 Killer of humanity. It is more murderous than leaky nuclear reactors, opium, or radioactive fallout. Nearly every American home carries it, either in its deathly white crystal state or in food products. (Incidentally, Kool-Aid and many other soft drinks are loaded with it.) As with other drugs, the addict claims he can quit when he wants to, but rarely does.

If you are thinking, *That's crazy talk, I'm not hooked,* check yourself with this simple experiment.

Repeat these words out loud:

For the next thirty days I will cut out all sugar in every form. No more desserts, cookies, sweet buns, or chocolate peanut-butter ice cream. No more Kool-Aid. No more soft drinks containing sugar. No more chocolate, Cokes, or Pepsis. No more cake, pie, Jell-O, or jelly beans. That's my own decision. I can do it. I'll show them. I'll prove I'm not addicted to the Great American Drug. So there.

Scary, isn't it? Makes your gizzard shrivel, doesn't it? Makes you wish you'd skipped this chapter, doesn't it?

Get the message? Sure you do. You're hooked if you're feeling uncomfortable, guilty, threatened, or beginning to hate Hill for writing all this stuff.

Remember, I'm not criticizing, I understand. I was where you are. I *do* understand. I was hooked, with no way out.

How did I get free? It was simple. Just for one day at a time I quit eating sugar in any form. No desserts or sweets of any kind. And thanking Jesus for His grace to do it without too much discomfort. And He did.

Not only did the sugar-low stupor go away, so did those ugly rolls of flab, all fifty pounds of them. They haven't come back, and that's several years ago. One pound a week dropped off. I feel many years younger. Even after driving six hundred miles in a day and ministering in the evening, I'm never exhausted.

Our sugar research revealed some amazing facts.

Refined white sugar, when eaten by human beings, is *lethal.* It is a nonfood, containing only naked calories. It's worse than nothing. It drains and leeches from the body precious nutrients required to detoxify and eliminate it from the system. It ferments in the stomach, producing alcohol plus burps (which is carbon-dioxide gas resulting from fermentation). If consumed daily it creates a state of overacidity. More minerals are drained from the bones and teeth in an effort to correct the imbalance in the body chemistry. Finally, in an effort to protect the blood, the body surrenders so much calcium that rapid aging and "death pallor" appear. That's why sugarholics look dull and pasty.

Sugar also does terrible things to kids. To test that statement, try this simple experiment. You'll be amazed at the results.

Remove all sugar from their diet for thirty days. Don't be surprised if their hypertension, nervousness, short attention span, and emotional upheavals diminish or disappear. Try it and report back. Many have been amazed that anything so simple can work so well.

Yes, you'll have to put up with plenty of "mouth." Addicts don't like getting clean cold turkey. Be patient and pray. You'll like what happens. So will they.

What do we use for sweetening? Whole, unpasteurized, raw honey. It's a complete, nutritious food, not a naked calorie.

What about brown sugar? Most, if not all of it, is white sugar spiked with molasses.

"For lack of knowledge my people perish" is repeated in many places in the Bible. And I nearly did; but I'm ahead of my story.

Choosing to ignore the advice of others more knowledgeable about these things, I proceeded along the gloppy road of destruction. I was hooked on the Great American Drug—white sugar. Giving it up was too painful, so I didn't.

The climax came in Bradenton, Florida, at a Christian retreat. I was scheduled for a week of teaching on the power of the Holy Spirit.

I assured those hundreds of King's Kids that Jesus can break every bad habit by the power of His Holy Spirit.

"Ask Him to do it, and admit you can't handle it on your own. Right now let's turn it all over to Him and in your own words tell it like it is."

Thus ended the morning service. Those who were honest with God found real release.

Amazingly, I was not one of them. I was still handling the sugar problem by ignoring it. Before midnight I had once again faced death at the hands of the Great American Drug.

The dinner party was delightful, prepared from the finest ingredients by a gourmet cook. The hostess had spared no effort in creating our favorite dishes. Fruit cup, sugar-cured ham with sweet, raisin sauce, sweet potatoes with marshmallows. And to top it off was my favorite gloppy: Black Forest cake (apologies to members of Overeaters Anonymous!).

Returning to my room to prepare for the evening message, I collapsed into the nearest chair. Listless, exhausted, with head swimming and emotions roller coasting, I was a real mess.

Drugged? Undoubtedly. It had become almost a nightly occurrence. My fat-racked body was in torment. No, it wasn't alcohol. I had been drinkless for many years. Then what caused that physical and emotional wipeout?

The Great American Drug had struck again!

It had been sugar—sugar all the way. Once again I was in the bottomless pit of sugar-low stupor.

"Okay, Lord, that does it. Please forgive me once more for mistreating this body temple. By Your grace and power, I'm quitting this sugar trip permanently *one day at a time*. Now please fix me, so I can speak at the meeting. Thank You very much. *Amen.*"

After lying down for a few minutes, I felt better. By God's grace I struggled through the evening service. Short of breath, perspiring profusely, knees wobbly, I somehow finished my message.

Afterward someone escorted me to the dining hall for refreshments. Suddenly things went black. I collapsed on the floor. Someone shouted, "Call an ambulance, Hill has passed out."

The rest of the evening is a blur, punctuated by wailing sirens and paramedics doing their thing. What happened? My body chemistry had overreacted to the Great American Drug—sugar.

Home again and another trip to the CICU on doctor's orders. Heart symptoms are never taken lightly. That could be fatal. The result? Another healing from Dr. Jesus. He seemed to say, "Hill, it's up to you to decide. Either obey Me or die. Which is it?"

How would *you* have voted? Maybe you need to cast that vote *before* big trouble hits. Most folks don't walk away from CICU three times!

How is it now? By God's grace I've been clean from the Great American Drug for many years, except for an occasional planned lapse.

"Hill, you mean you backslide now and then, like *we* do?"

Yes, now and then I set out on a planned "gloppy slip," after asking Jesus to keep me from overdoing it.

For instance, on each visit to Switzerland, I really pig out on Black Forest cake. They claim it's the world's best. Who am I to argue!

The power of the Great American Drug has been broken by Jesus. I can literally "take it or leave it alone."

If you are having sugar trouble, try turning it over to Jesus, one day at a time. By staying away from the first bite, sip, lick or nibble, just for one day, you too can be free "as only the Son can make you free."

For further scary things you should know about the Great American Drug, we recommend you see the Suggested Reading List in the back of this book.

11
Nick O'Teen:
Drug or Demon?

(Hill's Tobacco Battle—1915–1955)

Have you given up trying to quit smoking? Have you tried a lot of methods that didn't work? Are you fed up with guilt trips and criticism? Do you wish your friends and fellow church members would get off your back?

Cheer up, there *is* an answer. Before you finish this chapter, you'll know how to get free from the whole mess.

Is it a new formula, diet, or penance to suffer through? No indeed. It's not another willpower trip, either. It has to do with *God* power. It's kept me smokeless since 1955.

God is no respecter of persons. What He did for me, He will do for you, for His Glory.

Nicotine has been called the "dirtiest, ugliest, most devastating, and most highly addictive" of all drugs. It's also the hardest to quit. At least it was for me.

At age ten I smoked my first cigarette. My last one smoked me at forty-eight. For thirty-eight years I had no choice. Nicotine robbed me of the right to choose. I was instantly and permanently hooked. I couldn't "not" smoke.

Few drugs have the power of such instant and permanent addiction.

Does the noxious weed called *tobacco* contain evil spirits? Do they live in the drug nicotine? We don't know, but we have some thoughts which we'll share as we go along.

Here's the record of my nicotine trip.

South Norwalk, Connecticut, July 4, 1915

My parents were violently opposed to the use of tobacco in any form, especially cigarettes. They called them "coffin nails" and "devil sticks." My dad was especially down on them.

"Real men never smoke those filthy things. If I ever catch you smoking one of them, I'll fix you so you'll wish you hadn't." Then he added, "Grandfather Hill would probably be alive today if he hadn't been a heavy smoker."

My dad had huge hands which, when applied to the "seat of learning" (my rear end), left a lasting impression. But a no-no always opens the door to temptation; it soon surfaced.

I decided one little puff on a cigarette couldn't hurt me. How to go about it was a problem. Uncle C. was the only smoker I knew. He kept his cigarettes in his pocket. It wouldn't be easy, but I planned to steal one next time he came for a visit.

Then my great moment came. Uncle C. stopped by at dinnertime. He had just lit a fresh one when my dad called, "Come and get it!" Flicking the still-burning cigarette over the porch rail, he hurried inside.

I made a dive for it, took two big puffs, choked, became violently ill, and was instantly hooked on nicotine.

Forty years later I was still trying to quit smoking. Each coughing spasm brought up more blood. Walking up three steps nearly did me in. Breathing was a struggle. I wasn't long for this world.

The final year of my nicotine battle was really rough. Certain that death from lung cancer was not many cartons away, I set out to quit "if it killed me." It nearly did.

By then I had met God personally. I had turned my life over to Jesus. He had completely removed my craving for alcohol; healed my disintegrated spinal disc; and baptized me in His Holy Spirit. (It's in *How to Live Like a King's Kid*.)

I had plenty of proof that God was in the miracle-working business. But my nicotine addiction didn't respond. The harder I tried to quit, the worse it got. Even the thought of stopping caused great waves of nausea, dizziness, light-headedness, and panic to flood my insides.

If you're trying to quit, I understand your battle, I've been there.

Chances are you'll never make it on your own. Without help it is too much for us. No other drug has the power to so dominate a person's will, life, and attitudes as the devil weed tobacco.

Why is it called "devil weed"? Because it came about through the curse God placed on Planet Earth after the Garden of Eden incident. That's when Adam goofed, ate the no-no fruit, and brought death to all of Creation.

Take time out right now to read about it in the Book of Genesis, chapter 3.

Get the picture? Thorns and thistles (verse 18) includes the weed tobacco, part of God's curse and Satan's favorite tool for harassing the human race.

One account says that when Christopher Columbus visited America in 1492, his sailors soon copied the Indian custom of smoking the peace pipe. In a short time, they found it difficult or impossible to get along without it. They carried tobacco seeds with them back to Europe, and wherever else they traveled. That's how the nicotine curse spread throughout the civilized world. Tobacco thus became the first American export and surely the deadliest.

At this point, I can hear someone shout, "If God is a good God, why does He allow people to smoke tobacco?"

For the same reason He allows people to say *no* to Jesus, refuse salvation, and end up in the bad place.

God gives everyone free will to choose which way to go.

Satan's plan is to steal our free will and bind us to a life-style not of our choosing. As Jesus said, "The thief comes to steal, to kill and to destroy, but I came that you might have life and that you might have it more abundantly" (*see* John 10:10).

Many times I had quit smoking, but always the craving was with me. I had no peace with it or without it. That's not only addiction, it's obsession—total preoccupation with the drug nicotine. God power, not willpower, is needed to win over Nick O'Teen, the tobacco monster.

I asked Jesus to set me free from the tobacco habit. Nothing happened. How come? Many people lost the desire for tobacco when Jesus saved them. He did that for me with alcohol but not with tobacco. He could have, but there was a lesson I needed to learn.

Many Christians crave tobacco long after they quit using it. Some fight it day and night. Don't be discouraged. There's a better way.

If Bible threats, guilt trips, and ridicule worked, my story would be different.

One pompous church elder came at me with a really neat idea.

"Brother, if God intended you to smoke He would have grown a chimney out the top of your head."

Another laid this one on me. "Brother, are you sure you're saved?"

"That's what you get for seeking help from a bunch of self-righteous hypocrites," Satan whispered in my ear. I agreed wholeheartedly. And my attitude got sicker.

"You're probably hiding sin, and God is not hearing your prayer," one of them snorted. That one launched me on a really bad guilt trip.

A quarter-ton evangelist wheezed, "Brother, you're not supposed to smoke up the temple of the Holy Spirit with all that garbage."

It was all doctrinally true. They had Bible for it—but no one offered to pray for me. I needed Christian love and acceptance, not guilt trips.

Maybe you've given up, feeling that no one really understands. I've been there. I know the feeling. But don't let the bad mouths get you down as I did. That only delays your deliverance.

They finally got to me. I turned bitter and resentful. I threw a gigantic pity party, took my martyr pills, and sang the "poor me" anthem to whosoever would listen.

Then I began to look for weaknesses in my critics. It didn't take long. Their religious self-denial life-style had broken out in gross obesity—just what I needed to hang on them. How I gloated.

At the Wednesday-night prayer service I was ready for them. The service began with their favorite theme song, directed straight at me, in E-flat:

> *We don't drink or smoke or chew,*
> *And we stay away from sinners who do.*

"Look at that herd of elephants," I fumed. "What a mess of flabbos, chubbos, hippos, and blimpos. They couldn't fall if you pushed them. They'd just roll like a bunch of rotten eggs."

Can you identify with my feelings? That was only the beginning. Things went downhill fast, when they began calling me "Stinky Hill, our smelly brother."

"I'll show them I'm as holy as they are. I'll quit smoking if it kills me."

One year later it nearly had. From two packs a day, I was up to three. Real progress for the kingdom of darkness! I had fallen into Satan's trap, by taking my eyes off Jesus.

One day, Tom, a lab technician and deacon, showed me his collection of human parts, preserved in jars of alcohol.

"Hill, you smoke, don't you?" Not waiting for the obvious answer he continued, "Take a look at this mess in jar Number Ten. What does that look like?"

Eyeballing the greenish-brown, gloppy mess more closely, I replied, "Either a mashed buzzard or two pounds of spoiled sturgeon."

"Brother Hill, that's what's left of the lungs of Mr. What's-his-name who bequeathed his body to our lab for diagnostic purposes. See the holes and cancer-eaten areas? You'd better quit before it gets you too."

There it was again, another guilt trip. No one realized I couldn't quit. Self-knowledge, threats, promises, or even certain death have no mechanism capable of breaking the powers of drug addiction.

During this learning situation (that's what it turned out to be), I never stopped talking to Jesus about it. But I made the mistake of failing to listen for His response—like hanging up the phone in His face after entering my complaints!

I had forgotten that prayer is a two-way communication system, not a squall-and-run trip.

A year later both my attitude and habit were worse. Resentments, grudges, and unforgiveness gave me no peace.

One day as I asked Jesus for wisdom from on high, He brought to my attention something peculiar about the *pattern* of my smoking. It wasn't uniform as habits generally are.

From bedtime until after breakfast the next morning, I had no desire to smoke. Then for the rest of the day, until bedtime, I had no choice. The drug nicotine took over. I had no power to control it. I was totally hooked.

Throughout the day I was compelled to light one every fifteen minutes. Otherwise the shakes, dizziness, hyperventilation, and nausea wiped me out. Concentration became impossible. Often I found myself lighting one while another smoldered on my desk.

"Lord, I don't understand all this," I wailed. I need Your wisdom from above. Why does the craving stay away all night and come back after breakfast? Could it be demon power?"

One preacher said I needed deliverance from nicotine demons. He offered to cast them out. I didn't feel ready for that.

Without waiting for His answer, I continued, "Lord, whatever it is, I need power from on high to deal with it. It's killing me. Please give me power to quit this filthy habit."

In desperation I gave up, and for the first time listened for the Lord's answer. It came in that quiet inner voice of the Spirit.

"Hill, why do you want to quit smoking?"

"Lord, they're killing me."

"That's right, they are, but what's your real reason?"

Still not ready to be honest, I tried another angle.

"Lord, I'm the temple of Your Holy Spirit. I shouldn't pollute it with all this garbage."

"Yes, all that is true, but let's be honest for a change. I know your gut level motives, so you might as well come clean."

Wow! I was being a phony right in God's face, lying in my teeth to the great God of the Universe, thinking I was fooling *Him!*

"Okay, Lord," I answered. "You already know all about it, so I might as well be honest. I want to show those self-righteous church slobs that I'm as pure and holy as they are. That's my real motive."

Then I let it all hang out.

"Thank You, Lord Jesus, for putting up with my phoniness. Thank You for making things so clear by Your spirit of truth. I have no power in my will, even to desire or ask You to set me free from nicotine addiction. I'm so thoroughly hooked that doing without it is unthinkable. If it's up to me, I'll get up to ten packs a day, until the smoke starts coming out my ears.

"I can't face life without nicotine. That's all there is to it. In all honesty, I can't even ask You to do anything about it. The truth is, I enjoy every cancerous puff. I can't ask You to change it and really mean it. That would be another phony prayer. I've prayed enough of them. So I give up and dump the whole mess on You. Your Word says to cast all my cares on You because You care for me. I'm doing that right now. From now on, I'm going to enjoy every puff until You do something about it. Please take full charge of this whole mess. If I'm not sincere about all this, You just go ahead and do it anyhow. *Amen.*"

For one more week I smoked as much as ever. I refused all guilt trips from the "most holy brethren," who were still finger pointing.

One day I counted three cigarettes burning on my desk at one time.

"Lord, I'm sure glad that's Your problem and not mine. We've got a

real problem on Your hands. If You can't handle it, that makes two of us."
And He did.

One week later Jesus set me free from a lifetime of nicotine addiction.
Since 1955 I have been smokeless. Even the "reach" went away. Hard
candy and chewing gum, my former substitutes for smoking, were not
needed. Jesus did a thorough job when I applied the self-honesty or "surrender mode" of Matthew 5:3. It goes like this:

> *"Blessed are the poor in spirit: for theirs is the kingdom of heaven."*
>
> King James Version

Pleading poverty with God released His power; admitting my life was
unmanageable and that I was powerless to do anything about it, was the
key.

Once I asked Jesus for power to quit smoking, He taught me another
lesson.

"Hill, if I gave you power to quit smoking, you would soon become
Chief Pharisee and begin laying guilt trips on others less powerful. I'll not
give you power to become righteous, holy, sanctified, or wise. But I have
become all those things for you. Read My Word and you will realize it is
already yours."

And that's exactly what First Corinthians 1 says:

> *For he is made unto us wisdom, righteousness, sanctification and redemp-
> tion that as it is written if anyone glory, let him glory in the Lord.*
>
> *See* verses 1:30,31

God set me free by the method He prescribed for the demon-possessed
boy whom the disciples were unable to help. It's in Mark 9:17–29. Other
problem areas of our lives have responded to it.

Now PLEASE do not get nervous and tell folks that Brother Hill says all
smokers have demons. I'm doing no such thing. I'm telling you how Jesus
dealt with my own personal case.

Time out to read Mark 9:17–29.

This boy had suffered from demons since childhood. The disciples were
involved in the healing ministry. They certainly had prayed and laid hands
on him. Nothing happened.

"How come?" the boy's dad asked Jesus.

"This kind comes out only by prayer and fasting."

That's the prescription Jesus gave me. Three seventy-two hour fasts in a row. One each weekend for three weeks. It worked. I haven't had any desire or interest in tobacco in any form since 1955.

Remember, I'm not pushing a doctrine. This is my report on how the power of fasting can break habits of a lifetime.

We are told that abstinence and prayer are backbone principles of the Alcoholics Anonymous program. It translates into this simple Hill paraphrase for getting rid of old habits and hang-ups:

1. *Pray.*
2. Abstinence from (Stay away from) the first drink, snort, sniff, pill, shot, needle, dose, or nasty remark. Do it just *one day at a time*. You will be set free from whatever bugs you.

Try it and report back in ninety days. But make sure Jesus is in charge of your life and affairs. If you have any doubts, pray this prayer:

Lord Jesus, please come into my heart right now. Forgive my sins, cleanse me from all guilt, fear, doubt, and bondage to ———— [name your problem]. Take over my life and use it for Your own purposes. And if I'm not sincere about all that, please do it anyhow. Amen.

Now send a self-addressed, stamped envelope to us for your free copy of *A Trip Through the Bible in Twelve Months*. It also contains additional aforementioned goodies you will find helpful in everyday living. See the address in the back of the book.

FLASH...

Another theory about why cigarette smoking causes cancer

The September 10, 1984, issue of *Forbes* magazine, page 168, carried an article entitled "A Smoking Gun?"

It contained this scary report:

Some scientists are convinced that alpha radiation in cigarettes causes cancer. Can it be as simple as all that?

According to this source, Edward Martell at the National Center for Atmospheric Research in Boulder, Colorado, thinks so.

It further states that this hypothesis has been around since the early 1960s and divulges this sobering bit of information.

...Even one cigarette smoked indoors contains significant levels of radon 222, an invisible radioactive gas produced by uranium in the soil. ...
...One of these decay products, polonium 210, emits alpha radiation. ...
An alpha particle hitting a cell from a distance of less than a micron packs a wallop of about 20 to 30 times that of medical X rays.

It is also pointed out that the effect of this radioactivity in the bronchial forks amounts to about 8000 chest X rays for a person smoking a pack and a half a day for twenty years. Also, when the smoker coughs and swallows this throat garbage, cancer of the esophagus, stomach, and liver are possible.

There's lots more to cause serious thought about the effects of smoking and also to raise the question, "Why haven't we been told all these facts?"

We recommend that this article be read in its entirety.

Our purpose is not to put you on a guilt trip. *We want to be helpful.* If you're hooked and can't quit, remember I was, too, until I dumped the problem on Jesus Christ. That was nearly thirty years ago, and He still has it under control.

And now let's look on into Part II of this book and let Liz Rogers and her friends tell us how the female sector copes with alcohol and other drugs.

Part II

HERS

(From a Woman's Point of View)

by
Mary Elizabeth Rogers

12

How to
Lose Your Mind

Baltimore, Maryland, 1972

A fly buzzed around the hot, sticky classroom as twenty or so algebra-trig students tried to concentrate on the lesson.

"Today I shall prove De Moivre's theorem by using the method of mathematical induction," I began, holding on to the back of the desk chair to steady myself. With ears ringing and head pounding, I tried to ignore the dizziness, the hollowness, the unreality, and the terror that were mounting in gigantic waves.

Why was I so terribly frightened? I should be feeling better after my courageous decision three days ago to fire my shrink, throw away all the Librium and Valium, pour the liquor down the sink, and go on the wagon. But inside I felt insane, dead, numb, enraged, and hysterical—all at once.

I poured a cup of iced coffee from my thermos. Years ago I used coffee to steady my nerves: *Maybe it will work again,* I thought. My hands shook so badly, I could hardly pick up the cup.

"My God, I hope the students don't notice," I prayed.

I forced myself to continue: "Now we know that $[r(\cos\# + i\sin\#)]$ to the nth power equals. . . ."

The mounting terror had subsided for a moment and I was able to go on with the lesson. I had proved this particular theorem many times, and, so well did I know it, I had felt no need for a review the night before. I had been too sick anyway. Taking three aspirins, I had retired early, hoping a good night's sleep would help.

A good night's sleep! What a laugh. I couldn't remember the last time I had had a good night's sleep. Completely exhausted, I would lie on my bed, circular nightmares bedeviling my mind. I called it closed-loop dreaming: once it ended, it began again, and played through, only to end and start all over.

My nightmare menu consisted of three horrible hallucinations: either I was trapped in a sandpit with evil, little men holding my skirt, so I couldn't escape, or I was refighting the Battle of the Alamo on the Texas State Fairgrounds, or I was hiding from spooks in the Lehman family mansion on Junius Street in Dallas. Each was equally hideous, and every night was showtime for mad mental movies.

Last night had been one of the worst. Alone, I lay with my eyes staring at the ceiling, afraid to close them for fear of being overrun by the Mexican army. Then I heard *thump, thump, thump!* Someone was coming upstairs! I lay paralyzed with fear, as a large, gray, shadowy giant paused menacingly beside my bed, and then jumped onto my stomach.

If that was only a nightmare, why were my stomach muscles so sore this morning?

My hands were perspiring on the chalk, as I continued:

"Since this is true for n = 8, then it is true for 4n, which equals. . . ."

Suddenly something inside my brain went *squish* and my mind went blank—just like turning off the lights.

I stood there, holding the chalk stupidly, trying to multiply four times eight. I knew that something terrible had happened. The people in front of me looked like students, so I must be the teacher. Years of training came to my rescue, and I spoke evenly:

"Please excuse me, class. I'll be right back."

I walked the short distance to the classroom door, opened it, and collapsed in the hall.

That's all I remember.

"Mary Elizabeth, you've had a small stroke on the left side of your brain, affecting the right side of your body."

The Chinese neurologist's words trickled slowly out of a long pipe, or at least that's the way it sounded. Remote.

Once again my husband had been forced to search the medical lists for someone to help me, but this time he had hit paydirt. The short, slim Dr. Cheng was efficient and compassionate, but firm:

"You have a seventy percent chance of recovering the full use of your right arm and leg," he went on. "But I must warn you: *you are an alcoholic, and if you drink again, you will surely die!*"

The shock of his words hit my stomach. *Alcoholic?* Never to drink again? Even now I was in a state of acute misery which only another liberal dose of my "medicine" could relieve. Perhaps I could stop on the way home. . . .

The doctor continued, "You see this line?" He had drawn a vertical line on a piece of paper with a pencil.

"Yes, sir," I whispered.

"This line represents your spinal cord. Now I'm going to draw a coil about this line. This coil is your central nervous system," he said, looking at me.

"Now watch what happens when I erase spots on the coil. Do you see?"

"What?" I said fuzzily.

"The functions of your central nervous system have been seriously impaired. This is what alcohol has done to your body. You are short-circuited. The messages to and from your brain are interrupted," he explained.

"Oh?"

"Your decision to discontinue your medication and liquor 'cold turkey' could have led to your death. You should have been gradually withdrawn under close medical supervision. You were far too sick to do it alone."

I couldn't remember making any decision. Right now all I wanted was a scotch.

"Chances are you can recover *if you quit drinking once and for all,*" he repeated those terrible words.

The impact of what he was saying gradually took effect. My mind worked as though it were surrounded by mud, every thought oozing out with great effort. It was a toss-up which crisis was the worst: no brains or no booze.

Never drink again? How am I doing to do it? He didn't tell me how! He might as well have told me to hold my head in a bucket of water for the rest of my life. How do you *not drink,* when every cell of your body is crying out for alcohol? I needed a drink so badly at that moment that I would have robbed my own jewelry box to get it. But I was in no position to quibble.

Maybe when I get home, I can figure out something, I thought, trying to measure the walking distance to Al's Liquor Store. My brain slogged down and quit.

All the way home I begged my husband for a drink, but he didn't reply. Silently he helped me out of the car. Using a cane, I climbed the steps to my front door, my knee buckling under the weight. After settling me on the sofa, he left.

Alone. I was totally alone, except for my small poodle, Suzy. She was so glad to see me. She did her little pirouettes, twirling round and round, and jumped up on my lap to lick my face. She was, I believed, the only living being on the face of the earth that cared two cents for me. Waves of self-pity washed over me.

"Oh-h-h, Suzy," I moaned, "I'm an alcoholic."

I grabbed her and, with great racking sobs, buried my face in her soft fur.

13
The
Sweetheart of Sigma Chi

Dallas, Texas, 1945

What was a nice girl like me doing in a mess like this?

An *alcoholic!* Dr. Cheng said I was an *alcoholic!* That wasn't possible! I had been to enough movies to know about women alcoholics. I wasn't a lush like Susan Hayward in *I'll Cry Tomorrow;* nor did I bed down with strange men like Lee Remick in *The Days of Wine and Roses.* I wasn't a prostitute or a movie star. I was a schoolteacher!

I *couldn't* be an alcoholic!

I was forty-five, a wife, the mother of two grown children, and grandmother of two small grandsons.

I was at the peak of my career, having just received my master's degree in Liberal Arts from Johns Hopkins University.

I was a veteran high-school mathematics teacher, holding a Bachelor of Science degree from the University of Houston; a member of the Phi Kappa Phi honor society, and Zeta Phi Eta, the National Professional Speech Arts fraternity.

I had been a bibliographical research expert and submarine systems analyst at Westinghouse.

I had been awarded a three-year fellowship from the National Science Foundation for the study of higher mathematics.

I had taken drama lessons from Schuster Martin's School of Dramatics, starring with Aaron Spelling.

I had modeled jewlery from Linz's in Dallas.

My picture had hung in the rotunda of Southern Methodist University.

I could sing, dance, play the piano, swim, knit, crochet, sew, cook, paint, speak, write, teach. . . .

I had toured Europe and Hawaii, and cruised the Caribbean.

I owned a house, two cars, a camper, a place on the lake, Nieman-Marcus clothes, diamond rings, a mink stole, a silver tea service, color television—you name it.

Last but not least, I had been the *Sweetheart of Sigma Chi!*

Of all my accolades and honors, this last title was my favorite. As a popular S.M.U. sorority girl, I had had many beaux, but Paul, my favorite, entered my name in the annual contest to choose his fraternity's official "sweetheart."

There were two qualifications: the winner had to have blue eyes and blonde hair to accommodate their famous ballad:

> *. . . the blue of her eyes,*
> *And the gold of her hair,*
> *Are a blend of the western sky,*
> *And the moonlight beams,*
> *On the girl of my dreams,*
> *She's the Sweetheart of Sigma Chi.*

The fly in the ointment was the fact that I had green eyes and black hair. I didn't want to go to the Sweetheart Ball, because I knew I'd lose.

It was a grand affair. The selection would be made at the end of a dance at the Dallas Country Club. The lucky girl and her escort would burst through a big, red paper heart to receive a crown and a bouquet of American Beauty roses. The glory of the moment was unimaginable!

Having a big crush on me, Paul brushed aside my objections.

"I'll pick you up at eight," he said that afternoon.

Paul wore a black tuxedo. He gave me a white-orchid corsage. My long, black hair hung to my waist, curled in a page boy on the ends, and my strapless black-lace dress, which cost a hundred dollars at Nieman-Marcus, fit to perfection. I would be a glamorous (but gracious) loser. But

I had reckoned without Paul's influence. His father was a Texas oil baron.

At midnight the band struck up the fraternity's refrain: "The girl of my dreams is the sweetest girl. . . ."

We candidates and escorts lined up behind the twelve-foot paper heart, framed in a wire. We waited breathlessly. Who would it be? And then:

"Ladies and gentlemen, I present to you the 1945 Sweetheart of Sigma Chi:

"Mary Elizabeth Rogers!"

I gasped. The other girls gasped. I couldn't believe it! Me? Oh, the glory! I began to sob, as Paul and I burst through the paper heart.

> *. . . the blue of her eyes,*
> *And the gold of her hair. . . .*

The president of the fraternity placed a gold cardboard crown on my head, leaned down to kiss me, and said:

". . . . ."

"You are fantasizing the whole thing."

The familiar evil voice spoke in my ear. "Look at yourself. Go to the mirror and look at yourself."

Rising with difficulty, I clutched my cane and wobbled to the bathroom. The person reflected in the mirror was a stranger: a sick, pudgy, old woman, with a bloated, red face, blotched skin, and disheveled, dyed-black hair. She looked like Cruella deVille in *101 Dalmatians*—101 light-years away from the Sweetheart of Sigma Chi.

The low, taunting voice continued:

"You were never a sweetheart. You're too ugly for anyone to love. Nobody loves you. Your husband hates you. Your children hate you. You're a disgrace. You deserve to die. Why don't you kill yourself and get it over?"

I put my hands on my ears, trying to block him out.

"You need a drink. You can make it down to the liquor store. It's only three blocks. . . ."

"*Stop!*" I cried, clutching my cane. I paced the floor, knocking against the walls, imagining that I was being tossed by giant waves.

I tried to remember the woman I used to be: the daughter who washed dishes every night singing "God Bless America"; the college coed who loved to dance; the mother who put her little ones to bed with the "Hi-Ho" song; the teacher who loved her students. She was gone. I had never been her. *Who was I? Did I even exist?*

I spent the next days saying, *My name is Mary Elizabeth. This is my dog,*

Suzy. I live on Regency Circle. My children are Sylvia and Roger. These people know me. I must exist.

Mostly I was alone in my anguish. I kept walking the floor, crying, raging, fainting. *Does anyone care?* Only in incessant crying could I feel anything, and deep as the wound was, I preferred tears to nothingness.

My generation had been brought up to believe that doctors were gods, and that there was a pill for everything—for peace of mind, for sleeping, for relaxing muscles, for dieting, for breathing, for urinating—anything you want. Maybe there was a pill that would give me back my life. My doctors had given me pills: the wrong pills, the right pills, too many pills. They treated my symptoms and not the cause of my illness. I had followed my doctor-deities' directions explicitly. I had drunk the wine. I had taken the pills. I had had my psyche analyzed. I had spent a fortune. Now I was a loony tune. My medical messiahs had let me down.

The huge maple tree in my front yard began to shed its leaves. Still I cried and paced the floor, unwilling to believe that everything I had worked for was gone.

A knock came at the door. Cautiously I opened it enough to see two little children standing there in Halloween costumes.

"Trick or treat, Miss Liz!"

Jimmy and his little sister, Sandy, lived in the parsonage next door. Their parents left me alone, but the kids liked me because of Suzy. Handing them some fruit, I saw their minister-father running across my yard:

"Don't touch that fruit! Come away from that house! Haven't I told you never to go into this yard!" He whisked them away.

"Those Holy Joes! Everyone who ever lived there thought he was God Himself." His rejection added to my misery.

Cold November wind and rain blew around the house and my draperies were still drawn, the telephone unanswered, callers turned away. I could face no one. The humiliation and shame were so great. Numbness came and went in different parts of my body. The mental horror movies played day and night. Wild music and party sounds crashed in my head. Sounds of cats meowing and jungle birds cawing reverberated in my brain. I was afraid to close my eyes because the Stomach Jumper would attack me again. I couldn't control my mind. I didn't know where I was half the time. I wanted to do nothing, wanted to see no one.

Since my husband worked shift hours, I seldom saw him. Neither of us understood what was happening. We had no idea of the deathly struggle being waged—the warfare being fought in the unseen realm for one sick woman.

At one point in my frenetic pacings, when the noise in my head was overwhelming, I passed the dining-room buffet, where I used to keep the scotch. Suddenly the crazy noises stopped. Dead silence enveloped the room.

Then a wonderful Voice, which sounded like Liquid Love, spoke to me: **"Mary Elizabeth."**

I turned and looked into the living room. Seeing no one, I wobbled back through the kitchen, up the stairs to search the bedrooms. No one was there. As I sat on the bed, the noises returned, but diminished in sound, as if the party was breaking up.

Thanksgiving came and went. I couldn't face my daughter. I was too sick to visit my baby grandson, John; too sick to ride three-year-old Christopher on my back. I was ashamed for them to see me.

But the noises were almost gone. I thought I had broken the back of the demon by not feeding him his favorite poisons. Little did I know that he would continue to torment me for months. That feeling of unreality, as if everybody were far away at the small end of a telescope, persisted. My husband and I grew even further apart. We were like strangers who passed in the night, speaking in monosyllables.

Early in December a fight broke out. We blew up like the explosion after a long-spitting fuse. With gut-ripping words we emotionally shredded each other. He left for a few days, and I was alone again with a fear that surpassed fear.

I began pacing again, but had no spirit for it.

On a bright, cold winter's morning, December 7, to be exact, I gave up.

It was the moment of truth, the turning point. I would decide either to live or to die.

Dropping to my knees on the living-room floor, I uttered the first prayer I ever said in my life:

"God help me!"

It all started with a small glass of wine prescribed by a doctor to help me sleep.

The first glass set up a compulsion for another, and the progression of a phenomenon called "craving" took over. I was thirty-one when I began this downward spiral in Houston, Texas. At the age of forty-five, in Baltimore, Maryland, I almost died by abruptly stopping drinking. For fourteen frightful years, I was one of the estimated 12 million practicing alcoholics in the United States of America.

I drank coffee to pep me up. I drank alcohol to help me sleep. I took tranquilizers to calm my nerves. And all, except for the coffee, under the best medical advice.

During those years of misery and desperation, I lived with a feeling of impending doom. To ease it, I drank more alcohol and popped more pills. But one drink demanded another, and another, and another, until I was drunk again. In the hangover or withdrawal stage, I would swear off the stuff forever, and then be drunk the next night.

Scientists call alcohol an accident of nature. Preachers call it the devil's own brew. Doctors have called it a painkiller and anesthetic, and priests use it as communion wine. Actually, alcohol, a result of fermentation, or a conversion of sugar to carbon dioxide and alcohol, is caused by a reaction between yeasts and sugars.

Fermentation in barley makes beer; in apples, cider; in grapes, wine. Whiskey, gin, vodka, and brandy are distilled. Ethyl alcohol is the basic ingredient of all whiskey, wine, and beer. Other additives, plus water, give each beverage its distinctive flavor.

The amazing fact about ethanol, however, is that even though it is a poison when drunk excessively, it is not poisonous when taken in small amounts over a protracted period of time. That was the key to alcohol's success as a killer drug in my life. It made me feel super good!

Alcohol not only wooed my body, but its exhilarating effect on my brain, the computer of my nervous system, was the thing that made it attractive.

In *The Safe Way to Drink,* by psychiatrist William B. Terhune, the brain is compared to a central office that receives, records, and returns messages, and the spinal cord to the cable through which those messages pass, via nerves, conducting the action between brain and body.

Dr. Terhune says:

> *The cells of the Central Nervous System are very sensitive to those drugs which are able to reach them. The specific effect of alcohol on nerve cells is to dissolve the fat, increase cell fluids, and make the cells temporarily inactive. Every time you take a drink, you are putting some of your brain cells out of commission. Indeed, if alcohol did not have that effect, you would never drink it.*

I certainly didn't know that my brain cells were being put out of commission! All I knew was that I felt relaxed and happy after a couple of drinks.

Let's examine what happened after I sipped the alcohol dregs from the glasses of dinner guests in our home, when I was a child.

Within minutes, I felt a warmth spreading from my stomach to my arms and legs. The alcohol passed into my bloodstream from the stomach and through my heart to the rest of my body. When it reached my brain, I turned on like a light bulb!

I said, *"Umm, umm, good!"*

And that's why most people drink alcohol; they like what it does to them.

It's the same reason why people use any drug: refined sugar, nicotine, caffeine, tranquilizers, and so forth—they *like* the feeling they get from it.

After addiction sets in, it's too late. We're hooked and can't quit. Initially, however, the feeling is one of pleasurable acceptance.

This marvelous sensation depends on the amount of alcohol in the bloodstream. Because the brain and spinal cord contain a high concentration of blood, alcohol immediately affects the feelings, thinking, and body movements.

I grew up an only child in Dallas, Texas, during the depression. I don't remember a lot of drinking in my home, but rumors were that my paternal grandfather had a drinking problem.

One night my parents, Mabelle and Lehman Rogers, were expecting guests and had prepared special drinks for the occasion. My job was to serve the drinks, mind my manners, and disappear into the kitchen for cleanup. Kids were not pampered in those days, so I toed the mark.

When they finished, I collected the empties and carried them to the kitchen. Then I poured all the dregs into one glass and drank it.

"Umm, umm, good!"

Then from the decanter in the refrigerator, I poured myself another glass, adding water to restore the level in the decanter.

What a gorgeous feeling! I began to sing my favorite song, "God bless America, land that I love. . . ."

I placed no significance on the fact that I had sneaked my very first drink and falsified the evidence—one of the first symptoms of alcoholism.

The memory of that leftover cocktail stayed with me. Many years later, when "Dr. Sleepwell" prescribed a small glass of wine as a "medicine" to help me sleep, I was delighted to follow his instructions. Little did I know that from the "prescription" in 1958 to the 1972 "cold-turkey" crisis, I would take a tour of Tophet, the highway to hell.

14
Coffee With
Cream and $C_{12}H_{22}O_{11}$

San Antonio, Texas, 1950

Shirley Temple and I grew up at the same time. My grandmother was ambitious for me to be a child star, like Shirley, so I took dancing lessons, drama lessons, and "elocution" lessons. I recited poems before audiences of doting parents and grandparents. My dancing recitals were rewarded by huge bouquets of flowers, presented with much applause, with cards reading, "FROM YOUR SECRET ADMIRER." I didn't know it was my grandfather. I loved every minute of my stage life, and I knew what I wanted to be when I grew up. I would be a *star!*

I was good at it. At the age of two, before a full house at the Palace Theatre in Dallas, Texas, I recited "The Night Before Christmas."

I toddled out on the stage to thunderous applause. Making a little curtsey and holding my ruffled pink dress, I lisped, "I shall now recite for you *'The Night Before Christmas'* by . . . er . . . er . . . " I had forgotten the author's name.

Then I remembered!

"By Mary Baker Eddy!"

Laughter and more thunderous applause. It made the papers. In 1929 there wasn't much to laugh about, so I must have broken the monotony.

My Christian Scientist grandmother carefully cut out my "press notices" and pasted them in a scrapbook.

The newspapers called me a "child prodigy," and I *was* smart. I used to joke that when God was handing out brains, I thought He said "trains" and asked for a long, fast one.

That's what I got—a swift brain. I could memorize *anything*. Put a book in front of me, and in a short time I could recite it word for word.

It was really a trick. I was born with a photographic memory. All I had to do was to look at the page once and take a picture with my mental camera. *Click!* Then with my eyes closed I could read it on the back of my eyeballs. I could recall it whenever I desired, so that taking tests in school was a cinch for me. I copied, not from other students, but from the back of my eyeballs. Naturally I made top grades.

Later this memory trick was a mainstay for my chosen profession, teaching mathematics. Memorizing calculus formulas was duck soup. God had also given me a talent for number computation. But not knowing Him, I thought it was all my own doing.

The day came, however, when my tricks no longer worked. Twenty-five years later I discovered why. The reason was simple. Like the title of the 1923 song, I had the "Sugar Blues": ". . . I'm all confused, I've got the sweet, sweet, Sugar Blues. More Sugar! I've got the sweet, sweet Sugar Blues." ("SUGAR BLUES" Words by LUCY FLETCHER Music by CLARENCE WILLIAMS © Copyright 1919, 1949 by MCA MUSIC, A Division of MCA INC. New York, NY Copyright renewed. USED BY PERMISSION ALL RIGHTS RESERVED)

I was completely ignorant about $C_{12}H_{22}O_{11}$. I didn't know that my symptoms were due to the food I ate and the beverages I drank. They weren't due to some mysterious little "germ," lurking on doorknobs or toilet seats. I didn't know that sugar is a poison more lethal than opium and more dangerous than atomic fallout. I didn't know that sugar is a concentrated, crystallized acid.

I didn't smoke or drink, and I didn't date boys who did. But I didn't realize that teetotalers are often the biggest sugar gluttons. While bragging that liquor never passes our lips, we pig out on sugar which makes alcohol in our stomachs.

In *Nutrition Against Disease,* Dr. Roger Williams states that no one who follows good nutritional practices ever becomes an alcoholic. Doctors know, of course, that alcoholics frequently suffer from malnutrition, but Dr. Williams contends that it is a contributing factor to the disease and not merely a result of it. Through dietary manipulation, he turned teetotaling animals into compulsive drinkers. He created a "biologic thirst" for alcohol by feeding them the All-American diet, and plying them with coffee and soda pop. Could this be the reason for the ever-rising alcohol problem among high school and college students?

Could this be the reason for my down-the-road battle with booze? I don't know but I suspect it is.

I was ignorant that the consumption of refined sugar had brought about entirely new diseases with a veritable babel of names: paroxysmal tachycardia, cephalalgia, dementia praecox, schizophrenia, paranoia, catatonia, chronic urticaria, and so forth—words to freak out Scrabble players, and all of them symptoms of "sugar blues." If I went to a doctor with indigestion, he wouldn't tell me that it was due to something I ate. That's what I had already told him. But if he said, "You have a very intersting case of dyspepsia!" I would be impressed enough to pay the bill. Give a dog a bad name before you hang him.

No wonder Arab and Jewish physicians carefully measured out refined sugar in miniscule amounts in their prescriptions. They knew it was a brain blotter, offering the human mind and body a smorgasbord of destruction from exhaustion to hallucination.

Endocrinologists tell us that the brain is probably the most sensitive organ in the body. The difference between whether I felt good or bad, energetic or pooped, sane or insane, smart or dumb, loving or hateful, depended in a large measure upon what I put in my stomach. Whether I understood it or not, my head *was* connected to my body; my brain *was* a part of my whole physical system; the same blood which flowed in my legs also flowed in my brain; and the amount of glucose (sugar) in the blood must balance with the amount of blood oxygen. If my blood sugar level is low from cramming in too much refined sugar, my body cells, which *include* my brain cells, are starved.

"Whoa! That doesn't make sense!" you may be saying. "How can *too much* sugar bring on a *sugar low?"*

Here's what happens. When sugar pours in and the cells are starved, the brain goes into a crisis. Helpful Hormones pour from the adrenals, mustering a host of Chemical Commandos to fight the Sugar Bandits. Insulin Invaders from the Islands of Langerhans in the pancreas, whose work it is to neutralize the sugar level in the blood, report for the emergency. They rush in too fast and go too far, gobbling up all the Sugar Bandits in sight. Pancreas Pac-Man strikes again! As all sugar is removed, the glucose level in the blood drops dangerously low.

Then a second crisis follows. Pac-Man goes home and closes the door.

The adrenals are tired from too many emergencies. Other hormones must be found to reverse the damage done by the too eager Insulin Invaders. The body must be restored to an even keel, like a listing ship. Then another shot of Sweet Poison commands a repeat performance. My sugar habit determined how I felt at any given moment. Up and down. In and out. Good and bad. While the sugar was being absorbed into my blood, I felt "up." A quick high, a pick-me-up! I rushed around doing my work hastily because I knew it wouldn't last. Sure enough, this surge of borrowed energy was followed by the "downs," when the bottom dropped out of my blood glucose level. The sugar blues were onstage; tired, listless, requiring great effort to move or to think. My brain was susceptible to suspicions and hallucinations. I became irritable and nervous.

"Mary Elizabeth is high-strung," people remarked.

"No, she has a high I.Q. All geniuses are nervous," my grandmother would defend me.

I was not a Jumpy Genius; I was a Glucose Glutton.

Trying to cope with sugar-laden goodies, my body found itself in crisis after crisis. The new one began before the old one ended. At the end of a day, the accumulation was often a blockbuster. After years of such abuse, the adrenals got tired and refused to play. They were completely pooped from overwork.

My brain had trouble telling truth from fiction. Fantasies became real to me. Was I really the Sweetheart of Sigma Chi? Or had I made it up?

Under normal stresses of living, I went to pieces. I no longer had a healthy endocrine system to help me. The mental mastery of the photographic tricks became undependable.

I first noticed that my mental camera failed to click during a job as nurse's aide.

World War II was fought during my high school days and my contribution to the war effort was helping out the skeleton nursing staff at Jewish Hospital in Cincinnati, Ohio. My father was working there in a war production plant. At seventeen, I was more interested in winning boyfriends than winning the war, but there weren't many eligible young men around. They were all overseas, fighting.

At the hospital I carried bedpans, took temperatures, and ran errands for the skeleton nursing staff. The hours were long, and I was tired all the time. Skipping breakfast to catch the four A.M. streetcar for the two-hour ride across town, I snoozed on the hard, wooden benches. At the hospital cafeteria, I grabbed a supply of coffee and sweet buns. I relied on them to keep up my energy.

My green hospital uniform looked good on my trim, five-foot, four-inch figure. I watched my weight carefully, measuring my waist every morning. Scarlett O'Hara's was eighteen inches; mine was twenty-four inches.

Ugh! I'm getting fat, I thought, checking into the nurses' station.

I had a horror of gaining weight. All the movie stars were slim and beautiful. Boys only liked skinny sweethearts.

"Nurse Rogers," the head nurse ordered, "breakfast is coming up on the trays; please attend to Valerie."

"Yes, ma'm." Good! Valerie was my favorite patient. In spite of her pitiful condition, she never complained. And she had such faith! I carried in the tray and prepared to feed her.

Setting it down with a lurch, I sagged into the chair next to her, and laid my head on the side of her bed.

Another one of those crazy spells was coming!

"What's the matter, nurse? You look white as a sheet!" Valerie said anxiously. She was a polio patient, paralyzed from the neck down.

"Dear Lord, please help my nurse right now!" she prayed.

I raised my head to look at her, and my mind went blank. For several moments I had no idea where I was or who she was. Dizziness, followed by nausea, washed over me, and I fainted on the floor.

When I revived, I saw Head Nurse Bernstein standing over me, a disgusted look on her face. Knowing that I wasn't in love with my job, she thought this was a trick. But it wasn't.

"Go over to the nurses' dorm and rest for a few minutes, Rogers," she said grimly, hating to lose an extra hand.

"And eat some lunch! Eat a good lunch!" her motherly instincts came out.

I staggered over to the dorm, getting a Coke on the way.

"Twenty-four inches is too much," I muttered, thinking about my waist. "I'm not gaining another inch."

Eventually I got through the summer. With much starving, exercising, and sucking in, I got my waist down to twenty-two inches, four short of Scarlett's. My weight dropped to ninety pounds, accompanied by more fainting spells. Then my nurse's aide job thankfully came to an end.

Moving back to Texas, I prepared to enter Southern Methodist University as a freshman. I was young and tan and slim and lovely, just like "The Girl From Ipanema."

The war was over and the men came home. I dated boys, boys, boys; 4F boys, RAF boys, army boys, air force boys, and we all liked to eat the same things: chili, hamburgers, hot dogs, Cokes, Dr. Pepper, tuna fish sandwiches, potato chips, Fritos, Mexican food, coffee—the All-American diet.

I had a date at the co-op with Doak Walker, the football hero. We each had a hamburger, a Coca Cola, and a hot-fudge sundae.

I went out with Paul to El Chico's for enchiladas.

I dated Jim. We ate Italian spaghetti.

In between were malted milks, coffee, pastry, more coffee, candy, and more coffee.

My day began with coffee—huge jugs of it made with cream and sugar. I carried a thermos of it to class, and drank four or five more cups before noon. With no appetite for lunch, I tapered off on Dr. Pepper. At dinner I was tired and irritable. During spells of sleepiness, I would often sit down under a tree on the campus to "rest my eyes." I studied into the wee hours with the aid of more coffee, then was unable to close my eyes for hours.

I lived with my grandmother in Highland Park. Having hoarded sugar during the war ration days, she had bags and bags of it. She put it in everything she cooked—carrots, peas, turnip greens, corn, spaghetti sauce, and so forth. She scattered sugar on the top of pies and cookies. Generous amounts went into tomato relish and pickles. We loved her sweet, rich, fat, southern-style home cooking.

She made the very best tapioca pudding, my favorite dessert.

In my second year at S.M.U., spells of weakness and dizziness increased. With it came extreme itching and rapid heartbeat. My emotions were very fragile, and I cried when someone looked cross-eyed at me. Ordinary experiences of dating—"going steady" and "breaking up"—were heartbreaking events. When Paul and I "broke up," I was devastated for weeks, even though I had made the decision. Everything was a three-act drama.

I flunked a test in Spanish. Sweating, shaking, trembling, I forgot my vocabulary, and with humiliation pulled a *B*. The back of my eyelids were blank.

After I married in my junior year, one of the first things we bought was a coffeepot. It was always hot. I also learned to cook the same sweet, rich, fat, southern food I loved so much.

During my first pregnancy I suffered extreme nausea, bordering on eclampsia. After the obstetrician put me on a strict diet, I rapidly improved. However, morning nausea stayed with me for many years. Only recently have I begun to enjoy breakfast.

In 1950 I was pregnant with my second child. During a sizzling San Antonio summer, temperatures averaged above a hundred for weeks. I plied myself with iced coffee and not much else. Our tin-roofed garage apartment was not air-conditioned, and my little girl, Sylvia, and I suffered terribly from the heat. Nothing would stay in my stomach. I thought I would die.

When I was seven months along, I no longer felt the baby move. In January, 1951, my son, a hydrocephalus, was born—and died.

And I almost died with him.

Without realizing it I was one of 15 million coffee addicts in the United States, hooked on a heavy drug, Coffea arabica. I drank my morning drug, suffered the misery the chemicals caused, and self-righteously declared coffee to be the friendly, all-American beverage. Those who disagreed I labeled party-pooper health nuts.

My morning coffee was ready when I raised my aching head from the pillow, thanks to a timer, and I dragged through the day with a cup in my hand. I probably drank ten or twelve cups a day. I *had to*. Otherwise, I would start to sag. My coffee intake gradually increased until my habit was addictive and progressive.

On a family outing away from the coffeepot, I got a dull, throbbing headache, accompanied by the old familiar nausea.

"I've got to have a cup of coffee," I would groan.

"Let's get Mama her fix!" my daughter Sylvia would laugh.

Then would come the sweaty palms, the nervousness, the anxiety, the frequent potty breaks. Within ten or fifteen minutes after I had gulped down a cup, I felt better.

Does this scenario sound familiar? It ought to. The same thing is happening to millions of Americans—maybe to you.

I don't remember reading newspaper or magazine articles about the harmful effects of drinking coffee. No radio or TV ads ever crossed my path. Doctors never warned me about it. My obstetrician said nothing at all about what I ate or drank, only how much. I remember telling him that it was so hot I couldn't eat, but I could sip iced coffee. He made no comment.

Many coffee drinkers are not addicts. They are able to drink one to two cups a day and quit. But for millions of others the story is different. Two becomes three, which becomes four, and so on, until we are drinking out of control. We're hooked, trapped by a drug that dictates how, when, and perhaps, *if*, we live. Our lives are controlled by coffee.

Certainly mine was. Often I couldn't get my body and head to behave properly. When my stomach wasn't killing me, my head was. A tense hyper feeling always tormented me. But I never connected these symptoms with the coffee I was drinking.

"Mary Elizabeth is a bundle of nerves," people used to say about me. They were right. I was.

Actually, my problem was a double-barreled threat. The deadly culprits at work in me were two separate but related compounds: caffeine and coffee.

Let's look at them one at a time.

First, what is *caffeine?* Caffeine is an odorless, slightly bitter-tasting alkaloid chemical, found in many plants. While it can be manufactured synthetically, most caffeine is obtained from coffee, tea, and cocoa plants. The nuts from the tree, Cola acuminata, used in many sodas, contain about 2 percent caffeine.

Chemically, caffeine is called *1,3,7-thrimethylxanthine.* It belongs to a family called *methylated xanthines.* White like cocaine, heroin, and morphine, caffeine dissolves easily in water and alcohol. (This information comes from *Kicking the Coffee Habit* by Charles F. Wetherall.)

The xanthines in coffee, tea, and cocoa affect your body to different degrees. Caffeine is a powerful stimulant to your central nervous system, (CNS), represented by the coil drawn around the line by my doctor. On a day-to-day basis these chemicals disrupt the CNS, the cardiovascular, and respiratory systems, and foul the gastrointestional tract.

Instances of chronic CNS disturbances, tumors, facial lesions, stomach disorders, cancer, heart disease, ulcers, breast cancer, and other crippling and fatal illnesses have been reported.

Are you identifying with some of these symptoms from your own coffee drinking? Have you had that drugged up "hyper" feeling? How about stomach pains and nausea, maybe even heart problems, ulcers, or breast tumors?

If your symptoms are mild and you keep drinking coffee, they may improve, but you won't.

It's bad enough that caffeine is naturally in coffee. But worse, some manufacturers add caffeine to soft drinks, whether we like it or not. The

FDA Consumer of 1980 reports the United States government requires that caffeine be included in cola and pepper drinks and *permits* it to be added to other soft drinks, although the FDA admits it doesn't know how harmful caffeine is. (Chris Lecos, *FDA Consumer,* October 1980.)

Where does the caffeine come from that's added to soft drinks? From coffee, that's where! A chemical process using harsh cleaning-fluid type solvents separates the caffeine from the coffee beans. Then it is refined and added to a variety of drinks, foods, and medicines.

For a horror story read chapter 31 about Mary Lynn. She was hooked on Fiorinal, a caffeine-based prescription drug.

Caffeine hypes up the soft drinks your kids crave. I watched as a mother gave her youngster a can of Coke and then brought him into one of our meetings. As the caffeine and sugar hit his bloodstream, he squirmed and fussed for the next hour, tormenting his mother, the speaker, and others around him. Parents mean well, but hyping kids up to calm them down shows a lack of awareness.

Too much caffeine can kill you. Overdosing, called "caffeinism," causes a variety of miseries. Frequent urination (I never slept the night through), jitters, shaky hands, trembling, agitation, irritability, muscle twitchings (I had two around my eye and lip that drove me bananas), light-headedness, rapid breathing, rapid heartbeat, and cardiac problems.

For years I suffered from the "coffee itch," an intense irritation on my back. Coffee junkies often like to have their backs scratched.

Space doesn't permit going into the tragic cases of cola addiction. One poor woman, addicted to a popular cola beverage, consumed a case every other day. Sickly white and bloated, she was a cola junkie. Yet when I told my story about alcohol addiction, she turned away in disgust.

Why do we drink it? Like alcohol, we drink it to feel good. When you swallow coffee, it rolls down your throat, through the stomach, and passes quickly into the central nervous system. Its first target is the cortex and the medulla, stimulating such functions as breathing, blood-vessel dilation, and the operation of the vagus nerve. The vagus nerve provides energy to the larynx, lungs, heart, esophagus, and most of the abdominal organs.

The shot of caffeine jolts your whole system, and deceives you into thinking you've got a lot of get-up-and-go.

The next deadly ingredient in coffee is *coffee.* This may sound like double-talk, but remember the two separate parts we are considering: caffeine and coffee. The same tongue-twisting oil and acid compounds that are present in your friendly morning cup of coffee are also used in industry for such jobs as tanning leather and cleaning solvents.

These varying compounds are affected by the many processes the coffee beans go through on their way to the grocer's shelf. Therefore, no one is sure which components produce what ailment.

Nearly all studies point the guilty finger at caffeine, but no one knows how the oils, acids, and other compounds in coffee affect the drinker. They only know what it does. Many studies on heart disease and cancer classify decaffeinated coffee as being equally as bad as the regular kind.

Coffee drinkers are more prone to pancreatic and bladder cancer, heart disease, and breast cancer. It apparently makes no difference whether the coffee is regular or decaffeinated.

You may be asking yourself, *Am I hooked on coffee?* Only you can answer. Actually it's irrelevent. Because whether or not you are addicted, if you drink a lot of coffee, the oils, acids, and caffeine are still harmful to your system.

There's more to caffeine consumption than just coffee. Let's look at some soft drinks and their caffeine content, which stays fairly constant.

On the Poison Chart below tabulate the number of 12-ounce cans that you and the kids have been drinking.

POISON CHART

DRINK	MG. CAFFEINE	YOUR TOTAL
Coca Cola	64.68	_____
Dr. Pepper	60.96	_____
TAB	45.00	_____
Pepsi Cola	42.00	_____

As you can see, a couple of Cokes will inject about 130 mg. of caffeine into your system. Children, with smaller bodies, have more hyper reactions than adults. Perhaps the behavior you don't like in your children may be due to the hidden caffeine they're getting. Before taking them to a psychiatrist, remove the caffeine and sugar from their diets and watch what happens.

Expectant mothers especially should be aware of what caffeine can do—fibrocystic breast tumors and breast cancer; possible birth defects in their children, stillbirths, miscarriages, and more. Mother, if you are pregnant, kick the caffeine!

Don't wonder for the rest of your life if caffeine killed your baby, as I have.

15
Who Is God?

The death of my baby boy was the first real tragedy in my life. Completely overwhelmed with grief and physically weak, I had no spiritual resources at all to help me. If there was a God, I didn't know who He was.

The woman next door to my hot box came over to tell me about her religion. She brought her little boy and a timer, which she set before she began to talk. I never heard a word she said, because her little boy reminded me of the son I had lost, and I wept throughout the visit. Later I heard that she was a Jehovah's Witness. I had to admire her zeal. I was surrounded by churchgoers, but no one told me about Jesus.

As far as I was concerned, God was Somebody who liked other people, but not me. I had visited a lot of churches, but I never could put it together. When my grandmother, a Christian Scientist, got sick, she would dramatically announce that she was dying. The family never took her seriously, so I never took her religion seriously. I believed my grandparents went to church to dress up and see their friends.

Dallas, Texas, 1937
My other grandmother was into spiritism. One of the most vivid scenes I can recall took place in our living room. I was still in grade school. My grandmother, whom I called Big Mamie, and her friend, Mrs. Rice, frequently met to run the Ouija board, a new fad at that time. They stationed me, with my wirehaired terrier, Mr. Asta, beside them. I had a notebook

and pencil to jot down what their temperamental spook, Dr. Clover, had to say—if they could get him on the board.

Dr. Clover was Big Mamie's "spirit guide" into the next dimension. He talked to her regularly via the printed alphabet and numbers on a slab of wood called a Ouija board. Sometimes they had to entreat his presence for hours because he had turned them over to some stupid inferior spirits who didn't know anything. My grandmother wanted Dr. Clover, and *no one else*. He was the only spirit who could, or would, tell her what stocks to buy and sell. She took his advice and made lots of money.

"Dr. Clover, are you there?" my grandmother spoke softly.

We all watched the indicator. Even Mr. Asta, who normally slept through these sessions, sat with his ears perked up.

"We're waiting for you. Please talk with us. I need your advice," she continued carefully.

Dr. Clover had been known to display bursts of temper and tell her off. She had great respect for Dr. Clover, but not for many people. Although she loved her family, her own angry outbursts often outdid those of the spooks.

We kept our eyes trained on the indicator, but it didn't budge.

The phone rang. It was an emergency call for Mrs. Rice, and she had to leave. Gathering up her things, she turned to me.

"Mary Elizabeth, you take my place. You're ten years old, and it's time you had a 'guide' of your own."

She paused at the door. "Emma, ask Dr. Clover to get a spirit guide for Mary Elizabeth. Then she can take over when one of us is tired."

Her words filled me with alarm. I didn't like the whole thing. Whoever was out there, I'd rather they forget me. With a sense of foreboding, I slipped into Mrs. Rice's chair.

"Don't press down too hard, Mary," Big Mamie commanded. "Just barely touch it."

"I know, I know." I did know; I had watched these two women running Ouija for years. My fingertips hardly brushed the sides of the indicator.

"Dr. Clover, are you there?" my grandmother began again. "Hello, hello, anybody out there?"

Mr. Asta began to bark as a cold, clammy sensation swept into the room, and settled itself around us. A terrible fear gripped me.

Suddenly the indicator took off with the speed of lightning. It swung to the left and then to the right, from YES to NO, back and forth like a pendulum. It was Dr. Clover's signature when he was angry. I could picture him pacing back and forth across the room.

"Dr. Clover, is that you?" Big Mamie asked.

The indicator violently swung to YES.

"How are things out there?" my grandmother began pleasantly. I never understood why she kept asking that question because she never received a sensible answer.

"*R-I-C-E*" he spelled out.

"Mrs. Rice? She had to leave early."

"*No!*" the indicator swung violently to the right.

"Well, Dr. Clover, she's gone. What can I do? Mary Elizabeth is taking her place. You know my granddaughter, Mary Elizabeth?" she started to introduce me to the spook.

"*No!*" he repeated.

"You don't want her to take Mrs. Rice's place?" my grandmother was astounded.

"*No!*"

"But, why not, Dr. Clover? She's only ten years old but she's smart. She needs a guide. . . ."

The indicator went wild, making wide circles all over the board.

"Tell me why not, Dr. Clover!" Big Mamie demanded.

The indicator halted for a moment, and then very carefully spelled out these words:

"S-H-E-B-E-L-O-N-G-S-T-O-A-N-O-T-H-E-R."

"She belongs to another? Who?" she persisted.

But the Ouija board was silent. Dr. Clover was gone and all his spooks with him. I got out of Mrs. Rice's chair.

"Big Mamie, please don't ask me to help you with the Ouija board anymore," I pleaded.

"I won't, honey, I won't."

And that was that.

Of course, I knew that Dr. Clover wasn't God, but since he always talked about his "master," I thought he meant God. The churches I visited were never as interesting as my grandmother's sessions with the spirits. The preachers talked about religion, but Big Mamie seemed to have the real thing. At least things happened when she was around.

But *nobody* told me *anything* about the kingdom of darkness versus the Kingdom of light. They didn't know.

"For lack of knowledge My people perish," is God's warning.

16

Dr. Sleepwell's
Soothing Solution

Houston, Texas, 1958

"Doctor, I'm awake most of the night. I can't seem to get to sleep till early morning. Then I have to get up and go to work. My days and nights are turned around."

I drummed my fingers and tapped my foot. Dressed in a smartly tailored gray-wool suit, I looked the part of a successful educator.

"Why don't you try a small glass of wine before you retire? It'll relax you so that you can get to sleep."

The doctor had finished my checkup, and we were back in his office. He hadn't found anything that would explain my jerks and jitters. Like so many others, he told me, "You're just a nervous person."

"Is that all?" I asked, expecting a prescription.

"Try this and see if it works." He playfully took out his prescription pad and wrote on it: A SMALL GLASS OF WINE.

"Doctor, I don't drink at all. What kind of wine should I get?" I was puzzled.

He named a brand of good, red wine.

"That's the kind we drink at home. My wife likes it," he said.

Driving home I stopped at a wine shop and bought his "prescription." Then I went to Sakowitz, a Houston department store, and purchased a

Waterford crystal wine glass. If I was going to drink wine, I would do it in style.

Remembering the pleasant feeling I had in my childhood, when I drank the forbidden cocktail, I looked forward to my evening medicine.

Pouring the wine into the beautiful crystal glass, I drank it quickly.

"Umm, umm, good!"

The warmth hit my toes and started up my legs. My body became warm and alive. Then my head said, "This is it! I found it!"

I floated off to dreamland, thanks to the good "Dr. Sleepwell" and his Burgundy Bacchus. My Liquid Lullaby did the trick, and soon I couldn't do without it.

The next evening I had two glasses of wine, and they did for me exactly what the one glass did. No more, no less. Before the year was out, I was drinking a quart of wine before I went to bed, with no more effect than the one glass had.

Alcohol, the great deceiver! In those beginning years I never got drunk. Never wavered, waffled, quavered, staggered, stumbled, slurred words, or misbehaved.

"A girl with such high intelligence and superior credentials can certainly handle a little wine," I reasoned.

I didn't know that I lived in Fantasy Land, that an insidious disease was taking over my life. My body began to develop a *tolerance* for the drug in which I soaked it. Ethanol alcohol, C_2H_5OH, disguised as a friendly nightcap, had me on the hook. I was building an acceptance level, while mistakenly believing myself superior to other drinkers. No matter how much I drank, I didn't get intoxicated. At first.

I was Sanctimonious Sally who drove the other slobs home, lecturing them on the evils of inebriation.

"If you can't hold your liquor, don't drink!"

I didn't have to worry; I could hold mine. Self-righteousness was my signature.

"Now, of course, I drink wine because my *doctor prescribed it,* so that doesn't count," I rationalized. "I really don't *'drink.'* I just take my *medicine* like a good girl."

Doctor Sleepwell was the "God of my body," and over the years I was to pay him great homage, not to mention money. I didn't understand that, where my body was concerned, *I and I alone* am responsible to the Lord. Here is the Lord's advice:

Have you forgotten that your body is the temple of the Holy Spirit, who lives in you and is God's gift to you, and that you are not the owner of your own body? You have been bought, and at a price! Therefore, bring glory to God in your body."

See 1 Corinthians 6:19, 20

"Mama, what's in that bottle?"

My seven-year-old son, Roger, pointed to a fifth of Teacher's Scotch sitting on the kitchen counter.

"That's my medicine, Rog," I tried to brush him off.

"But won't that make you drunk?" he persisted.

"Of course not, honey. That's why it's called Teacher's. It's made especially for schoolteachers, so they won't get drunk!"

The lie came to me as quick as a wink. It sounded good and it satisfied Rog, so he quit bugging me.

I had switched from wine to scotch and soda, reasoning that one would put me to sleep as easily as the other. I was drinking more now, especially after coming home from a rough day teaching algebra-trig at the high school.

I won a three-year fellowship from the National Science Foundation to study higher mathematics in the Evening College of the University of Houston. Because of this honor, I had my picture in the newspaper: a local yokel made good.

My schedule was enough to break the back of a strong bull. I got through the days with coffee as a pick-me-upper and scotch as a calm-me-downer. Up and down. Up and down.

Up in the morning. Aspirin for headache. Pot of coffee. Fix family breakfast. Drive Sylvia to junior high, Roger to elementary school, and myself to the high school where I taught. Coffee in the teachers' lounge. Teach five classes and do other work. Pick up kids. Coffee at the 7-Eleven. Fix supper. Several scotch and sodas. Give the house a lick and a promise. Drive to classes at U.H. Concentrate on higher mathematics. Drive home. Couple of "relaxing" drinks. Do homework. Grade papers. Take "medicine." Bed about one or two A.M. Up at six-thirty to do the same thing again.

Workaholic. Coffeeholic. Budding alcoholic.

Soon after the Teacher's Scotch incident, Roger's first-grade teacher, Elaine, also a personal friend, called to say she wanted to talk with me about his work. When our teacher-parent conference was done, she walked with Rog and me out to the car. He began playing with a chum.

"Liz, do you teach any of the McDugle children?" she asked. The McDugles had eleven kids in the Houston schools.

"Yes, of course! I've taught one every year since I've been here. This year I have Bobby in my general math class."

"Well, I have little Donnie and I feel so sorry for him. They all come to school so uncombed and dirty, often with no lunch."

Her voice lowered, "You know both their parents are *alcoholics*. You wouldn't believe the stories I hear about them."

Unknown to us, Roger was listening behind my skirt.

"Oh, Mrs. Webster, I know what they can do!" he piped up. "They can drink Teacher's Scotch *like my mama does*, and then they won't get drunk!"

The conversation ended abruptly, and our friendship eventually cooled. My school district had a small-town flavor, with women teachers held in great respect. I was put on their Suspect List. Elaine's husband was also my principal, and he began keeping a closer eye on me. My drinking had become public knowledge, and I chafed under the "unfair" treatment.

17

Sipping at the Circus

Baltimore, Maryland, 1968

The icy February wind swept over the harbor, causing our car to sway, as we drove over the Hanover Street Bridge. It was too cold to be out, but we had two good seats for the Ringling Brothers, Barnum and Bailey Circus, whose main attraction was my dream man, Gunther Gebel-Williams.

Carrying a large satchel purse, I walked unsteadily up the Civic Center ramp, my husband holding my elbow, and made straight for the ladies' room.

"Wait here, hon, I'll be right out."

I hurried in and closed a stall door behind me. Getting a bottle of whiskey out of my purse, I quickly gulped down several swallows and waited for the burning to subside, before I drank more. The trembling in my legs disappeared, and equilibrium returned. I was all set—at least for another hour.

I loved everything about the circus: the acrobats, the high-wire performers, the trained dog acts, the flying trapeze, all of it. But the main reason I came was to see the star of the show, that magnificent tiger trainer, Gunther Gebel-Williams.

We settled in our seats and my husband ordered hot coffee and pretzels from the vendor. Barely sipping the coffee and nibbling the pretzel, I didn't want to take the edge off the "high" I had maneuvered in the rest room. It was so hard to keep the uppers separate from the downers; my poor body didn't know whether to perk up or slow down.

The performances were superb, as one act followed another. I made a couple more trips to the rest room, finishing off the pint. I couldn't remember when I had had such fun. It was almost time for the main attraction. I hurried back to my seat.

There was Gunther! In pink tights with a scarlet-sequined jacket, his long, blond hair flying, Gunther led a gaudily decked elephant to center ring. Then he carefully let a fierce tiger out of his cage. With whip and shouted instructions, he ordered the tiger to jump upon the back of the elephant. Then, in a series of leaps, he climbed on the back of the tiger!

"Three natural enemies have come together in one act, ladies and gentlemen: an African elephant, an Indian tiger, and a man. Give them a big hand!" the ringmaster exclaimed.

Wow, what a man! I peered at them through a rosy haze, as the vision of a man on a tiger on an elephant went in and out of focus.

Gunther and I have a lot in common, I thought. *He likes tigers, and I like cats.* (I had fourteen cats at home.)

Suddenly I had a great idea!

I giggled, "I'm going backstage and give him a couple of tips on how to train a tiger. Heh, heh, heh."

"Wha-a-t?" shouted my husband over the noise.

"Nothing." The finale began, and I gathered up my satchel and stumbled up the steps, calling over my shoulder, "You wait here. I'll be right back."

Down the aisle I staggered, to the back of the Civic Center Auditorium, and down the stairs to a lower level.

Opening the door, I found myself on the floor where the elephants were tethered to small iron stakes.

What magnificent beasts! I wobbled between them, patting their legs. "Good work, Jumbo! Nice job, Sambo!"

What a glorious adventure!

"Lady! What do you want?"

I glanced around, seeing no one, but felt a tug on my dress. Looking down I saw a midget—a very mad midget.

"What do you want?" he again demanded.

"Take me to Gunther Gebel-Williams," I said grandly, gathering myself into a royal posture.

"Oh, yes, ma'm," he said, "follow me, please."

We wove around the elephants, past other performers and animal cages, arriving at some big double doors.

"Right through there, lady," he directed.

"Thank you, my little man," I said loftily, giving him a dollar for his trouble.

I swept through the double doors, which clanged behind me, and a cold blast of air hit me in the face. I was out on the street behind the Civic Center without a coat in minus-fifteen-degree weather.

I had been bounced by a midget!

I woke up on the couch, sick as a dog, barely able to make it to the bathroom. Throwing up was a morning ritual. Even brushing my teeth started my stomach churning again.

The clock told me the bad news—late for work again. Should I call in sick? No, better not. I had too many sick days already on my record.

I poured a cup of coffee, hands trembling, and head bursting with pain. Perhaps several cups would calm my nerves.

The house was silent. Both my children had left home last year, and my daughter was pregnant with her first child. I ought to be joyful that I was going to be a grandmother, but I was too sick to care. My husband had gone to work, and I desperately needed a drink. That night at the circus almost did me in!

With great effort I showered, noticing several mysterious bruises on my arms. I dressed, and drove the short distance to the high school, where I was the senior algebra-trig teacher. Fortunately I had the first period free, so, if I was lucky, my tardiness would go unnoticed.

Entering the main office, I went over to my letter slot to check for mail. Sensing that someone was standing behind me, I turned and came face-to-face with the principal.

"Mary Elizabeth Rogers, may I see you in my office immediately?"

My heart lurched, and began to pound. Feeling weak and dizzy, I followed him into his office.

"Have a seat, please." He indicated a chair.

I collapsed into it.

He came right to the point. "Have you been drinking this morning?"

"Of course not! I *never* drink in the morning! How dare you suggest such a thing!"

"Nevertheless, there is a distinct odor of alcohol on your person," he persisted formally. "I warn you that this cannot happen again, and a written copy of this conversation will be put in your teacher's file."

I began to cry, "But, Mr. Northrup, I *really* haven't been drinking this morning. Maybe it's Listerine that you smell."

That *was* the truth as I saw it. What I didn't realize was that the large amount I had consumed the night before was now coming out of my system, through my breath and the pores of my skin. Since arising, I had drunk nothing but a pot of coffee, but the combination of stale alcohol and caffeine made me stink all over, like all drinkers, smokers, and drug users.

Mr. Northrup finished writing the memorandum and handed it to me, but my eyes were too blurry to read it.

"Sign it, please."

"No, I won't sign it. You're very unfair, Mr. Northrup. I assure you that I am *not drunk,* just sick," I cried.

"Are you sick *again?* You have used eighteen sick days since the school year began, and it's not yet Christmas."

"Yes, I'm sick *again,* and today will be number nineteen. I'm going home! I shouldn't have tried to come to work anyway, in my condition. I think I'm coming down with the flu." Crying, I gathered up my things.

"And I'm *not* signing that paper!" was my parting shot.

I knew my rights. We hadn't lived through the Sick Sixties without learning that service professions have clout. I was a member of the local teacher's union. They would be hearing from me. And they did!

How I gloated the day Mr. Northrup was transferred. Yes, the case was decided in my favor. Unjust? Sure. It happens all the time. That's why drunken drivers continue to kill innocent people and get away with it. "Might is right," as the old saying goes.

Today I realize that Mr. Northrup was trying to help me, but the only trouble was, he didn't know how. He tried shame and humiliation, coupled with threats. That rarely works, as it serves to put the alcoholic on the defensive, causing him to redouble his cover-up efforts.

18
The Miracle at Quebec

Baltimore, Maryland, 1971

The sun baked North Charles Street, as I inched forward in the 5:00 P.M. traffic for my weekly appointment with Dr. Helen Santez-Montego. At forty-five dollars an hour, the Sorbonne-educated Spanish lady psychiatrist picked my brains to find out *why I drank so much.* In six months of treatment we had only discovered the tip of the iceberg, but in the meanwhile I had doubled my intake of Chivas Regal. Better make hay while the sun shines. I figured that once she determined the cause, I would exclaim, "So that's why!" and then I would be able to drink with my husband like a lady! Parking my car, I limped into the Belvedere Hotel cocktail lounge and ordered a double scotch and soda. My big toe was throbbing. I had stubbed it on the cobbler's bench the night before, as I danced with an imaginary Fred Astaire to the tune of my favorite heartbreaker, "Yellow Bird." Years before an old boyfriend and I called it "our song." Dredging up memories, some real, some fanciful, I played that song every night, seeking a little bit of love in my lonely life.

At the first strains of the calypso beat, my family would leave, bored to death. My kids used to threaten to break the record. I threatened back, so it was a draw. I was still in the same rut: home from work and pour a couple of doubles to relax; fix supper with the aid of more drinks; off again either to Johns Hopkins night classes or to the shrink, fortified with more liquor; return home late to keep a drinking and dancing date with Yellow

Bird. In the past couple of years of nightly staggering around the living room, I had broken all ten toes.

I was greatly discouraged with my lack of progress with Dr. S-M. She was my last hope. If a high-priced, Spanish psychiatrist with a hyphenated name couldn't cure me, who could? When our sessions first began, I told her that I needed help to control my drinking, so she asked me how much I normally drank in one week.

"I have no idea, Doctor. I never kept track."

"Pleeze, Mees Rogers, next week write down how moch you consume. I must know."

I did what she said and tallied five "fifths" of scotch, which I reported at the next appointment.

"Feeths? How moch is a feeth?"

"A fifth of whiskey, doctor. A fifth."

"How moch ees that in cubic centimeters?"

"Who knows?"

"You are a math teacher, Mees Rogers," she admonished.

The telephone rang. The clock ticked away, and so did my forty-five dollars, with her incoming telephone calls included in the bill.

Our next session I reported that a fifth of scotch was 757.58 cubic centimeters and that five of them were 3787.9.

"You dreenk four t'ousand cc of leequor each week!"

"I guess I do."

"Mees Rogers," she said somberly, "you have a drinking problem."

"I know. That's why I'm here."

Anticipating more of the same trivia, I finished my scotch at the Belvedere and took the elevator to her office in the building next door. It looked like I was in for a long wait. Her 4:30 patient, a short, fat, young woman with long center-parted hair and granny glasses, was still in the waiting room, crying.

"The doctor is at the hospital on an emergency. Do you want to wait or make another appointment?" The receptionist did not look up.

My God. All that time wasted in a hot traffic jam.

"No, I'll be back next week. Same time."

The little, fat girl was still bawling, as I limped out the door and down the elevator. I needed a drink to face this new crisis: no shrink for a whole week. She hadn't helped me so far, but I was developing a dependency on her, comforted by the knowledge she was available. Besides, I needed another prescription for Valium; I was almost out.

I had been reluctant to add pills to my routine. But Dr. S-M assured me that the mild prescription would help me through those terrible anxiety attacks.

Back in the Belvedere lounge I swallowed another little yellow pill and ordered a drink. The doctor had cautioned me about mixing pills and booze, but today was an exception. I *needed* both. After a while my toe stopped hurting.

I tried to remember in which parking lot I had left my VW. My mind refused to cooperate. Locating the VW, I got in and drove unsteadily back the way I came.

Suddenly I remembered passing a church earlier. The Shrine of Saint Jude. My friend, Harriet, had told me that Saint Jude was the patron saint of hopeless cases.

That's me, I thought, as I wheeled the car around into the church parking lot. I got out and limped inside.

As my eyes adjusted to the cool, dark interior, I spotted Saint Jude's statue in the corner, surrounded by little candles. He had a look of compassion on his painted face, and I stood, looking up at him, unsure of what to do.

"Can I help you, my dear?" Turning, I came face to face with the oldest living human being I had ever seen. He looked like the Dalai Lama in *Lost Horizon,* only in Catholic attire.

The combination of sedatives (alcohol and Valium) was taking effect. I was unable to talk.

"Can I help you, dear?" the old priest repeated, putting his arm around me kindly. "Did you hurt your foot?"

His loving touch set me off. I began to sob.

"Drink . . . need help . . . please help me."

"Wait here." He hobbled off, leaving me alone.

I lay down in one of the empty pews.

If I die here, at least I'll go to heaven, I thought, the ceiling of the chapel fading.

Shaking. Someone was shaking me.

"Here, drink this." The old priest was back, offering me a glass of water. He thought I was thirsty.

I sipped it. "Liquor . . . too much liquor," I tried to explain.

"Ah, I see," his eyes lit up with understanding. "You look like a nice girl."

Helping me to my feet, he headed me toward the door.

"You'll be all right, my dear. Drink only a little wine with your meals. Just a small glass of wine."

A small glass of wine. That's how this nightmare started, but how was it going to end?

I wanted *out*.

Quebec, Canada, 1971

"I don't care how much it costs! Buy it anyway! You like to drink as much as I do! Don't you want to have a good time on this vacation?" I yelled at my husband as he angrily stomped back into the Canadian liquor store.

A bottle of scotch cost five dollars more than it did back in the States, and our vacation budget was already strained from the high living we were "enjoying" at the Chateau Frontenac. The beautiful, old castlelike hotel, overlooking the Saint Lawrence River, should have been the setting for an ideal holiday. Instead, we were fighting, as usual, over my drinking.

I was weak and run-down following an exploratory operation, which left me with a long vertical scar from my navel down to forever, ruining any future bikini beauty. Fortified with little yellow pills from my Spanish shrink, I had started out on a drinkless vacation with the best of intentions.

I had gone on the wagon before. Many times. Sweat out a few miserable days and then stay dry for a while to prove to the nags and nitpickers that I've got this thing under control. My present dry spell was the result of a week's stay in Johns Hopkins Hospital, plus several weeks' recuperation. Of course, I had only switched one drug for another: painkillers and Valium for alcohol. But in my ignorance I believed that my so-called drinking problem had somehow disappeared.

The hospital emergency was weird. During a family dinner, a terrible twisting pain had gripped my stomach. Groaning, I slipped to the floor and lay there writhing in agony. The ambulance screamed all the way to the hospital, where four specialists questioned me. They punched and probed my belly, unable to diagnose my problem. None of them asked if I had been drinking. No blood or urine samples were taken. Finally, they decided that I should undergo an exploratory operation. I was wheeled into an emergency operating room and cut open to see what was inside.

Nothing. Nothing abnormal was there. While they were at it, however, they clipped off my appendix, just to have something to do. Many years later I learned about alcoholic gastritis, and by that time, I was able to joke about it: "Did you know that I have been operated on for alcoholism? Too bad. I'm still an alcoholic. They didn't get it all."

My shrink visited me at the hospital to see if I was suicidal, but she found me in neutral. Actually I didn't mind my stay. The painkillers kept me remote, and I had an unexpected furlough from the classroom. A spirit of invalidism began to set in.

Both my surgeon and my shrink recommended a vacation. Hey, great! All this attention was worth the scar on my stomach.

My husband asked me where I wanted to go.

Quebec. I wanted to go to Quebec, but I didn't tell him why. He would have thought it was a flaky idea. And maybe it was. But I couldn't forget a conversation I had had with my best friend, Harriet.

Also a math teacher, Harriet was my confidante and adviser. We usually stopped at the Lancer's Pub at the end of the week for a couple of drinks to hash over classroom clashes. She was a devout Catholic, and I was secretly envious of her religious life. I was neither a Protestant, a Catholic, nor a Jew. I was a nothing.

One Friday afternoon, after several rounds of drinks, I tackled her theology:

"Harriet, what's the name of that shrine over in France?"

"Do you mean Lourdes?"

"I guess so. The one where Audrey Hepburn saw the Virgin Mary," I kidded her.

"Who's Audrey Hepburn?" (Harriet was not a movie buff.)

"She played Saint Bernadette. Or maybe it was Jennifer Whatshername."

"Liz, Saint Bernadette saw a vision of the Blessed Mother near a French town called Lourdes. Ever since then people have been going to Lourdes, some of them being healed miraculously."

"Do you believe in miracles?" I asked sarcastically.

"Yes, I do," she said quietly.

I thought about it.

"Too bad it's in France. We could use a miracle mill over here!" I ordered another drink.

"There's one up in Canada," she said casually.

"Really! Where?"

"Outside of Quebec. Sainte Anne de Beaupré."

"Does it work for non-Catholics, too?" I asked jokingly.

"What do you need a miracle for, Liz? You've got everything you could possibly want."

I laughed and changed the subject.

Harriet was always telling me how lucky I was, but the truth of the matter was that she had several things I really wanted: she had peace of mind; an imperturbability in the face of any crisis; a stability; she had a connection with God that I greatly admired; and, last but not least, she had the ability to take a couple of drinks and *stop*.

I had none of those things.

I stored that piece of religious information in my mind. *If all else fails,* I thought, *I will go to Quebec and get a miracle.*

Now I was here in Canada, and my dismal situation hadn't changed. I had brought myself with me. Panic and unknown terror had also accompanied me. The rooms of the castle closed in on me, and I became afraid of fear itself. My anxiety attacks had become so intense that I was often immobilized, paralyzed. Unable to be alone, I drowned the ones nearest me with words of guilt, self-pity, and remorse. I seesawed between complete dependency and total anger. One moment I would ask cloyingly, "Do you still love me?" and the next moment I would rage, "Don't touch me!"

I spent hours talking, pacing, reading, trying to bathe, trying to sleep. I wandered through my past, crying over old wounds, unhealed hurts, unresolved relationships. Talking incessantly, I would tell anybody everything. My past became more real than the present. Probably my "medicine" was rooting out those things I had repressed.

I didn't know what I was frightened of. What was it? I had a loving daughter who stood by me; a husband at wit's end; a job that I loved; and a Spanish shrink. But people finally got tired of my complaints.

What more could I do? I was doing everything I knew to help myself, but my emotions got worse instead of better. Both doctors had advised me to keep the Valium in my purse, but cautioned me about drinking. "The two don't mix well," they said. I had carefully followed their instructions, but this new peak of terror was more than I could bear.

Valium is a peculiar drug. It is neither an upper nor a downer. It silently levels things out. It gives no high, no rush, no boost, but only a dullness of soul. Doctors call it safe and sane, and millions of prescriptions are written for Valium every year. I was in good company. Many of the women teachers I worked with popped those little yellow pills. We were the intelligent ones, the dedicated ones, but we needed chemical help to get through the day.

Valium, however, doesn't always work. My prescription was for only four mg. a day, but upon arriving at the castle, I doubled my dosage and still found no relief.

I *had to have a drink!*

So I had won the argument. I got my expensive bottle of Canadian whiskey, secluded myself in my hotel room, and proceeded to drink to oblivion.

I was only dimly aware of the passage of time. I awakened alone, full of remorse, guilt, self-pity, and terror. All my Baltimore enemies had followed me to Quebec.

The hotel stationery told me where I was. Quebec, I was in Quebec. And I needed a miracle. *Bad.*

Holding onto the walls, I wobbled into the bathroom to brush my teeth. No go. I did my usual calisthentics, a waist-bend over the commode. I heard my husband come in and slam the door.

"I can't stand it. I'm taking you home," he said wearily.

"No," I pleaded. "No, please. Just one more day. I promise not to drink anymore. I want to go see a cathedral."

"A cathedral? *You* want to see a cathedral? Not a bistro? A pub? Not another fancy watering hole?" he sneered.

"Listen to who's talking! You enjoy those joints as well as I do!"

"I used to enjoy a quiet drink in a nice setting but not anymore! You've ruined it! Why can't you drink like a lady?"

The fight was on again, but I had no stamina for it. Besides, I had to get to the cathedral. This was my last chance. I began to cry.

"I don't know why I can't drink like a lady. I'm sick. I know you won't believe that but I am. I'm sorry, too. I don't know why I act like I do. If you'll only take me to Sainte Anne's, I promise not to make any more trouble for you."

"Where is it?" He gave in.

The twin spires of the beautiful, old cathedral, Sainte Anne de Beaupré, jutted up against a blue sky, decorated with white, fleecy clouds. My mental camera, which hadn't worked in years, took a picture. I can close my eyes today and see it.

Helping me up the steps, my husband left me to do solo sightseeing. It was just as well; I knew what I was going to do. I stopped at a souvenir booth.

"Where do you go to get a miracle?"

The girl looked at me and smiled.

"Over there." She pointed to a crowd around a table.

I made my way to where they were. Yes, I was in the right place. There was a man on crutches . . . a woman in a walker . . . a young girl in a wheelchair . . . a pale-looking baby, lying in a stroller. These people definitely needed miracles.

The adults were writing on a circular ledge, supported by a pole through the center like an outdoor umbrella table. Attached to this pole, in a little glass box, was a relic. The marker said that it was a piece of bone from the arm of the Virgin Mary's mother. *She must be Sainte Anne,* I thought. That's *interesting, but so what?*

While I stood puzzling over bones and miracles, a nun handed me a slip of paper.

"This is your petition, my dear," she smiled.

"What's a petition?"

"You write your intentions to Sainte Anne," she said, moving on.

What did she mean? I guessed I was supposed to write down what I wanted. Disappointed, I took a stub of a pencil, filled in my name and address, and wrote these words:

> *Dear God, I want the following things: 1. a happy marriage; 2. to see my son again; 3. help with my drinking problem.*
>
> *Sincerely,* MARY ELIZABETH

I read it over, feeling even more depressed. Was this all there was to it? I don't know what I had expected, but it certainly was more than this.

Suddenly I felt someone breathing on the back of my neck. I turned to see the amused face of my husband. He had been reading over my shoulder.

"What do you call that?" he asked contemptuously.

"I call it a *dead letter!*" I said disgustedly, shoving it through the petition slot.

Going to the rest room, I swallowed down three Valiums and went out to the car.

So much for miracles, I thought. *If there was a God, He didn't have one for me.*

But little did I know that the wheels of God, which grind very, very slowly, had started to turn for me.

The impossible takes a little longer!

19

The Temple of Amun

Linthicum, Maryland, 1972

Suzy's nose nudged my leg, interrupting my intense concentration. 11:00 P.M.! I had been working on my term paper for three hours straight without a break. The ice in my drink had long since melted, giving the scotch and soda a warm, flat taste. I swallowed the rest of it and went to the kitchen to mix another one.

My toy poodle, Suzy, and I were the only ones at home. My husband was on the night shift, and I very seldom saw him anymore.

Suzy whined, twirling on her hind feet for attention.

"Do you want to go out, little girl?"

She ran to the door, and I went outside with her. It was a cool April night, and I stood there, sipping my drink, looking up at the stars, pleased with my progress.

I was writing my final term thesis, prior to graduating next month with a Master of Liberal Arts degree from the Johns Hopkins University, one of America's most prestigious halls of ivy. Not only would this degree give me status among the intelligentsia but it would also significantly increase my salary, and add to the framed collection of degrees and honors hanging on my wall.

Suzy rooted around under the brilliant pink azaleas near the picture window.

"I have worth. I am smart. I am good," I chanted, practicing my affirmations.

My new psychiatrist, the Greek Dr. Dimitri, had assigned these mantras to compensate, he said, for a poor self-image. I was lost, he told me, and, for sixty dollars an hour, he was helping me find out who I was. Once I made contact with this paragon of virtue, this wonderful person hidden inside of me, I wouldn't need to boost my sagging ego with alcohol.

He also switched my prescription from Valium to Librium. It seemed to help. With the aid of Librium and a smart shrink (who recognized my good qualities), my drinking, though not stopped, had leveled off. I was certainly grateful for that since this was my last year at Hopkins, and I was enrolled in the most popular course on the campus: Dr. Janet Bernhardt's "Ancient Egypt."

Five years previously I had put my name on a waiting list for this course taught by Dr. Bernhardt, who is not only a favorite Hopkins professor but also America's leading Egyptologist. Her class is limited to twenty-five students in their final year of master's studies. So popular is her course, reservations for it must be made in the freshman year.

My mid-term grade was *A*, thanks to the mental camera which was improving since I had been off Valium. Dr. Bernhardt had asked only one question on the midterm exam.

"Draw the map of ancient Egypt." Hah! That was duck soup! With closed eyes I "saw" it in detail on the back of my eyelids, . . . every bend in the Nile, every wadi, all the towns, and so forth.

Drawing maps was my forte. It took me a half-hour to sketch it, and I left while the others were still figuring out the location of Thebes. The professor told me that in all her years of teaching Ancient Egypt, mine was the most detailed map she had graded. It wasn't easy to make an *A* under Dr. Bernhardt, but I did it! That should prove one thing at least— my so-called drinking problem was a figment of my husband's imagination. So what if I did have a few didoes to my credit? He had no room to talk. He was no saint.

I had waved my term grade under his nose.

"Look what Liz the Lush did!" I mocked.

He made no reply. Since my quirky Quebec escapade, I hadn't given him any more ammunition. Changing shrinks and medication seemed to stabilize my emotions and behavior.

I had been, more or less, in control of my drinking the last year. I *had to be.* Dr. Bernhardt's class met on Tuesdays and Thursdays, and *I had to be sober* during those crucial hours. More than anything else, I wanted to complete her course, and with it, my master's degree program, graduating with sober flying colors. Carefully planning ounces and hours, I *arranged* to be alert and abstinent at 8:00 P.M. every Tuesday and Thursday, with aspirin and Librium easing the headaches and heartaches. Eight months down and one to go. I could make it!

Suzy's barking broke my trance, and I called her inside.

Back at the dining-room table I poured myself another scotch and picked up my term paper to read what I had written.

> *The temple of Amun at Karnak, on the east bank of the Nile, just north of Thebes, grew out of a modest shrine that was erected in the twelfth Dynasty for the god Amun when he was a local deity.*

I don't know why I was hung up on shrines. They intrigued me. Given the first choice on the list (because I was the top student in the class), I chose the magnificent Egyptian shrine at Thebes as the subject of my final thesis. Ever since I read Richard Halliburton's adventure books as a child, I have wanted to visit Egypt, the Pyramids, and the shrines. Dr. Bernhardt's course was the next best thing to being there in person.

I read on. "Thutmose I, Hatshepsut, and Thutmose III laid out the basic features. . . ."

Wow! What a super paper this is! Dr. Bernhardt is going to blow her mind! If she thought my map of Egypt was good, wait till she reads my paper on the temple of Amun, I thought. *Maybe I'll become a famous writer.* I reached for another drink.

Suddenly I had a great idea!

"Harriet oughta know," I gushed sentimentally. "She's my bes' frien' so I oughta tell her first," I told Suzy, dialing Harriet's number.

"Hello," she answered drowsily.

"Harriet, hi, Harriet . . . my dear frien' . . . I wanna tell you sumpin' wunnerful."

"Liz, is that you? Have you been drinking?"

"I've been writin' my paper!" I yelled indignantly.

"Liz, it's almost midnight. What do you want?"

"Put on your robe, old gal! I'm comin' over!" I banged down the phone, and gathering up Suzy and my term paper, I got into my VW.

Slowly I drove the ten miles to Harriet's house, keeping my eye on the rearview mirror for the police. Usually staying close to home during drinking bouts, this particular late night excursion was an exception. I wanted no fuss with the fuzz. Hassling with a husband and dickering with doctors had been the extent of my public disgrace. That stupid principal who tried to pin a bum rap on me to ruin my teaching record learned his lesson!

The lights in Harriet's house were ablaze, and the front door open. I walked in to the aroma of coffee, just as Harriet came out of the kitchen with a large, steaming mug.

"Here, Liz, drink this."

"Do you have any scotch?"

"You don't need any more scotch, kid. You need coffee! Here!" she shoved it at me.

I took a few sips to pacify her.

"What do you want? I have to get up at 6:00 A.M." She looked at me worriedly.

I took my term paper out of my large purse.

"I have here what ish probably gonna be THE MOSH FAMOUS document in hishtory! My thesis! *Ta-Da!*" I waved it around. "You're gonna be the firsht to hear it cause you're my besh friend."

"I should be so lucky," she groaned. "Honey, let me put you down on the sofa . . . you're tired . . . been working hard . . . we can read it in the morning. . . ."

"*No!* You're gonna hear it *now!* Beshides, Suzy's out in the car 'n' I'm goin' home after this."

I began to read the paper: "Thuh tempul of Amnoon of Crow Neck, on thuh eash bank of thuh Nile, jush norsh of Thebes, grew outta a modesh shrine . . . shrine . . . oh-h-h, Harriet . . ." I blubbered, thinking of the Canadian caper.

"Liz, honey, drink some more coffee. Why don't you lie down on the couch?"

"No, I'm gonna finish thish and go home." I plowed through the rest of the paper, Harriet yawning.

"Well, whaddaya think of that? Ishn't it stupendush?"

"Yeah, Liz, okay. Have some more coffee."

"*Okay?* Ish that all you can say? I don't think you were paying attenshun! I gonna read it to you agin."

"NO! I heard it the first time!"

Suddenly I had a good idea!

"Come on, Harriet, have a drink with me—just one drink and I'll go on home," I wheedled.

"That's a deal," she quickly agreed.

I followed her to the kitchen, where she mixed two weak drinks.

"Here," she said, handing me the watery libation, which I gulped down.

Sipping hers slowly, she urged me several more times to stay with her, but I refused. My mind was on the bottle of Chivas Regal on the dining-room table back home. When she got up to go to the bathroom, I dashed out to the kitchen and glugged down more whiskey.

"I'm going now!" I called to her, going out the door.

"Liz, please. It's 2:00 A.M.! Stay overnight. I'll fix you a good breakfast in the morning . . ." she called after me but I was already gone.

Cautiously I inched the Volks around the subdivision of Country Club Estates, with Suzy licking me on the cheek. One street looked like another, and they all went in circles. I passed Harriet's house a couple more times, and slowed down trying to focus on the street sign.

"I'm lost, Sue," I giggled, remembering Dr. Dimitri's diagnosis. He had given me a list of "affirmations" to remedy the situation. "Just talk to yourself and reprogram your mind," he said. "You are better than you think, so let's have another drink!" I sang loudly, overcome with gales of laughter.

Ga-lump! Suzy and I hit the ceiling. The car had bumped over a curb and come to a halt in some grass.

Dazed, I sat staring straight ahead.

Suddenly I noticed a gum-ball machine in my rearview window. Fascinated, I watched the red and blue lights go round and round.

"Lady, are you all right?" a face appeared in the side window.

"Uh. Yeah." Suzy started barking.

"Get out, please, and let me see your license." He opened the door for me.

Good grief! It was a highway patrolman!

Gathering up my bag and stuffing my term paper inside, I climbed out and stood swaying in his headlights.

"Get into my car, lady," he said.

"Okay, offishur."

That's so nice of him, I thought. *He's going to drive me home.* I got in the backseat, and we started off.

"Oh-h-h, we furgot, Suzy!" I yelled at him.

"She'll be all right," he assured me. I took his word for it, and waved bye-bye to her.

For the first time I noticed that there was another policeman sitting next to me.

"Whash your name, young man?" I felt friendly.

"Frank Smith, ma'am." He sounded like Jack Whoosits in *Dragnet.*

"Dum-de-dum-dum," I laughed, nudging him. "Get it?"

He didn't reply. We rode along in silence.

Suddenly I had a great idea! I fished my term paper and a little flashlight out of my purse.

"I've gotta real treat for you boys." I cleared my throat, "Lishen to this: thuh tempul of Amen at Crow Neck, on the eash bank of the Nile, just norsh of Fibbs, grew out of a modesh shrine . . . shrine . . . Offishur! This ishn't my house!"

We had arrived at a brightly lighted police station, and they helped me out of the car.

"Whaddare we doin' here?" I asked curiously. *Maybe they're sending a special squad car back for Suzy?*

We went inside to meet another policeman. He looked at me through slitted eyes and read me my rights as a citizen.

"Lady, you are under arrest for Driving While Intoxicated," he intoned. "Do you have anything to say for yourself?"

Waves of helplessness and panic I had never felt before engulfed me. My knees buckled and I sank down on a bench. I cast about in my mind what I could say for myself, but pain had wiped it blank. I could only think of *one good thing in my favor.*

"Yesh, offishur," I said, drawing myself up regally, "I am the Shweetheart of Shigma Chi!"

20

Bottom
of the Bird Cage

Baltimore, Maryland, Spring 1972

The house was ominously quiet. Suzy sat on the sofa next to me, her head hanging low, following my every movement with her big, brown eyes.

My husband was on the telephone upstairs in his bedroom with the door closed. After hours of effort, he had bailed me out of the pokey, retrieved my car, recovered Suzy from the dog pound, and driven me home. And he hadn't been in any mood to listen to "The Temple of Amun."

Who was he talking to now? Maybe another shrink, or a hospital, or a lawyer. . . .

As I heard him coming down the stairs, I froze. He was angrier than I had ever seen him, but was trying to control it.

He had a very sensitive job with the U.S. government, and I was ruining his reputation. He told me that more than once. We had been invited to many parties on the famous Washington "cocktail circuit," where celebrities rub elbows with lesser luminaries; where lobbyists twist the arms of congressmen in their cups; where the business of the kingdom is done. My orders were, as always, to drink like a lady. I could dress like a lady, behave like a lady, and talk like a lady, but for some unknown reason, the whole act went up in smoke once I took the first drink. Try as hard as

I could, I *could not drink like a lady.* Invariably I got embarrassingly bombed, saying and doing stupid things I couldn't remember the next day, humiliating him in front of his bosses. My theme song for the past couple years had been "You Always Hurt the One You Love," and I went around chanting, "I'm sorry; please forgive me," like a broken record. But this last transgression had blown the top off the mountain. I doubted that our marriage, already badly bent from boozing, would ever recover.

One look at his face told me to stifle the I'm-sorry-please-forgive-me routine. Better keep my mouth shut.

"Your lawyer's name is Walter Thompson, and here's his number," he muttered, throwing a slip of paper at me. Then, dangling my car keys, he said, "You're grounded."

"Grounded!" I exploded. "How do you expect me to get to work or to classes at Hopkins? Walk?"

"That's your problem," he shouted, slamming out of the house.

I ran after him, but he was gone, leaving me once more in more misery than I could handle.

"No problem, Sue, I'll take a cab to work!" I said defiantly.

Raging anger swept over me at the injustice of it all. Who did he think he was, telling me I couldn't drive my own car? He wasn't so high and mighty! He drank, too. We used to enjoy drinking together, but I couldn't control it anymore. The fact that he could infuriated me. How could he act like a Holy Joe when he drank the same stuff I did? Why was I the one stuck with going to shrinks and doctors while he got off scot-free? It wasn't fair!

"Come on, Sue," I said, putting her leash on, "I know one place that's within walking distance."

It was Al's Liquor Store.

But I had forgotten that it was Thursday night, my semi-weekly rendezvous with Dr. Janet Bernhardt.

The class was already in session when I cautiously opened the classroom door. Stumbling over someone's feet, I flopped down into the nearest chair-desk. I had never been late for class before.

"The invasion of the Egyptian delta region by the 'Hyksos' was really an infiltration by Palestinians, glad to find refuge in a more peaceful environment. Most of these Palestinians were Semites, and scarabs have been found inscribed with the name 'Ya-kob,' probably the patriarch Jacob," Dr. Bernhardt intoned.

Seated in the back of the room, I covered most of my face with my hand, faking a studious pose. This was not my usual place. Normally I sat on the front row, so I could be the first to answer questions, but tonight I was drunk. And I knew it. However, master of the cover-up, I was confident that if I sat in the back and kept my mouth shut, no one would know.

Suddenly I got the hiccups.

"Hic . . . hic . . . hic!"

"The term, 'Hyksos,' was a word used by the Egyptians . . ." the professor continued.

I started to giggle.

"I wonder if the 'Hyksos' got the hiccups?" I nudged the student next to me.

She glared back. (Hopkins students are seldom frivolous.)

The professor stopped talking and looked back at me.

"Did you say something, Miss Rogers?" she asked.

I had made a juvenile boo-boo. No one talks when Dr. Bernhardt teaches.

"No, ma'am," I snickered.

The whole class turned and looked at me. I giggled again. She frowned and went on.

"From your last assignment, can someone tell me the significance of the Hyksos invasion for the ancient Near East?"

"Hic . . . hic . . . hic!"

My giggles were out of control. I couldn't help myself. I put my head down on the desk, laughing uproariously.

The professor stopped again and deliberately put down her chalk. No one moved as she walked back to my desk, raised my head, and stared into the face of her disgustingly drunken disciple.

Her amazed look of repugnance branded itself on my brain, and my mental camera went "click" for the last time.

"Perhaps you'd like to be excused," she said formally, and, sniggling uncontrollably, I gathered my things and left.

For problem drinkers like me blackouts are often a blessing, blotting out the memory of blunders made while under the influence of alcohol. However, I was not to be allowed to forget my foolishness. Sobering up the next morning, remembering every degrading detail, I suffered great remorse and guilt. Embarrassment and humiliation tortured me as the picture of Dr. Bernhardt's face stayed embedded on the back of my eyelids. I couldn't get away from it. Even in my sleep her look of loathing haunted me.

And now, garbed in black mortarboard and gown, waiting with the rest of the graduates for the processional, I could see her again. I half-expected her to come up and yank me out of the line, forbidding me to graduate. But she didn't show up.

It was a beautiful spring day, blue skies, perfect weather, but inside me a storm was raging. Tossed about by twenty-foot emotional waves, my face contorted trying to control it, my heart pounding rapidly, I was coming to the end of my resources. This was it. I had had it. The suffering was too great. I had done everything I knew to get help, to no avail.

A bad seed. Like the Patty McCormack movie, I was a bad seed. No matter what I did, it was wrong.

I had met with Dr. Bernhardt's class one more time to take the final exam. But I couldn't write or think. My hands shook so bad that I could hardly form the words with the pen. I covered less than a half-page in a blue book and handed it in. I couldn't look her in the eye.

Crisis upon crisis had piled up. My lawyer, Mr. Thompson, was in contact with my doctor, trying to work out a medical defense. Graduation was an iffy thing, considering the fact that I must have failed the final. My children had decided not to attend anyway, and the rejection hurt. My husband was incommunicado, working, gone, wherever.

At the last moment he appeared, to drive me to the university. *He must be somewhere out there in the crowd,* I thought. The music began, and we graduates slowly marched across the lovely campus. We took our seats on the grassy area in front of the Milton Eisenhower library, and President Steven Muller addressed the assemblage.

This is my big moment, the dream of my life come true, I thought. *This is what I've worked five long years to achieve.*

The president's voice was far away. I was in a dream world which had turned into a nightmare.

Everyone should be proud of me, but they're not. They hate me. Everybody hates me. I hate myself. Tears ran down my face as wave upon wave of self-pity washed over me.

"... you graduates will be the leaders of the community, the successful businessmen, scientists, artists ..." President Muller was saying.

An evil voice spoke clearly in my head, "They will be the leaders, all right, but you won't. You'll be dead. This is the last day of your life."

"Yes," I whispered to him. "This *is* the last day of my life." A strange peace suddenly engulfed me, as if the whole thing were out of my hands.

Once again the music was playing, and we were marching. It was all over. I had switched the tassle from one side of my mortarboard to the other. I was now a "Master of the Liberal Arts." I had only to pick up my diploma and go home.

The end was near.

The hands of the kitchen clock were at midnight as I put the top back on the fifth of Chivas Regal. I looked at my diploma on the table.

"The Johns Hopkins University, upon the recommendation of the faculty . . ." I laughed scornfully.

"I wonder if that includes Dr. Bernhardt," I snorted, finishing the rest of my glass.

I had drunk nearly the entire fifth of scotch but I felt nothing. No high, no low, nothing. Even the liquor had turned against me.

"Now! Hurry, do it now!" The voice in my head broke in again.

I got up to leave. Lucky thing I found a spare set of car keys. Suzy raced to the door with me and whined. We both went out into the warm, starry night, and she leaped into the Volkswagen ahead of me. Paying no attention to her, I listened to the urgent voice telling me what to do.

"Down the street and turn left."

I obeyed the instruction.

"Up the hill and then stop."

Again I did what he said.

I was at the top of a steep hill on Charles Street. Down the hill in the distance was a row of trees bordering a brook.

"Let go! Let go!" the voice urged.

I took my foot off the brake and the little VW shot down the hill at breakneck speed.

Halfway down the hill I lost consciousness.

21
More Lives Than One

Baltimore, Maryland, 1972

> For he who lives more lives than one
> More deaths than one must die.
> WILDE, *The Ballad of Reading Gaol*

I opened my eyes and at the foot of my bed was a figure, dressed in a Mexican soldier's uniform. He kept fading in and out of sight. He looked like my husband, but I couldn't be sure.

"I hope you die," he said.

"I hope I do, too."

I closed my eyes and drifted off.

Still alive—a failure even at suicide. I wasn't even badly hurt, but all of my ribs were cracked, and I had a brain concussion. Doped up on some kind of painkiller, I was unable to speak clearly.

"You're a miracle!" my student, Teresa, told me. She said she heard my car crash across the street from her house, and ran outside. The VW had somehow slithered between the trees, rolled over twice, and landed upside down in the creek.

"I recognized your car immediately, Miss Rogers, so I called to you, and you climbed right out of the window!" she went on excitedly.

"I did? . . . can't remember a thing." I mumbled. That was the truth; mercifully my mind was a blank.

"What happened?" she asked curiously.

"I *can't remember!*"

"Well, it's a miracle you're alive . . . that's what the guys with the tow truck said. The entire car was crushed except for a little bubble where your body was. Somebody's looking out for you!" she exclaimed earnestly.

I didn't reply. The one question I wanted to ask filled me with dread.

Finally I got up the courage: "Did you happen to see my dog? . . . my little black poodle?"

"No, Miss Rogers, I didn't . . . I didn't see any dog."

"Oh, Teresa," I cried, "what time is it? Where am I?"

"You're at home! It's afternoon . . . you'll be okay," she patted my arm. "I can stay with you awhile."

"Thank you, honey," I couldn't hold my eyes open. They had given me some Demerol at the hospital, after patching me up. Then they sent me home. No one had known of my deranged decision; they assumed I had had an accident. Teresa had driven me to and from the hospital, and I didn't remember a thing.

Where was Suzy? I drifted off into a strange dream:

"Miss Rogers, I have bad news for you," the white-clad psychiatrist with a goatee, holding clipboard and pen, said solemnly.

"What is it, doctor?"

"Because of your drinking, your dog has a serious personality disturbance. We have tested her and she has schizophrenia."

"Oh-h, what can we do?"

"She must undergo psychoanalysis immediately. I will call on her each day at the dog pound. That will be a hundred dollars an hour."

"Oh-h, thank you, doctor! What is your name?"

"Dr. Clover."

I awoke with a start! What a nightmare! I tried raising my head from the pillow.

"Ow-w-w!" I screamed.

Teresa came running up the stairs to my room.

I was crying, "Oh-h, please help me! Help me up!"

She pulled me gently, and with enormous pain, I managed to get out of bed and walk.

"It's almost 9:00 P.M., Miss Rogers. I'm going to have to go," she said, handing me a pill with a glass of water. "Take this sedative before I leave."

I swallowed it down.

"You go on, Teresa. Thanks . . . thanks for all you've done." I couldn't think of the words to thank her.

She kissed me on the forehead and left.

Alone. I was alone again. It seemed as if I was always alone. But this loneliness was a dark, black pit, and I was teetering on the edge of it . . . any moment I would fall in. I didn't know that acute symptoms are the soul's way of saying that you are frightened, lonely, loveless, depressed. I didn't know that chemicals could bring on such exquisite pain. I would rather *do* anything than experience these emotions of loss, fear, anger, sadness—*anything.*

The worst thing about mental agony is that you can't get away from your own head. Only unconsciousness would accomplish that relief.

With agony of movement, I reached for the plastic container of Demerols. I twisted it one way and another, but it had a kiddie-proof lid, and I couldn't get it off!

Total anger and frustration swept over me. *"Somebody" had His eye on me for sure. He wouldn't let me live, and He wouldn't let me die!* I wanted *out.* A play about the futility of living, which I saw several times, said it perfectly: STOP THE WORLD! I WANT TO GET OFF!

I shook my fist at the ceiling:

"Who are You? What do You want?" I shouted.

Silence was the answer.

Suddenly, down at the front door, I heard the barking of a little dog.

22
Reality
in the Rose Garden

Linthicum, Maryland, Fall 1972

Another shrink.

This one put me back on Valium, which he said I would probably have to take for the rest of my life. These stronger drugs did curb my drinking to some degree, but again I lived in a dull, hollow, hopeless half-life. The summer of 1972 was spent either in his air-conditioned office or behind drawn draperies in my house, with Suzy and Tinky, my Siamese cat, to keep me company.

My weight was up to 140 pounds, and I resolved to slim down, get a tan, and get in shape before beginning a new school year. Refusing all meals but one small salad a day, I existed on a tight regimen—Valium, lettuce, sunbaths, shrink. My aim was to be a middle-aged version of "The Girl From Ipanema."

"Tell me about your childhood, Miss Rogers."

The psychiatrist leaned back in his chair, taking notes on a clipboard.

Dr. William Wellington Shaw had been recommended to my husband by one of his government bigwig friends. Short, fat, and beardless, he never looked me in the eye.

"Dr. Shaw, do I have to? Can't you get the information from your colleagues? I've gone over and over the same thing so many times, but it's never helped my drinking problem. I *must* have help, or my husband will leave me. He wants me to drink like a lady, and I've got to learn how! Can you help me with *that?*"

"How much do you drink, Miss Rogers?" He never looked up from his notes.

"Do you want it in quarts, fifths, ounces, or cubic centimeters?" I asked sarcastically.

"Why do you feel threatened, Miss Rogers?" still not looking at me. More psychobabble!

"I feel threatened because you are charging me seventy-five dollars an hour, and we're going round and round the same barn!" I shouted at him.

"I see," he intoned, "and you feel angry, belligerent, upset."

"And infuriated, irate, indignant, and irritated!" I yelled.

At that he looked up. Good! At least he was alive!

"Dr. Shaw, do you want to play Scrabble?!" I asked resignedly.

"No, Miss Rogers, why do you ask?"

"Word games! We're playing word games, just like my father and I used to do!"

"Ah-h-h! Tell me about your father, Miss Rogers." He was back on solid ground, head down, taking notes again.

"Oh, my God."

I couldn't sleep. Night after night I lay open-eyed and totally exhausted. How ludicrous!

This insane insomnia was the reason I sought help years ago, and now I'm worse instead of better.

After thousands of dollars and hundreds of hours in doctors' offices I still couldn't sleep.

The Valium caused tics and tremors—twitching and shaking in various parts of my body. I couldn't walk straight without holding on to the furniture or a wall. The worst symptom was slurred speech. I *had* to do something about that. *No way* could I go back into the classroom, staggering and babbling. I *had* to have a clear mind to teach mathematics. Now that I was on a higher pay scale, thanks to my new master's degree, my work had to be more, not less, efficient. I was afraid that I might have promoted myself out of a job. The teachers on higher pay scales didn't last long. They were too expensive to keep on the payroll. Hassled daily, they were under constant scrutiny. On-the-job tensions were tremendous.

The end of September found me tan and trim at 120 pounds. The high school had a new principal who was trying to pull the faculty back together. Maybe under him I would have a better chance at survival in the educational rat race.

Entering the side door of the high school that morning, I stopped by the auditorium, as always, to greet my friend Toby, the head of the Art Department. She was an alcoholic. Everybody knew about her drinking problem, and the tragedy which caused it. But we all loved Toby, who was often included in the after-school get-togethers at the Lancer's Pub. Calling ourselves the Quiz Kids, Harriet, Alene, Toby, and myself, teachers of math, music, and English, enjoyed our outings together.

"How are you feeling, Toby?" I asked, sinking down into a chair, my own head dizzy. It was early, so I had time to chat.

"Liz, I'm just making it one day at a time. The pain is so bad this morning, I don't think I can stand it." Her appearance was pitiful. It hurt me to look at her. Arthritis had so swollen her body that she could barely move.

"What are you doing about it?"

"Daddy put me on the 'gold treatment' but it doesn't seem to help." Her father was a famous physician, member of a presidential advisory committee.

"I'll pick you up after school. We'll go to the Lancer's Pub and celebrate the end of the month! Okay?"

"Okay!" her eyes brightened. "A couple of drinks is the only thing that eases this pain!"

(A couple of drinks, hah! Toby always got loaded.)

"See you later!"

I walked carefully up the stairs to my own classroom, steadying myself on the wall, when I thought no one was looking. I had tapered down to two Valiums—one in the morning and one in the evening, maintaining a precarious balance of mind and body.

That afternoon when the Quiz Kids arrived at the Lancer's Pub, the waitress, expecting us, served us our usual drinks without asking. I began with two double Southern Comfort sours.

"Toby, you're limited to three martinis," we told her. From experience we knew that after three, she would start retelling the story of her little daughter's death, crying out of control, causing a disturbance.

"Bring them all at once then. This pain is terrible."

The waitress brought our drinks, and Toby and I gulped ours down thirstily. The others were sippers, especially Alene. She could nurse a drink for an hour, the ice melting in it.

Within ten minutes Toby and I were ready for more, and I beckoned the waitress to bring another round.

"Liz, no more for Toby . . . remember?" Harriet said.

"Aw-w-w, Harriet, you're a party pooper," I jibed.

"Then you're responsible for driving her home, not me!"

"Okay, okay, I'll take Toby home!"

And take her home I did. The two of us were bombed out of our gourds, but I carefully inched my new white Mustang around Linthicum to Toby's big, country home. Even though I was drunk, I couldn't forget the shame and humiliation of the police-station incident. For a healthy fee my lawyer had put up a successful defense, and I was free to drive again. The downhill "accident" was charged to "failing brakes." No tickets were written.

With much laughing and falling, we stumbled upstairs to her bedroom, and I helped her to undress. I had done this many times before, and I knew where everything was. I went to the bathroom to get a wet washcloth. Returning, I saw that she had passed out on the bed. She lay there, drunk, swollen, partially nude, pitiful.

Suddenly a Voice said to me:

"But for the grace of God, there you are."

Immediately I was cold sober. I whirled around to see who was standing behind me, but there was no one there! I searched through the other bedrooms, ran downstairs through the kitchen, living room, dining room. No one.

Where did that wonderful Voice come from? It sounded like Liquid Love. I wanted to hear it again.

I went outside to the rose arbor in her backyard and sat down on the swing to try to put things together. Suddenly, it seemed urgent that I make a decision. I had to decide, right then and there, whether I wanted to live or die. I couldn't go one more minute, not one inch further, until I faced this "moment of truth."

The past fourteen years played inside my head like a technicolor movie. I saw the years of pills and drinks and shrinks—all those wasted years. I remembered a long-forgotten poem but couldn't recall who wrote it: "Some men die by shrapnel/Some men die by flames/Most men just die inch by inch, playing little games." That was me ... I had spent most of my life fantasizing, spinning my wheels, playing little games.

Inside my head came this question: *What have you done with your life?*

The chips were down, I couldn't lie. *Nothing,* I thought. *I'm forty-five years old and I've done nothing worthwhile with my life.* Every effort had been to get something for myself: a higher salary, a bigger house, a better car, a higher degree, everything for me. I was the center of my own world. No need to ask who my God was. I was my own god.

"What can I do?" I asked in confusion.

An idea formed in my mind.

"For starters, you can give up your crutches: you can dismiss Dr. Shaw, flush the pills down the toilet, and pour out the liquor."

"That's what I'm going to do!" I resolved, as I left the security of the rose garden, and drove home to meet the consequences of my decision.

I didn't know that I was too sick; too addicted to these chemical substances; too addicted to alcohol, to withdraw safely without medical help.

My quality decision brought me to the brink of death.

23

The First Day
of the Rest of My Life

Linthicum, Maryland, December 1972

With heart pounding, and high with the resolve born of desperation, I went through the house from top to bottom, gathering up all the bottles of wine, scotch, beer—everything that contained alcohol. Some of it belonged to my husband, but I took it anyway. I went to the sink, opened each one and poured it down the drain. Gone!

The little evil voices said, "You'll die, you fool! You'll be sorry! In ten minutes you'll be in agony!"

"Shut up! I'm sick and tired of you!" They were quiet.

Again, I went back through the house, to the medicine cabinet, in my drawers, in all my purses. I gathered up all the vials and little plastic containers of pills. It looked like a small drugstore on the sink. I flushed them down the toilet. Gone!

Again the clamor of voices in my head began.

"Shut up, I told you!" They were quiet again.

Only one more thing to do—say bye-bye to Dr. Shaw. But it was too late; his office would be closed. *I'll call tomorrow,* I promised myself. *I'll get a good night's sleep and call him in the morning. Tomorrow is Saturday.* This would give me two days to recuperate from the withdrawal agonies of quitting pills and booze. Monday I would go to work feeling better.

I undressed and went to bed, alone, as usual, except for Suzy, who had followed me on my housecleaning mission.

I closed my eyes and mercifully went to sleep. It was to be my last night's sleep for six months.

Saturday I got out of bed, and did my usual morning exercises over the toothbrush.

Monday I'll be able to brush my teeth without upchucking, I thought. How naive I was!

I made a pot of coffee, filled a mug, and went back to bed. The hair on my head hurt. My scalp felt like it was on fire.

"Sure, it's going to be tough," I told myself, "but you can make it. This is the end. No more booze or pills—*Ever.*"

Gradually strange things began happening in my head—whirring noises, ringing and whistling sounds. I got up and paced the floor.

Around noon I called Dr. Shaw's office. He wasn't in, his receptionist said. I told her to scratch my name off his schedule, I wouldn't be coming back, and hung up. I didn't have the nerve to listen to her response. I took the phone off the hook. By early afternoon a creeping sense of anxiety came into my head, and little jolts of pin-pricking electricity darted all over me. I tried to breathe deeply. My body suddenly went cold. I broke out in a clammy sweat.

These symptoms continued on and off, in waves of nausea, dread, and fear all day Sunday. The accompanying emotions were indescribable, all rushing together at once. Every part of my body was affected—my eyes, ears, mouth, stomach, arms, and legs. My mouth jerked spasmodically, and I let out little screams that scared me. Suzy whined and moaned, crying in her own way for me. Toward the end of the day, I began to feel some relief. I was able to hold a little water on my stomach. I hadn't eaten for two days, only drunk coffee.

I have to go to work! No more absences! I'm working under a new principal. I want to make a good impression, I thought.

I thrashed around in bed most of Sunday night, closing my eyes only to see strange animals coming at me. Waking with a start, I decided that sitting up with the light on was preferable to being devoured by ghostly animals.

Monday dawned hot and humid. Slowly I dressed, drove the mile and a half to work, parked, and entered the building. The ceiling sloped down to brush my head and I ducked to miss it. I reeled toward the auditorium, but Toby wasn't there.

"She's absent again!" her assistant said with a knowing look.

Extreme paranoia overcame me, and I rushed away from him.

What is he thinking? Who's looking at me? What are people saying about me?

Thoughts of shame and humiliation washed over me. Oh, how I wanted a drink, but my resolve stayed firm. I remembered the experience in the rose garden, and gritted my teeth in determination.

Slowly, as the walls of the stairwell closed in on me, I climbed the stairs to my second-floor classroom.

I didn't suspect that today's classes would be the last I would ever teach.

So we come once more to the beginning, that fateful hour in the algebra-trig class, when my head refused to work, when I collapsed outside the door, and was taken to Dr. Cheng, a highly qualified specialist in nervous disorders, one of the many people God used to save my life.

Compassionate but direct, he laid it on the line.

"You *are an alcoholic, and if you drink again, you will surely die.*"

He explained how dangerous it was to withdraw abruptly from alcohol (and later, Valium), after using it for fourteen years. He showed me drawings and illustrations of what alcohol had done to my central nervous system, and gave me a 70 percent chance of recovery, better than he really believed. Because of his kindness, I listened to him.

In 1972 there were not as many recovery centers as there are today. The fashionable one nearby charged two thousand dollars for four weeks. I couldn't afford that place, but I should have had some kind of medical help. I went home and literally shook myself sober, every cell in my body crying out for the alcohol and Valium it was used to getting.

September, October, November, and then that memorable day, *December 7, 1972,* the moment when my new life began. Those three months in a living hell changed my life. I have never been the same since. Old values passed away. Problems and events I thought were earthshaking, became trivial. All my Hollywood dreams and Highland Park goals were just so much ticky-tacky. Family tragedies and difficult relatives became unimportant. The pride, passions, and opinions I had clung to were torn away from me. December 7 was the first day of the rest of my life.

What made that day different from all the others? What took place then that hadn't happened before? What made the difference?

Only one thing—I gave up.

I knelt down and cried out, "God help me!"

"Just that simple?" you say.

Yes, it's that simple.

The Law of the Paradox turned my life around. I didn't know that I had to surrender to win. If someone had told me that, I would have called him crazy. Nevertheless, God's laws work whether or not I know about them or believe in them. When I was a toddler, learning to walk, falling down and skinning my knees, the Law of Gravity was in effect, although I couldn't even pronounce it.

So this spiritual principle, the Law of the Paradox, says I have to surrender to win. Certainly no one likes to surrender. People like to *win*. Surrendering means that I lost, that I was a failure, that I was doing something wrong, that—heavens to Betsy—I might have been at fault! So, surrendering doesn't seem like winning. *But with alcoholism it is.*

Only after I came to the end of my rope, on the bottom of my bird cage, up against a stone wall, nowhere else to go, nothing else to try, nobody else to blame, did I surrender. The fellowship of Alcoholics Anonymous defines it as "ego deflation at depth."

That's where I was.

Certainly I had been given hints of God's mighty power working in my behalf. Ever since I wrote my "Dear God" letter in Quebec, my mental wavelengths had tuned in a Voice which sounded like Liquid Love. I first heard Him in Toby's bedroom, when He said, "But for the grace of God, there you are!"

He continued to talk to me in her rose garden, when I determined to throw my booze and pills away. He gave me the courage to carry out the assignment, sending me to a knowledgeable physician for treatment, and encouraging me through the months of withdrawal hell. It was all necessary in bringing me to this great turning point in my life—*my surrender to God.*

The Bible puts it this way in Acts 2:21:

Whosoever shall call upon the name of the Lord shall be saved.

I had never read the Bible, so I didn't know this principle. Nevertheless, it worked for me anyway. That day I became a "Whosoever."

It was the first day of the rest of my life.

24

The Character
in the Cream-Colored
Cadillac

Linthicum, Maryland, December 7, 1972

Immediately a knock came at the door. At least, it seemed like "immediately." When I opened it, there stood a fancy dude in a three-piece gray suit. His cream-colored Cadillac was parked in front of my house.

"Is there someone here having trouble with booze?" He looked at me and smiled.

My waist-length black hair had been unwashed for weeks. In my mismatched blouse and slacks, my red face swollen and blotched from so much crying, I looked like the wreck of the *Hesperus*. I began crying again.

"Yes, that's me," I sobbed.

He came in, sat down on the sofa, and introduced himself.

"My name is Al, and I'm an alcoholic. You called for help?"

"Help?" I whimpered, puzzled.

"I guess you don't remember," he said matter-of-factly. "You telephoned our group this morning, but there was no woman available to come to your aid, so here I am! You'll just have to put up with me."

"Oh." I had no idea what he was talking about.

"What's your name, honey?"

"Liz," I blubbered.

"Well, Liz, as I said, I'm an alcoholic," he went on, paying no attention to my crying. "I got your call at my office. I have a law practice in downtown Baltimore, but I came out to share my story with you the same way that Bill, my sponsor, shared his story with me when I called for help fifteen years ago. You have to give it away to keep it, you know!" he laughed.

An alcoholic? This well-dressed lawyer? It couldn't be! Everyone knew that alcoholics were either bums, prostitutes, or movie stars. And if he was an alcoholic, it certainly didn't bother him, the way he laughed! I could see that he was no one to be afraid of, so I stopped crying, dried my eyes, and listened.

He told me his story. He said that he had been a successful Baltimore lawyer but couldn't control his drinking. When he took one drink, he always had to have another, which led to another, then one more, which led to another one, and so on. So he always ended up "bombed out of his gourd." He said he was compelled to get drunk every time he drank, no matter how much he wanted to do otherwise. Finally he drank himself out of a marriage, three children, a beautiful home in Hunt Valley, and his law practice, and ended up a skid-row bum on Pratt Street.

He paused to catch his breath.

"What happened, Al?" I asked anxiously. It was the first time in months I had thought of anybody but myself.

"Same as you. I called for help." He lit a cigarette and waited for me to digest what he had said.

What an amazing story! And almost the same as mine, except I had been a successful teacher with a brand-new master's degree when the ax fell. *If this impeccably attired, intelligent professional says he's an alcoholic, maybe Dr. Cheng was right—maybe I am, too.* Suddenly the idea didn't seem so bad.

"Well, you're sure no skid-row bum now! What happened after you called for help?" I smiled, completely at ease with him.

"Fellow from the group talked to me," he took a drag on his cigarette. "Old Bill . . . he died sober . . . and he told me his story, same as I'm doing for you. But he told me one thing I didn't know. He told me that *alcoholism is a disease.*"

"A disease!" I exclaimed.

"Yes, that's right—a disease. He told me that alcoholism is a progressive, fatal disease and that, unless arrested, he was doomed to die a horrible death. He said that alcoholism is a total tyrant, crushing the spirit and inflicting an obsession on the mind and a craving on the body. Its victims are locked into a point-of-no-return death sentence.

"Then he asked me if I could manage to stay sober until 7:30 that evening, and I said I guess I could. He got me to a Recovery meeting that night, and I have been sober ever since. Got my practice back, and doing better than ever by applying the principles the group taught me."

"And you *never* drank again? How did you do it?" I asked incredulously.

"The same way you did, honey, I gave up. I asked for help." He smiled at me approvingly.

"You may not know it," he went on, "but you are on the road to recovery. You don't *have to drink anymore.*"

"I don't *have* to drink?" That was a new twist!

"That's right. You can if you want to, but you don't *have* to. You have a choice. Just for today, you can choose *not to drink.* The choice is yours. But you've already taken the first step," he declared.

"I have? What's the first step?"

"You asked for help. You admitted you had a problem. That's the first step to getting well: admitting you're sick," he said encouragingly.

"Sick!" I snorted. "That's the understatement of the century! But what do I do now?"

"Can you go without a drink until 7:30 tonight?"

"Certainly!"

He got up to go.

"Then I'll have a woman pick you up tonight and take you to your first Recovery meeting. Marty's an alcoholic and she lives in Glen Burnie. Be ready at 7:30."

"A meeting tonight! But I haven't been out of the house in months! I look like. . . ."

But he was out the door. I followed him as far as the driveway and watched him get into his cream-colored Cadillac. He rolled down the window.

"Don't forget, Liz. Today's the first day of the rest of your life!"

With a wave he drove off. I never saw him again. I walked up the front steps, surprised that I was climbing them without my cane. Somehow I felt stronger. I thought, *If I'm going to some sort of meeting, I had better get a bath!*

A small flicker of hope entered my heart. Maybe I was going to get well after all.

What took place on that cold December day that had never happened before?

I had gone to doctors, psychiatrists, and priests. None of them had suggested I had a disease. Why didn't they know? I had spent thousands of dollars for their so-called expertise. Then a Baltimore lawyer, himself a recovered alcoholic, came to my door. In thirty minutes he gave me more hope than I'd had in years. What was the cause of this miracle?

Because a miracle it was! I never drank again!

There are several factors involved in successfully carrying the message of sobriety. The first one is that it's not so much *what* is said but *who* is saying it. When Al carried the message of sobriety to me, it was *one alcoholic* talking directly to *another alcoholic*—birds of the same feather.

You see, long before a victim of alcoholism walks into his first Recovery meeting, he has probably asked for help from many other sources. Or maybe others have sought help for him. But all such helpers are *superior people*—doctors, shrinks, nurses, bosses, husbands, wives, ministers, priests, policemen, judges, parents, or whoever. Even though not verbalized, the degraded position of the alcoholic and the superior status of the helper is always understood. Overtones of disgust, disapproval, and distrust are always there. But for the first time in fourteen years, I heard a new song: "You can make it!" Instead of nagging and criticism ("Why did you do that?" and, "Why don't you do this?"), I heard the voice of a brother sufferer, saying, "This is what I did."

With "brother" Al, I let down my defenses entirely. I wasn't afraid of him. I knew he understood me and wasn't judging me. I trusted him not to hurt me, which was a miracle in itself, since I had been betrayed so many times.

If Al had not said, "I am an alcoholic!" I would not have listened to him. But because he laid down his reputation, his life, I'm alive today. That is the very reason why, in the face of much criticism and persecution, and after years of sobriety, I still say, *I am an alcoholic*. The scepter has passed to me, and I have the privilege of carrying the message of recovery by saying to another victim, *"My name is Liz and I'm an alcoholic."* Only if I wear the letter *A* will the suffering victim listen to me.

Another factor in the miracle of recovery from that ancient death-dealing enemy, alcoholism, is the unique maneuver of treating the physical symptoms *first*. If one of your children fell and gashed his head, would you set him down and lecture him on safety rules, or would you first stanch the flow of blood and bandage the wound? Even the most thorough diagnosis of his mistakes would do no good if he died. No. First things first! The horse *must* come before the cart.

So, as a beginner in sobriety, I was told that I had a progressive disease which, unless arrested, would kill me, and that the first step to take after calling for help was to make a decision *one day at a time* to stay away from the first drink. But the choice remained with me. No one could make the decision for me, and no one could make me carry it out. No pressure was put on me, no finger pointing, no reproaches. The ball was tossed into my court, and I had to play it.

First things first. My physical symptoms were treated on the very first day of my recovery program, when Al asked me if I could stay away from a drink until 7:30 P.M. *Not one* of my doctors or psychiatrists *ever* suggested that I stop drinking for any period of time, until Dr. Cheng told me it would kill me. Only later, and with much help and in great detail, were my deplorable mental and spiritual conditions treated.

In Father Martin's chapter we learned that alcohol is a drug closely related to ether. If a surgery patient, coming out from under anesthesia, babbles obscenities or behaves strangely, the nurse doesn't call a psychiatrist to analyze his psyche or a priest to confess his sins. No, she would wait for the ether to wear off and the patient to come to his senses. The same is true for the alcoholic patient. The alcohol must *leave* his body and mind first *before* effective work can be done with his mind, emotions, and spirit.

You see, I had to learn that alcoholism is a three-part illness: *bankruptcy of the spirit, obsession of the mind, and addiction of the body.* Perhaps I should clarify what I mean by a "bankrupt spirit." I do not mean that I didn't *have* a spirit. Everyone has a human spirit. What I meant was the absence of the Holy Spirit. And even worse, possession of a wrong spirit, the spirit of alcoholism. All this was part of the learning program started when Al came to call in his cream-colored Cadillac and arranged for my first lessons in recovery.

I must have seen the name of Al's group in a newspaper or on television. He said I called them, but I don't remember doing so. My head wasn't hitting on all cylinders, and the memory of those crucial days is dim. I'm telling what I can recall, but one thing I know for sure: God chose that group of recovered alcoholics, beginning with Al, to save my life.

These wonderful recovery principles, which I would learn later, were waiting for me as I bathed, washed my hair, dressed, and sat down to wait for Marty to take me to my first meeting.

25

"Whom the Gods Would Destroy . . ."

Pasadena, Maryland, December 1972

Fearfully, I entered the large room, where some sort of reception was being held. Well-dressed men and women were laughing and visiting with each other, drinking coffee and munching cookies. *Perhaps it's a church meeting,* I thought, standing inconspicuously in a corner.

Just as Al promised, Marty, a stylishly dressed woman, old enough to be my mother, picked me up. She told me that after her husband died two years before, she began drinking around the clock. Her minister recommended this program six months ago, so she was a newcomer, too. I promptly dubbed her "Mama Marty."

"Six months! That's a long time!" I exclaimed, beginning to relax.

She smiled. "When did you have your last drink, Liz?"

"Sometime in September. I don't remember too well." I wasn't about to tell her of my stroke.

As we pulled into the yard of a little, white, country church, my heart began to pound. Since I didn't bring my cane, my right knee kept giving out, as we walked up the sidewalk.

This is like the last nine yards to the electric chair, I thought. *Who are these people? And what am I doing here? I'm certainly not as bad as they are! Good grief, these guys are* alcoholics!

Already I had begun to rationalize and minimize the seriousness of my predicament.

"Certainly *you* couldn't be an alcoholic!" my sick head assured me. "You have too much education. You're too well bred. What would your parents say if they knew you were here?" In agony, I waited for the ax to fall.

A woman in a Harris tweed suit, with a southern accent, came over and held out her hand.

"Hi! My name's Nancy. I'm an alcoholic from Texas."

"Texas! So am I! My name's Liz," I replied shakily.

We shook hands. She sure didn't look like an alcoholic.

"Come on, the meeting is about to start." We sat at a large table in the middle of the room, and she put her arm around me.

"You'll be okay, honey. I was scared stiff at my first meeting, too," she assured me. "Let me get you a cup of coffee."

"Thanks." She reminded me of Al, calm and cool.

She put a steaming cup in front of me, but I had the shakes so bad that I spilled it on the table.

"Don't worry about it, everyone spills coffee around here," she chuckled.

"Nancy," I whispered, looking around, "where are all the alcoholics? Al said this was a Recovery meeting."

She laughed.

"It is, honey," she said, patting my arm, "we're *all* alcoholics here."

"All these people?" I asked incredulously. "They don't *look* like it!"

"Well, we are! We are alcoholics who *don't drink.*"

"Alcoholics who *don't drink?* I never heard of such a thing. If you don't drink, how could you be an alcoholic?"

"Liz, alcoholism is a disease. For most of us in this room, with the exception of the newcomers, the disease has been arrested. I've been sober for seven years now . . . sh-h-h, the meeting's about to start!"

The man at the head table pounded his gavel and opened the meeting by saying, "My name is Larry, and I'm an alcoholic," and he began to read the bulletin of events for the Greater Baltimore Area, announcing the locations of several Christmas parties and the New Year's Eve Dance. I was amazed at all these activities.

"Hey, Nancy," I whispered, nudging her, "what do you guys drink at the New Year's Eve party?"

"Coffee!"

"Yuck!" I chuckled, beginning to enjoy myself.

Larry then introduced the speaker who said, "My name is Matt, and I'm an alcoholic." He told his story the same as Al had done; how he first started drinking at an early age; how the progression of the disease crept up on him, so that he didn't notice how much he consumed; how he hit bottom and called for help. Then he said something that really frightened me. He said that he continued to get drunk at regular intervals, and that he couldn't maintain his sobriety for any length of time. He announced the subject of the meeting was "How do *you* stay sober?"

"Hey, Nancy," I nudged her again, "why do you allow this guy to belong to the group if he still drinks?"

"*Anyone*, wet or dry, who has a problem with alcohol, can attend these meetings. We have all levels of sobriety here, from none to twenty-one years," she whispered back.

"Wow! Twenty-one years! Who has that much sobriety?"

"Harold H. Sh-h-h, listen now."

One by one, Matt called on the people sitting at our table. Each gave a short talk on how they maintained their sobriety. One man said that he attended the meetings regularly. Another said that he "put the cork in the jug." A girl named Peg said that she lived "one day at a time." Another woman said she depended on a Higher Power to keep her sober.

"Nancy!" I whispered in a panic. "What if he calls on me?"

Before she could reply, Matt pointed at me.

"How about you, honey?"

"Oh-h-h, my name is Liz, and I'm new," I stammered.

"You're new? Well, I have a little token for you," he said, reaching into a box and handing me a red poker chip.

"This is your twenty-four-hour sobriety chip. If you feel an urge to drink, just put it under your tongue. When it melts, you can have some booze!" Everybody laughed.

I don't know what I expected at a Recovery meeting, but it certainly wasn't a bunch of characters like this. I put the chip in my purse. Today, almost twelve years later, it occupies an honored position in my jewelry box.

Then Matt called on Nancy, and she began to talk.

"My name is Nancy, I'm an alcoholic and an 'anger-holic.' I don't have a problem with booze anymore, but I have a real problem with anger. I get furious with my husband who doesn't understand the nature of alcoholism and still expects me to drink with him. He continually throws up my past mistakes, even though I've been sober seven years. So I have to pray for him every day, or it's back to the bottle for me. I can't afford temper tantrums or brainstorms if I want to stay sober. If I get the PLOMs, I have to work with others to take my mind off of the Big Me. I have to avoid self-pity at all costs, because a Pity Party leads to resentments, and resentments are the number-one reason why alcoholics drink. The only cure is forgiveness."

Wow, she hit the nail on the head! I could see that we had a lot in common. My husband threw up the past to me, too, but *forgive him?* That was a new idea. I hadn't had a lot of practice at forgiving anybody for anything. None of my relatives were big on forgiveness. As a matter of fact, I couldn't remember anybody ever doing it. It sounded like a weakness instead of a virtue.

When the meeting ended, we all held hands and said the Lord's Prayer together. *Perhaps Al is right,* I thought. *Maybe today is the first day of the rest of my life.* Sensing a power surging through the circle of hands and trying hard not to cry again, I repeated the long-forgotten words. I never before felt such peace.

"Well, how did you like your first meeting?" Nancy asked, as the others gathered around to talk to me.

"I loved it, but I don't think I'm eligible to join your group. You see, it was a doctor who prescribed the wine that started me off. I'm not a *real* alcoholic!"

"Has your life been messed up in any way because of booze?" Nancy asked.

"Almost ruined!" I admitted truthfully.

"Then you qualify! It doesn't make any difference *how* you got here, just so you *got here.*"

"Incidentally, what are the PLOMs?"

"Poor Little Old Me. A Pity Party. Slurping Sorry Soup. Munching Martyr Pills. In other words, feeling sorry for yourself all the time. You can waste your life living in Pity City."

"Very interesting, but what about this forgiveness thing? Is that part of the program? If it is, you can count me out!" I said with feeling.

"You got a burr under your saddle?" she smiled.

"More like a cactus! My husband talks like I'm the Drunk of the Decade, but he still drinks himself! What a hypocrite!" I said vehemently.

"Liz, you'll never stay sober unless you forgive him. That emotional anger will work in your gut to keep you drunk and miserable," she said.

"I'll never forgive him! You don't know what I've been through," I exclaimed.

"Look, here's my telephone number. Call me tomorrow. But for tonight, I've got some homework for you," she said, writing on a three-by-five card.

"What's that?"

"It's a Forgiveness Prayer," she said matter-of-factly. "When you get home, make a list of all the people you're mad at and decide which one you hate the most—your Number 1 Stinker. Then kneel down by the side of the bed and say this prayer out loud. Just read it off."

She handed it to me and gathered up her things.

"See you tomorrow night at Jumper's Hole."

"Wait a minute, Nancy! How much do I owe, and who do I pay?"

"Nothing!" she laughed again. "This program's free."

"Free? Nothing's free!" I exclaimed.

"You've already paid the price of admission by suffering. Your dues are giving it away to others. Freely you have received, freely give." She waved good-bye.

"Oh, good-bye, Nancy! Thank you! I'll see you tomorrow!"

Mama Marty introduced me to several others before we left. On the way home we made arrangements for the next night.

"How long do I have to attend these meetings before I'm cured?" I asked her, knowing what she'd say.

"A cured ham gets smoked," she laughed. "Alcoholism is an incurable disease; it can only be arrested one day at a time by staying away from the first drink." She sounded just like Al. "Just keep coming back."

"I think I will!" I said. I didn't tell her I was dying of loneliness and wouldn't miss these meetings for the world.

Upon arriving home, I noticed my husband's car in the driveway. He must be back from his business trip! As I said my thanks to Marty and watched her drive away, I felt as if I had lost my last friend. Fearfully, I went into the house to confront my husband.

"Hi, how was the trip?" I asked tenuously.

"Where have *you* been . . . to the Lancer's Pub?" he asked sarcastically.

"Lancer's Pub!" I yelped indignantly. "I've been to an alcoholic Recovery meeting! I haven't had a drink in months, and, what's more, I'm *never* going to drink again!" I added self-righteously.

"A likely story," he snorted, heading for his bedroom.

"Please believe me, hon. I know these people can help me!" I pleaded. He turned on the top step and sneered at me.

"I'll be waiting for the other shoe to drop," he said, closing the door.

"I'll drop it on your head!" I screamed after him.

Angry tears came to my eyes, as I went out to the kitchen to get a cup of coffee. There, on the countertop, was a fifth of Canadian Club!

"Oh, God, help me!" I cried, turning away.

I sat down on the sofa, and from my purse I got out the little three-by-five card Nancy had written. I read these words:

God make me willing to be willing to be willing to forgive my husband.

"Never, never, never, never, never in a million years!" I shouted, throwing the card across the room.

Suddenly, more than anything else in the world, I wanted a drink.

26

The Postcard

Linthicum, Maryland, December 1972

Sipping the third cup of coffee, I went over my Mad List again. Husband, mother-in-law, grandparents, parents, son, the high-school principal, several teachers I worked with, innumerable students, and the neighbors. Especially those religious snobs next door.

The list was endless. It included almost everybody I knew. I was mad at the world. They had all dumped on me. My present mess was all their fault.

"Oh-h-h, I forgot! The shrinks!" I said, writing down the names of the Chinese shrink, the Greek shrink, the American shrink. Also the doctors who took out my appendix, and so on.

"Ah, ha! The mortgage holder of my Houston house!" I put him down, remembering how he refused to give me an emergency loan after it was wrecked by a flood. He was Number 253 on my list, which was just beginning to roll!

What'll I do when I'm finished? I thought. I decided to tell Nancy what I had done so far.

"Great, Liz! I'm proud of you! Keep going."

"But what happens when I'm finished?"

"You're going to forgive them. That's why you're making the list," she explained, patiently. "Did you use that prayer I gave you last night?"

"Uh, no." I didn't tell her I'd lain awake all night, fighting the urge to drink.

"Why not? It doesn't cost anything to kneel down and say a couple of words . . . just a little ego deflation."

"Nancy, I don't *know how* to pray. I don't go to church. I'm not a Protestant, a Catholic, or a Jew. I'm a nothing."

"That doesn't make any difference in our program. Church denominations aren't important. As a matter of fact, people like you who have no formal religious training sometimes catch on quicker than those who do. You don't have anything to unlearn," she said.

"Oh?" I said, encouraged.

"That's right, you may have an advantage over others."

"Well, if God writes on me, He'll be using a blank piece of paper," I laughed. "But, Nancy, I feel funny talking to the air, to someone I can't see. How do I know there's anybody out there?"

"Did you turn on a lamp last night? Do you watch television? Do you breathe?" she asked.

"Sure, but so what?"

"Electricity is invisible; so are electromagnetic waves and air, but you must have faith that they exist."

"So what are you getting at?"

"Try it, dummy. Just try it."

"Okay, okay, I will." I was annoyed with her. I'd show her that I could do it. Tonight I would say that prayer if the Spy King would stay off my back.

Mama Marty picked me up, and on the way to the meeting we discussed what Nancy had said.

"I've gone to church all my life," Marty said, "so I'm okay. I don't need a drunk to tell me about God."

"But, Marty, Nancy said this program has nothing to do with church affairs. Aren't there any stinkers you need to forgive?"

"That's none of your business! My church will take care of that!" she exploded.

I dropped the subject, confused about church attendance versus God. Until now, I had taken it for granted that if you wanted to know God, you had to go to church. Nancy had given me a new idea. She assured me that my lack of religious hang-ups would help me to make faster progress.

The Recovery meeting was much the same as before. I met many new people, among them a very classy lady named Ann-Marie, who had been sober five years. She and I talked for nearly an hour after the meeting about Mad Lists.

"I had a long list, too, when I got honest with myself. Have you prayed for yours yet?"

"No, but I'm beginning tonight. The only thing is, I don't know how," I complained.

"It's easy, Liz. Just talk to God like you're talking to me," she said encouragingly.

"Ann-Marie, how do you find God?"

"Liz, always remember this: *if you search for God with all your heart, you will surely find Him.*"

"But, Ann-Marie, HOW do you search for God? I don't belong to any church."

"Churches are places where people fellowship with each other, but one's relationship with God is personal. I happen to belong to a church, but you can find God anywhere, if you really want to. What do you think people did before churches existed?"

"I never thought about it!"

"Well, think it over. Pretend there's no such thing as a church building. How would you try to contact God?"

"I don't know! Holler for Him, I guess," I laughed.

"You've got it, kid," she smiled.

"Just talk into the thin air?"

"Liz, God is invisible. He's a Spirit! You can't see Him. You have to trust He's there."

"A Spirit!" I exclaimed. A light turned on as I remembered Big Mamie's Ouija board. Dr. Clover was certainly a real spirit, but I didn't mention him to Ann-Marie. Suddenly I felt good about the assignment. I remembered how Big Mamie talked into "thin air," so I resolved to do the same.

That night, alone in my bedroom with Nancy's card in hand, I knelt by the side of my bed, feeling very foolish. Clearing my throat, I said:

"God, make me willing to be willing to be willing to forgive my husband."

I waited, and then dialed Ann-Marie's number.

"Well, I did it, but nothing happened. What'll I do now?"

"Liz," she said wearily, "do it again tomorrow night."

"How long do I have to keep doing it?" I complained.

"How long have you been mad at him?"

"For years!"

"Then it'll take a while to root out the bitterness."

"Well, I sure don't want to be called a religious fanatic!" I declared. "One of those holy rollers!"

"Here's another thing to remember," she said evenly, "people who call names and make fun of those seeking God are called bigots."

"I don't want to be called a bigot either, so I'd better shut up," I laughed, as we hung up. She was easy to talk to.

I continued going to meetings and kneeling by my bed, praying for the boss. Finally one night I changed the prayer:

"God, I am willing to forgive my husband!"

The next evening he asked, "Are you going out again tonight?"

"Yes, they told me that newcomers need to go to ninety meetings in ninety days, so that's what I'm doing," I replied defensively.

"Uh, well, I think I'll tag along, if you don't mind."

I almost fainted from shock.

"Sure! Come along, if you want to." I played it cool.

That night my hand was trembling, as I drank my coffee, conscious that he was sitting behind me. The speaker was a woman who told how she used to hide her bottles in her snow boots. I felt a tap on my shoulder:

"I bet there are a dozen bottles of your scotch still hidden in the basement!" he snickered in my ear.

My face turned red, but I didn't reply because Ann-Marie was looking at me. I burned, trying to think of a good comeback.

"Half of them are probably yours!" I could say, or,

"People who live in glass houses . . ." or,

"When I find them I'll give them all to you!" or, . . .

I continued steaming about his remark, missing what the speaker said. By the end of the hour, I was nearly in tears.

After the meeting I introduced him to someone, and pulled Ann-Marie over to the side to tell her what he had said.

She laughed. "Maybe there *is* some booze in your basement!"

"There's booze all over the house," I declared indignantly, "but it's *his*, not mine! How do you expect me to stay sober if I have to look at his liquor all the time?"

"My husband, Butch, stared at my booze for five years, until I finally decided to stop drinking. He had a choice: drink with me or stay sober. He chose sobriety. You have the same choice. You can drink with your husband, or come to meetings and stay sober."

"But why me? Why should *I* be the alcoholic? Why not him?"

"I don't know."

"But that's not fair!"

"Nothing's fair, Liz. Haven't you found that out yet?"

"You mean, God's not fair?"

"That's right, God's not fair. If He were fair, I'd be in hell. God's more than fair. He's merciful," she said, writing something on a card.

"I never thought about it that way. But I still don't know how to handle the Spy King *or* his liquor."

"Okay, Teacher Liz, here's your homework," she said, handing me another three-by-five card. "Continue your Mad List prayers, but add three steps to your program."

Good grief, I bet these people carry those cards in their pajamas, I thought, as I read what she wrote:

> *Allow him to drink: live and let live.*
> *Let the insults pass: do not reply.*

I looked at her: "You're telling me just to let go of the whole thing, as if it didn't exist?"

"Oh, I forgot! Give me the card back," she exclaimed, adding something else to the list.

It went like this:

Let go and let God.

It was easier said than done. I had never practiced letting go of anything. Of all our family fusses, feuds, misunderstandings, and heartaches, no one forgot a minor detail of the smallest drama. Missed birthdays, inappropriate gifts, thoughtless words, inconveniences, all were constantly paraded before the culprit. The court was always in session, and the verdict was always, "Guilty!" *I don't have a chance,* I thought, wallowing in self-pity.

And what about that postcard? Thumbtacked to my kitchen bulletin board was a thirteen-year-old insult. It came during the worst crisis of my life, the near-death of my son and the loss of my beautiful Houston home in the 1960 flood. Everything I owned was ruined by the stinking snake-filled waters of Sims Bayou. With nowhere to go, my husband, daughter, son, and I lived in the only undamaged room of the wrecked house, the den.

Critically ill with rheumatic fever, my son was hospitalized, and I divided my time between a rat-and-snake-infested house and his bedside. That crisis, together with the death of our first son plus money shortages, was the straw that broke the camel's back of our weakened marriage. With many ugly accusations and much bitterness, we went our separate ways.

I rented a garden apartment on the Southwest Freeway and began the miserable, lonely life of a divorced mother with two children to support. Increasing my drinking, I came close to a complete breakdown. Two years later I met the Spy King. After a hasty courtship of dinner and theater dates, with lots of drinking, we married and moved to Maryland to continue his career with the Department of Defense.

In the midst of the Flood-and-Sick-Son Situation, I received a postcard from a close relative. It made no mention of the flood, which completely wiped me out. Nothing was said about the condition of my son, no offering of help. Instead, the message was a giant-sized complaint about a minor request I had overlooked in the midst of my catastrophe. My volcanic response was probably an escape-valve reaction to everything else. This poor soul had always been neurotic and had delighted in wounding me at every opportunity.

A maddening person who never could be reasoned with or depended upon, he never gave me any support. Instead, he bombarded me with hurtful criticism, constantly rained on my parade, and kept my emotions in constant turmoil. The three shrinks agreed he was the cause of all my trials and troubles. I would be a normal person, they said, if it weren't for him.

So I tacked that offending postcard to the wall. When I moved, it moved. Whenever guests came I led them to the kitchen to see Exhibit *A*.

"You poor darling," they would sympathize dutifully. "You're a modern-day miracle, succeeding like you have under such handicapped conditions."

"It wasn't easy," I would whimper.

Therefore, it was a toss-up as to who should have the honor of occupying Top Dog on my Mad List—the Spy King or the Postcard Writer. Both had tried me to the limit, expecting the impossible, never pleased with my efforts, filling me with anguish and guilt. I could never please them no matter what I did. How can I live in the same world with such destructive and heartbreaking people?

I called Ann-Marie to pour out my complaints.

"How old is that postcard, Liz?" she asked.

"Thirteen years."

"You've been reading that postcard every day for thirteen years?" she asked incredulously.

"Yes! I don't want to *ever* forget what he did to me!" I exclaimed bitterly.

"Honey, you're sicker than he is," she said gently.

"What do you mean?" I began to cry. "At the worst time of my life that man stabbed me again. You're not very sympathetic!"

"You've had thirteen years worth of 'sympathy,' and you're no better for it. You've got a colossal case of the galloping PLOMs!" she chuckled.

I thought about adding her to the list, but she was the only one willing to help me. Aggrieved, I didn't answer.

"Liz, stop pouting and start praying. How're you coming with your homework assignment?"

"I've ignored his booze and buttoned my lip," I answered snippily, "but I don't know *how* to let go and let God. It's a handy little slogan, but *how does it work?*"

She was quiet for a while.

"Maybe we ought to talk about your commitment step," she said thoughtfully. "I don't think you'll go any further without it."

"What do you mean—*commitment step?*"

"Don't you want to settle this thing once and for all?"

"Settle it! Nobody can change that man!"

"That's right, but you can change yourself."

"How?" I asked dubiously.

"You can *let go of it.* Forget it. Accept the fact that he is a sick person, and there's nothing you can do to change him. The Serenity Prayer says: God, grant me the serenity to accept the things I cannot change [that's your Postcard Writer], the courage to change the things I can [that's your attitude], and wisdom to know the difference.

"But the first three words, Liz, are *God, grant me.* You're asking God to do it. In order to do business with God on a lifetime basis, you need to commit yourself to Him, turn over your life and affairs to Him, and let Him manage them. Then you have the right to ask Him to grant you serenity and to bring forgiveness to your heart. Without Him you can't do it.

"It's the biggest step in our program," she went on, "but once you get past this one, the rest is clear sailing. I'm going to suggest that, during the first two years of your sobriety, you pray daily for every person on your

Mad List, to practice Live and Let Live (that is, mind your own business), and to come to believe in a Higher Power and make a commitment to Him.

"That ought to keep you out of trouble for a while," she added, chuckling again.

"*Two years!*" I shouted.

"Yes, it will take at least that long to begin your personality change. My Big Sister in the program told me that the old Ann-Marie would drink again. She said that my old value system, my old dreams and goals would all have to be reexamined.

"Tell me, Liz," she went on, "what do you want to be when you grow up?"

"When I grow up? Ann-Marie, I am forty-five years old!"

"Come on, honey, what dream have you always had in the back of your head?" she asked playfully.

"I wanted to be a movie star and live in Highland Park, Texas," I admitted sheepishly.

"And what did you turn out to be?"

"A Linthicum, Maryland, algebra teacher! Yuck!" I laughed.

"Now it will be interesting to see what the Lord wants you to be!" she said enthusiastically.

"What do you mean?" I asked anxiously.

"The Lord has His own plan for your life," she said mysteriously.

"The Lord? Who is the Lord?"

"I've giving you two years to find out. If I tell you, then it will be *my* Lord, not *yours.* Look for Him, Liz. When you find Him, He will be *yours.*"

27
How to Find God

Linthicum, Maryland, 1974

Where would *you* go to find God, if you were a Linthicum, Maryland, algebra teacher with no religious background?

One place I *wouldn't* go was to a church. Middle-aged, mentally confused, divorced, female alcoholics are about as welcome as navy-blue socks in a load of white wash. So I went to the public library. You can find *anything* there.

I read *The Lives of the Saints, The Power of Positive Thinking,* Billy Graham's *World Aflame,* and *The Sermon on the Mount.* But it was a book called *God Is Fabulous,* by Frances Gardiner, which intrigued me more than the others.

This Houston businesswoman whose story was so much like mine was a real kook, but she had a bold, courageous faith in a fabulous God who could answer prayer! As I read, hope that I wasn't chasing rainbows slowly began to rise up inside me.

She urged the reader to try Him out! She assured me that He loved me as much as her. Then she encouraged me to do something really far out: to ask for something personal but important, and not to tell anyone about it. When you get it, she assured me, you'll know God gave it to you. You'll know He's real.

I decided to try it by asking Him to do something impossible. I'd put in an order for a long nail on one of my fingers.

All my life I had chewed my fingernails down to the nubs. My grandmother used to bribe me with money to stop, but I never could. So I had the world's worst-looking hands. If there was a God who answered prayers, growing a fingernail would be the critical test. I didn't want to bother Him with ten. Just one.

I laid the book down and said aloud, "God, if You're interested in me, please grow one long fingernail. Thank You." Then I forgot about it.

Urged on by Ann-Marie, I continued to "look for God." I went to summer camps, lectures, and seminars. I listened to inspiring convention speakers and gruff radio preachers. I went on my first retreat! And I watched TV.

My favorite TV preacher was Pat Robertson, of "The 700 Club." I seldom missed his morning show. His message, however, was pretty radical. He insisted the only way to find God was by asking Jesus Christ to come into your heart.

But on TV News were pictures of long-haired, bearded, bedraggled hippies, smoking pot, and wearing Jesus T-shirts. They were called "Jesus Freaks," an epithet which, along with "Religious Fanatic," and "Holy Roller," I wanted to avoid at all costs. Maybe I *was* an alcoholic, I conceded to my fellow addicts in the Recovery group.

But nobody would ever call me a **Jesus Freak!**

"My God! Not another one of *those* meetings!" my husband yelled. "You're turning into a Jesus Freak!"

Slamming the door, he left for work. I was devastated. I couldn't make him understand that the Washington cocktail circuit was a no-no for me. Not only could I *not* drink like a lady. I couldn't drink *at all.* And now the thing I had most feared had come upon me. I was dubbed a Jesus Freak! That was the last straw.

I called Ann-Marie and Nancy and Mama Marty. No one was at home. I was alone again. No one cared. Self-pity, frustration, and anger boiled up inside me.

"God, help me!" I cried, kneeling on the floor.

No sooner were the words out of my mouth, than a knock came at the front door. Covered with goose bumps, I peeked out the crack.

Standing on the porch was a short, pleasant-looking, gray-haired lady who introduced herself as Lois Nelson:

"Howard and I just moved in next door. We'd like you to come to a Bible study at our house tonight," she said smiling.

"You mean next door to me?" I asked, pointing at the parsonage where the religious snobs had lived.

"Yes, that's right. It begins at 7:30. I hope you can come."

"Well, I'll see," I responded doubtfully.

That *had* to be God. During the ten years I had lived next to the parsonage, none of the numerous ministers who occupied it was friendly. Yet after *one prayer* I was invited to a Bible study!

"Good grief, where's my Bible?" I wondered.

At age seven my Grand-Aunt Bessie had given me a little white leather one with gold edges. I hadn't seen it in ages, so I pulled out boxes, looked in drawers, and finally found it in a closet. I dusted it off, and with trepidation waited for my very first Bible study, *ever.*

We were a mixed bag, Heinz-variety of disciples—a pair of Catholics, two Methodists, several Church of the Brethren, and one nothing—*me.* Margie, the leader, carefully presented the lesson, sensitive to the group's reactions. Like Pat Robertson, she taught us from the Bible that Jesus was the Son of God. Some of the group nodded, others kept mum, but I smarted off:

"But what if the Bible is wrong?"

"The Bible can't be wrong. It's the Word of God," Margie said, groping for words.

"You don't actually believe the story of Jonah and the whale? Or that those men walked around inside a fiery furnace?" I smirked.

"If it's in the Bible, I believe it."

"Can you *prove* that the Bible has no mistakes?" I asked.

She stood up and gathered her things.

"We'll have to continue this next week, I have to go now," she said, weaseling out of my questions. Just as I thought, it was all a house of cards.

I was the last to leave.

"Liz," Lois said, taking my hand, "Sears has a Beginners' Knitting Class starting Thursday. Why don't you and I take it together? I don't want to go alone."

"Oh, that would be great! I'd love to!" I replied, eagerly.

She looked down at my fingers.

"What beautiful nails you have! But you'd better file them or they'll snag the wool."

Startled at her words, I held up my hands and stared with complete amazement at *ten long fingernails.*

God had certainly proved Himself to be real, but what about Jesus and the Bible?

That was too much for me to swallow all at once.

My marriage began to emit death rattles. Recovering from alcoholism and searching for a Higher Power were not the fun and games he had bargained for when we were wed. Career-minded, we enjoyed drinking parties and dinner theaters. Before my stroke we had been devotees of the high life in the fast lane. Now the fun was over for me, but he was still flying. With nothing in common, we were strangers, isolated under the same roof.

I came home late one night after a meeting, detained by a beautiful redheaded young woman, who asked me for help. Her husband had knocked out her front teeth, leaving the inside of her mouth raw, so she kept her lips together when she talked. When I kidded her about it, she giggled for the first time. She said her name was Laura. Though I didn't know it, I had a friend for life. I spent an extra hour telling her what I knew about the program.

"Where have you been . . . to Midnight Mass?" he jeered.

I kept my lip buttoned.

He poured himself a drink and sat down.

"Or at the library reading the Bible?" He was having fun.

I said nothing.

"Probably the Lancer's Pub!" he roared aloud.

That did it! I blew up.

"I'll have you know that I've been sober fifteen months!"

He just kept grinning at me.

"I'm waiting for the other shoe to drop," he smirked.

Unable to control myself, I ran crying to my room and threw myself across the bed, ready for another Pity Party. But then I remembered Nancy's directions—substitute another activity.

"No PLOMs tonight, Lizzie!" I muttered, turning on TV. There was Pat Robertson on the screen in a late night rerun of "The 700 Club."

"Why don't you kneel down where you are right now and ask Jesus to come into your heart? Give Him your problems and let Him solve them. They're too much for you. He loves you so much that He died for your sins. He paid the price for you, so that you can be a member of God's family. Invite Him into your life today!"

He finished by assuring me that Jesus wanted me to belong to Him. I remembered Big Mamie's spook, Dr. Clover. He said I belonged to another. Maybe he meant Jesus!

But this program was taped! *There's no use praying with a taped rerun!* I thought. *It wouldn't work.*

I pointed my finger at Pat Robertson and said: "Okay, preacher, if you ever come *live* to Baltimore, Maryland, I'll pray with you!"

Early morning sunbeams peeped through the budding branches of the big maple tree in the front yard, as I decided to stop faking sleep and get out of bed. I had tossed and turned all night, unable to let go, much less let God.

Nancy and Ann-Marie must know something I don't, I thought. I had played and replayed those hurtful words all night, knowing that I was only increasing my misery, but unwilling to quit. I waited until the Spy King left. Then Suzy and I ventured out of the bedroom.

"I'm a prisoner in my own house, Sue," I declared bitterly, seeing empty years stretching endlessly ahead.

"I'm sober, but so what? I have no future. My career is gone. My brain won't work right. What good is a math teacher who can't even multiply beyond the four tables?" I began to cry again, and Suzy whimpered, too.

"I'm sick of crying! I'm tired of dropping things and stumbling! I'm bored to death with this house!" I sobbed.

The telephone rang, and I tried to compose myself.

"Hi, Liz. Laura here, are you busy? I need to talk to you! I'm scared to death!" She said all in a rush.

"What's the matter?" I said, drying my eyes.

"Ronnie's been out drinking all night. When he comes home drunk, he always beats me up. What'll I do? I can't afford to lose any more teeth!"

"Gee, I don't know. You're near a shopping center. Why don't you take a hike for a couple of hours?"

"That's a great idea. Thanks, Liz."

Laura's call brought me back to sanity. Considering her situation, my own didn't seem so bad. At least I had my front teeth.

Let go and let God, I thought, and flipped on the TV.

There was Pat Robertson's smiling face.

"Good morning, everybody. This is 'The 700 Club.' We are broadcasting *live from Baltimore, Maryland. . . .*"

What did he say? I stood there transfixed with a skin full of goose bumps. This was too far out to be a coincidence! *Had God really heard me promise to pray if Pat ever came* live *to Baltimore?* I wondered, as fear gripped my heart.

"Oh, woe is me! Today is the Day of Salvation! What am I getting into? A dull, religious life? No more fun? No more lipstick, jewelry, or pretty clothes? Good grief, I'll never smile again!"

But it was now or never. A great urgency to decide came over me, as it had in Toby's rose garden.

"Just turn off the TV and forget it." It was Satan whispering in my head.

"No, I'll just try it and see if there's anything to it," I told Suzy.

Pat was saying: ". . . and I invite you to step out in faith today and ask Jesus to be your Saviour. Now just kneel down in front of the TV set. . . ."

I knelt down with Suzy beside me.

". . . and say these words after me: Jesus, I believe that You are the Son of God. . . ."

"Jesus, I believe that You are the Son of God," I repeated after him.

". . . and that You were crucified for my sins, were dead and were buried. . . ."

I repeated that, too.

". . . and that on the third day You rose from the dead, that You ascended into heaven and now sit at the right hand of God the Father."

I kept repeating after him.

"Jesus, forgive me for my sins, come into my heart and save me. Thank You for doing it! Jesus, You are the Lord. You are now my Lord! Praise the Lord!"

". . . and You are now *my Lord.* Praise the Lord." I repeated the words after him exactly.

Kneeling there on the floor, I tried to determine if I felt any different than before. Nothing *seemed* changed.

"You can't be a silent Christian! You've got to *tell* somebody!"

"Fat chance I'll *ever* tell anybody about this, Sue," I said ruefully, struggling to rise. My body ached all over.

"Go to the phone and call the number on the screen," Pat continued. "There's a TV counselor in your city ready to take your call. He or she will counsel with you and tell you what to do next. Tell them you just received Jesus as your Saviour. You've got to tell somebody right now."

"Well, Sue, maybe it won't hurt to call the counselor," I said, dialing the number. I was so lonely, I was even willing to risk the humiliation of a religious snub.

"This is Warren at The 700 Club!" A man's deep voice came over the telephone.

"Hello. My name is Mary Elizabeth Rogers, and I just received Jesus as my Saviour. . . ."

"Praise the Lord!" he shouted.

"But, Warren, I don't feel any different," I cried. "I feel terrible! My brain doesn't work right, my right arm and leg are weak. I drop things and stumble. My career is finished, and I don't have any money. . . ."

I told him all about my problems. The death of my baby. The flooding of my Houston home. My son's critical illness. The miserable divorce with its resulting bitternesses. The suicide attempts. My present disastrous marriage. On and on I went for about an hour.

"And *now* I'm an alcoholic!" I cried, reaching the end of my tale. "I don't want to live but I can't even kill myself."

He was silent for a minute. Then he said:

"Well, honey, you've had a hard time!"

"Yes," I whimpered. "I've had a *hard* time."

"But the *good news* is that Jesus has forgiven all your sins and will never remember them any more. You can begin life all over again today!" he exclaimed.

"No, I can't! It's hopelessly messed up!"

"That's Jesus' specialty, straightening out messed up lives! But you need the power of the Holy Spirit to help you live with Him!" he boomed.

"I do?" I asked uncertainly.

"Are you ready to receive the Holy Spirit?" he shouted.

I held the phone away from my ear, certain that the neighbors a block away could hear him too.

"I guess so," I said, closing my eyes.

"Father, in the name of Jesus, I thank You for my new sister, Mary Elizabeth! I thank You that she is a new creature in Christ Jesus! I thank You that she is born again! I thank You that all her sins are forgiven!

"And now, Jesus, I ask You to baptize her in the Holy Spirit! Immerse her in Your glorious light! Endue her with power from on high! Do it now! In Your precious name!

"Hallelujah! Hallelujah! Hallelujah! . . ."

And as Warren was shouting his prayer to heaven, a remarkable thing was happening to my body. Beginning at the top of my head and proceeding slowly down to my toes, and then back up again, waves and waves of warm and wonderful electricity flooded over me. It was so marvelous, I wanted it to go on forever. Then I began to shout along with Warren:

"**Praise the Lord! Hallelujah! Glory to God!**" I yelled, waving my free arm in the air.

"You've got it, honey, you've got it!" he shouted.

"That's wonderful! What have I got?" I shouted back.

"You've got the Holy Spirit!"

"Praise the Lord!" I yelped and Suzy started barking.

After we had cooled down a little, Warren advised me to find a church which would teach me about Jesus. After further words of encouragement, he hung up.

I began to dance around the room, praising Jesus, Suzy following. Suddenly I wanted to know everything there was to know about Him! Where was that Bible? I wanted to read it now more than anything in the world! It would tell me about Jesus! Why, I'd even go to Louise's church and risk the flack if they would tell me about my precious Lord.

Then I stopped in amazement. My arm and my leg! They were working! I bent my knees and flexed my arms. No more weakness and fuzziness! My body was completely normal!

"I am healed, Sue!" I said, in awe. "Jesus must have healed me when Warren prayed."

I began to cry again, only this time for joy. Jesus loved me so much, that He restored my body. He had made me normal again. I was completely overwhelmed by His love for me. I knelt down again and said these words:

"**Lord, I promise You, whomever You put in front of my face, I'll tell them what You did for me.**

"**And if You have a job You need done, Lord, send me!**"

The date was March 8, 1974. Little did I know when I made that vow what the Lord had in store for me.

28

The Kook in the Cast

Glen Burnie, Maryland, Fall 1974

I put down my pen and leaned back to read what I had written. Filling up a small spiral notebook, I had come to the end of a detailed, personal inventory of my character defects which I had begun seven weeks earlier. A summary of my faults read like this:

1. *Hate and resentments:* An accumulation of grievances reaching back to my childhood, fueled by a family feud, and fed daily by my own sick thoughts and words.

Antidote: Pray daily for each person on the Mad List. I had begun to do this and my emotions (the mental barometer) had greatly improved, but still had a long way to go for good mental health. Recovery is not an overnight phenomenon.

2. *Self-Pity:* Accompanies resentment. They are the original gruesome twosome. Where you see one, you always see the other. I had constantly entertained myself with Pity Parties. My address was Pity City, USA. I drank Sorry Soup and popped Martyr Pills. I had a gigantic case of the PLOMs—the Poor Little Old Mes.

Two Antidotes: (a) An attitude of gratitude.

I began to thank God for blessings like my food, clothes, house, children, and so forth, realizing with a shock that I had never lacked for the necessities of life, even living luxuriously most of the time. But I had *never been grateful* for any of these gifts from God, only complaining that they weren't good enough and always wanting more, more, more. And

(b) Working with others.

I began helping newcomers in the program. Laura and I were becoming good friends, but, though she loved me, she still couldn't stay sober over any length of time. Working with her, I became grateful for my own sobriety. I found that I couldn't carry the message to Laura and entertain self-pity at the same time.

3. *Self-Justification:* "It's not my fault. The blame lies with my grandparents, my parents, my aunts and uncles, teachers, principals, neighbors, friends, children, husband, ex-husband, ministers, priests, shrinks, the State of Texas, the State of Maryland," ad nauseam. The finger pointed away from me—always at someone else. I was always scapegoating.

Antidote: Self-honesty, open-mindedness, and willingness to change. For the first time I reviewed the old feuds to find out the part *I* played in starting them and fueling them. In varying degrees of guilt, I saw that lack of communication and dishonesty, coupled with fear and jealousy, had kept the fires roaring. As the truth came to me, I resolved to make amends as best I could. (Another whole book could be written on "making amends," so I'll save that for the future.)

4. *Self-Condemnation:* As a result of the interior garbage, I didn't like myself. Who wants to live in a mental garbage dump? I thought I wanted out of the world, but I just wanted out of my own mental processes.

Antidote: Admitting these faults to myself and another person, praying that God forgives me, and then forgiving myself. I discovered that Jesus is the great Garbage Remover. It's His specialty, ridding me of physical, mental, and spiritual garbage.

But I have to put it out where He can get at it.

He won't break into my house and steal it.

So I collected my garbage by listing it on paper. Here's how I did it. I divided my life into seven segments of time:

a. Birth to first grade
b. First grade through high school
c. College years
d. Married years till the flood

e. Flood through divorce
f. Drinking years in Maryland
g. December 7, 1972 till now—the sober years

Keeping a pad and pencil handy, I took one segment at a time, asking God to bring to my remembrance the people, places, and things He wanted me to deal with. For a week or so, I concentrated on that single time frame, writing down each incident that I needed to confess and pray about. Each time frame filled several pages of notes.

Here is an example:

Birth to first grade:

Fear of "bad man" in movie
Tormenting the maid
Sassing my grandmother and others

First grade through high school:

Hurting Mary Clair and others

This last situation had really bugged me for years. My girl friend Betty and I used to make fun of Mary Clair's acne. Because this poor little fifth-grader's face was badly scarred, we decided one day to "have fun" at her expense. Cutting out an ad for Cuticura Soap (advertised as an acne "cure") and hiding it in her desk, we waited until she came in from recess. As she opened her desk and read this taunting ad, she crumpled in tears on the floor. I can still see her cringing in pain at my cruelty. Many times I wished I could undo that wrong. Forty years later Mary Clair's misery still haunted me. Now I wanted to get rid of it.

Ann-Marie was the one who had guided me through this crucial step. She called it "housecleaning of the soul."

Every business manager takes an inventory once a year to see what's worth keeping and what isn't. Since this was my first try, like all beginners, I saw only the bad stuff. But over the years, I've developed enough humility to see my strengths, as well. The first time around I attempted an inventory of my entire life. Then I continued updating it, adding things I had overlooked or forgotten.

I really sweated blood. It's not the greatest experience in the world to read, "I lied about this"; or, "I stole such and such"; or, "I hate so and so"; written in your own handwriting. But this personal "printout" started me on the road to self-honesty and inner peace. I had never leveled with anyone before. With the shrinks, to whom I paid thousands of dollars, I had merely philosophized. How could I expect them to help me if I didn't tell them the truth? It was plain that I had blamed all my sins on other people, and if I wanted true recovery, the buck had to stop at my door. No scapegoating was allowed.

Ann-Marie and Nancy explained the basic problem. Our natural desires have become warped and our emotions deformed in the process of living. No human being, however good, is exempt. So we have to make a vigorous and painstaking effort to discover what these liabilities are and to look squarely at the unhappiness they have caused others and ourselves. Unless I was willing to do this, they said, I would find little sobriety or contentment.

"It's like spring housecleaning," Ann-Marie explained. "You deal with dirt from the attic to the basement, one room at a time."

"What do you mean by 'a room'?" I asked.

"A time frame in your life. Let your first 'room' be the time frame from birth to first grade."

"Oh, I see. Divide my life into convenient periods of time and deal with each separately?"

"That's right. You've got the idea!"

"What do I write down? My sins? My mistakes? What?"

"Don't label them! That will only confuse you with religious terms! Here's the rule: *If you can remember it and if it bothers you, write it down.*

"Obviously, you can't write down something you don't remember. And if it doesn't bother you, you won't remember it anyway. Be sure to include *all close relatives,* because all of us have had family fusses. The main purpose of this inventory is to live a peaceful life with those we love."

"I've been praying for my entire family since my first day in the program, Ann-Marie! Remember all those three-by-five cards you gave me?"

"Yes, and I'm proud of your persistence. How're your emotions nowadays?"

"The hate is mostly gone. Just comes back in flashes," I admitted.

I was getting the hang of emotional honesty, which is the backbone of the program.

"That's normal," she said. "I've been praying for my mother-in-law for six years, and I can honestly say I have about ninety-five percent relief from frustration."

"But I picked up a new one last night!" I said hotly. "That old *kook* embarrassed me so much I could have died!"

"Maybe you'd better tell me about it, Liz, and get rid of it now. There's a saying that goes like this: 'You can't prevent a bird from landing on your head, but you can keep it from making a nest in your hair.' "

"You guys have a saying for everything!" I laughed, and proceeded to tell her about the kook with a broken leg.

It happened in a crowded, smoky church-basement meeting the night before. I was anxious to get out into the fresh air. Then the chairman called on a tall, white-haired man with a crew cut. His right leg was in a cast, propped up on a chair.

"My name is Hal Hill and I'm an alcoholic," he began, and told the story of his involvement with alcohol over a period of twenty-nine years. His tale was similar to many others, and I listened with half an ear, until I heard him say:

". . . and Ed said, 'If you don't have a God of your own, borrow mine. If you can't believe, make believe. Fake it till you make it.' So I asked his God, Jesus, to come into my heart."

Jesus to come into his heart?

Wow! That was the first time I ever heard anybody in the Recovery program talk about Jesus. I strained to get a better look at him across the smoky room. Wearing a baby-blue sweater (which matched his eyes), Hal spoke with a confidence born of much experience. He seemed oblivious to the reactions of some who were frowning and muttering over his Jesus talk. Some of them got up and walked over to the coffeepot. Others just shut their eyes in pain.

But I nearly exploded with excitement! After the meeting, I went over and sat down next to him.

"I liked what you said!" I began, smiling at my newfound brother in the Lord.

"You did, huh?" he said gruffly.

"How long have you known Jesus?" he squinted at me.

"Since March 8, 1974!" I said defensively, wondering what was eating him.

"And I just got baptized three months ago!" I exclaimed, whipping out snapshots to show him.

He looked at them indifferently.

"So you believe all that Bible stuff?"

"Of course I do! Why?" I asked, confused.

"Then pray for my leg . . . it's killing me!" he groaned.

Oh, oh, now he had me on the spot! I didn't know how to pray in public, especially for a leg in a plaster cast.

"I sure will—as soon as I get home!" I said, getting up to go.

"Oh, no, you don't," he said, grabbing my arm. "Pray *now!*"

"*Now?*" I whispered, looking around the room at the sneering drunks who were waiting to see the fun.

"*Now!*" he boomed.

This is where the rubber meets the road, I thought.

Was I playing religious games, or did I really intend to serve Jesus? My promise to Him was on the line. I could leave and keep my popularity. Or I could pray for his leg, now, out loud, in the name of Jesus, and lose my reputation.

Which was it going to be?

I took a deep breath, put my hands on his cast, and closed my eyes. Then in a loud, firm voice (like Warren at "The 700 Club"), I said:

"Be healed, in the name of Jesus!"

A burst of laughter exploded behind me. I heard someone say, "My God, we've got two Jesus Freaks in the program now!"

Like it or not, I had cast my lot with the Lord.

When I looked around, the other Jesus freak was gone with not even a thank-you ma'am. Red-faced, I left too, feeling alone and persecuted.

"He could have at least thanked me," I complained to Ann-Marie, "but that clown wasn't even friendly."

"Hal's an old-timer with twenty-three years in the program, Liz. Maybe his leg was hurting."

"You're right, maybe so. I'll put him on the list," I sighed, unwilling to add more names to the monster.

But, old-timer or not, the next time I saw that kook in the cast, I planned to give him a wide berth.

29
A Landmark for Laura

Hanover, Maryland, Sunday, July 4, 1978

As I backed the car out of the driveway on the way to church, the Lord spoke:

"Instead of your regular group, go to Calvary Chapel."

I turned the wheels and headed east instead of west, wondering what the Holy Spirit was up to. He was always way out ahead of me, zigging when I was zagging, changing the subject, talking over my head, keeping me on my toes. Just when I thought I had Him figured out, He was in another classroom teaching a different subject.

Actually, I was surprised He even spoke to me this morning, considering the way I had blown up. But He acted as if nothing had happened. I'm glad God doesn't pout like I do.

For the past four years, night and day, I had bent His ear about my fractured marriage, which had finally fallen apart like a broken yo-yo. In a last ditch attempt to salvage it, I wheedled the Spy King into repeating our marriage vows before the church, hoping that social pressure would force him to stay.

But last night he had taken off for parts unknown, leaving me dangling, and I was mad at Jesus for letting it happen. A four-year-old baby Christian in a spiritual temper tantrum, I had thrown the Bible across the room.

"Okay, Jesus, You and I are through!" I cried, feeling thoroughly rejected and deserted. "I thought You said You'd never leave me or forsake me!"

What was my real motive for wanting to keep the marriage intact?

As a divorced woman, I would be one of the "untouchables" in the Christian church; a second-class citizen in the Kingdom of heaven, consigned to such service as bake sales or the Cry Room. Phooey on that! I wanted to be a woman evangelist; winning people to the Lord; healing the sick; casting out demons; working miracles. Exciting things like that. I hadn't listened to hundreds of hours of Norvel Hayes's tapes for nothing! But with two broken marriages I would be lucky to get a job as janitor.

After tossing and turning all night, I apologized and told the Lord I was reporting for duty.

The first two assignments Jesus had given me in 1975 were far from glamorous. Number 1 was teaching alcohol recovery to low-bottom drunks in the damp basement of a halfway house in the slums of Brooklyn, Maryland.

"You are to help them with the steps of recovery, tell them about Me, and intercede for them," He ordered.

"Okay, Lord," I agreed.

The second assignment was slightly more glamorous. The "kook in the cast" turned out to be the well-known Christian author and speaker Harold Hill, whose first book, *How to Live Like a King's Kid,* had just hit the bookstores, and who needed a part-time secretary to answer the mail. I volunteered for the job.

"You are to consult Me about every letter and then do what I tell you," the Lord directed.

"Right on!" I shouted, excited at the prospect of working with *The* "King's Kid," as Hal was known throughout the Christian church. His disposition hadn't improved, but the thrill of knowing a celebrity made up for it. Then as the King's Kid continued to write more books, the number of weekly letters increased to several dozen. So I bought an electric typewriter and took a typing course. But the letters kept pouring in, and I was always behind in my correspondence. By 1977 the first book (*How to Live Like a King's Kid*) was on the *New York Times* best-seller list. Sales were skyrocketing. I had obviously gotten in on the ground floor of a good deal.

(Aside: the miracles the Lord performed in that halfway house and through those letters deserve another complete book.)

My excitement mounted as I pulled into the parking lot of Calvary Chapel.

"Something good is going to happen to you."

As those happy sounds drifted out the windows, I felt a thrill of anticipation.

Pastor Tony Spero opened the service.

"A guest speaker was scheduled to bring the Fourth of July message, but last night the Lord told me he wasn't coming. And shortly thereafter, he called and canceled. So I was unprepared to preach, but as the choir sang, the Lord spoke to me.

'This is Independence Day, the day to be set free from bondage. I want you to preach on "Freedom From Bondage" to someone special in the congregation.'"

Wow! that's me, Lord! I thought jubilantly. *Today's the day we'll kiss and make up and live happily ever after!*

I was second-guessing the Lord, as usual. He had something far more important in mind. The life of a suffering alcoholic hung in the balance.

After the service I rushed home, but *he* was still gone and the house was quiet. After a couple of hours the phone rang. It was Mama Marty:

"Liz, when was the last time you saw Laura?"

"I don't know—a couple of weeks ago. She's out drinking," I said.

"She called for you. She's in bad shape. I don't know if she's going to make it this time. Her liver's about gone," Marty said worriedly.

"Well, I don't know what to do. I'm waiting for a phone call," I said, confused.

"Liz, you'd better get over there now! You're the only one who can handle her when she's drunk."

"Okay, okay," I said, torn two ways.

It was worse than we thought. Poor Laura was as drunk as a skunk and critically ill. My helper, Bob, and I worked to get her dressed and in the car, while she twisted and screamed in an alcoholic frenzy. I drove to the hospital, while Bob subdued her. Then we carried her into the alcoholic ward, left her at the Admissions Desk, and hurried out. They admitted only sobered-up drunks, but I wasn't about to take Laura back home to die.

"Lord, please help Laura. Let the hospital accept her and let this be the last day she drinks, in Jesus' name," Bob and I prayed.

I went home to wait for my miracle, but the only change that occurred was in the sky. It was brilliantly lit with bursts from roman candles and skyrockets. My faith had dropped down to my toes. I went to sleep wondering if I had really heard from God.

The telephone's ringing woke me up.

"Miss Rogers, did you leave a patient named Laura at our facility yesterday?" a crisp voice asked.

"Yes, I did," I admitted, "can't you please keep her? She needs help or she'll die!"

"She's far from dead, Miss Rogers!" the nurse said dryly. "She's reading the Bible to the other patients, telling them that Jesus set her free. Can you come and get her?"

Jesus set her free?

The message from Pastor Spero must have been for Laura, instead of me. I was full of mixed emotions, happiness for whatever had happened to Laura, but deep disappointment that God had passed me by.

"I'll never be able to understand the Lord," I told Suzy, as I backed the car out of the driveway.

When I got to the hospital, Laura rushed up and hugged me.

"Oh, Liz, you were right! Jesus does love me!" she cried.

"How do you feel, honey?" I asked dubiously, remembering yesterday's struggle.

"I feel great! As soon as they put me to bed, Jesus appeared and began talking to me! Jesus! Talking to me!" she exuded, her eyes bright with happiness.

"What did He say?" I asked, cautiously.

"He told me He was setting me free, that I would never have to suffer any more!" she said excitedly.

I was silent. Jealousy gnawed at my heart.

"And He gave me a lot of directions, like taking out my false teeth so I wouldn't choke! Can you imagine? Jesus was interested in my teeth!" she laughed.

"Yeah," I said, deeply depressed.

"Liz, I'm ready to go to an Alcoholics Anonymous meeting tonight! I think I can make it now. For the first time since I can remember, I don't want a drink!"

I stared in wonder at my beautiful redheaded friend. I was looking in the face of a mighty miracle of God.

That was many years ago. Laura never drank again. Jesus set her free.

30

The King's Kid
From Kentucky

Glen Burnie, Maryland, July 1978

The hot, smoky basement room was crowded with A.A. members and friends who had come to hear one of their favorite women speakers.

The chairman opened the meeting.

"This is the Pasadena meeting of Alcoholics Anonymous and our speaker tonight is Laura."

Sitting on the front row, I winked at my nervous friend and settled down to hear her story. Laura had explained to me that in accordance with the traditions of the A.A. program, she would tell what it used to be like, what happened, and what it's like now, thus fulfilling several steps of the famous A.A. Twelve Steps. Tonight she would concentrate on Step One, the Admittance Step. The sooner she could admit to the problem, the sooner her recovery could begin.

"My name is Laura, and I am powerless over alcohol. I am an alcoholic with a completely unmanageable life," she began bravely.

"I was born in Evansville, Kentucky, in 1942 in a one-room log cabin, and I was 'birthed' by a midwife. When I was three years old, Daddy moved us to Baltimore where he took a job in a shipyard. My daddy was a jolly, handsome man before most of his stomach and his bowels were removed, and then he became thin and sickly. I got rheumatic fever, so Mama had to nurse us sick folks and work, too. She had a

209

real hard time, and I remember my folks as strict and serious. I learned to clean house when I was in the third grade in East Baltimore, where we lived in the Polish sector. My parents emphasized cleanliness and honesty. I was never allowed to get dirty. My dress always had to be real clean and neat, and I had to curtsy and say, 'Yes, ma'am,' and 'No, ma'am,' and 'Thank you.'

"But I was a rebellious child and willing to pay the price. I got lots of spankings and had my mouth washed out with soap because I didn't want to do all that stuff. I was a lonely kid, too, because I could only play with clean kids, and there weren't many of those around.

"I had my first drink with my girl friend, Julie. She was twelve and I was thirteen. That's when I had my first sexual experience, too, with my high school boyfriend, Ken. My parents found out and I was 'put in irons,' so to speak, but I escaped anyway. Every weekend we could, we got drunk. We'd go out hitchhiking and get men to buy us something to drink. And they would. I never, never had trouble getting booze. My red hair, good figure, and big mouth kept me drinking for twenty-three years until I almost died.

"When I was fifteen, I met an 'older man of twenty-two,' and I stayed out all night with him. My parents called the police, but it was too late. I got pregnant, and we married.

"That was the beginning of the lean, hard years with Ramsey. He was my first husband and father of my daughter, Valerie. He had a very high IQ—very intelligent—but he didn't want to work, so he went into crime. Ramsey was a crook best of all, and only earned meager wages when he had a legit job.

"I was the best fifteen-year-old mother I knew how to be. I kept Valerie in starched dresses like my mama did for me. I ironed fourteen dresses a week, sterilized her bottles, and anything that touched her mouth until she was fourteen months old. Then her father went to prison for forging and counterfeiting government checks. He was sentenced to five years, but he got out in three on a writ that he wrote himself—that's how intelligent he was.

"But while the case was pending, he paid for me to go to a beautician's school, which I did, putting Valerie in a nursery.

"I was brokenhearted that I had to live with my parents again, and I wrote Ramsey letters on beautiful stationery, until I found out that he was keeping another girl friend in another apartment. That really tore me up, and I began drinking heavily and going out to bars. My mother took over raising Valerie, and that was the end of my motherhood experience. I just gave up trying to do good, and started living to drink and have fun.

"I also started taking dope—with needles—heroin, speed, and one time, Dilaudid, and I got involved with Ramsey's old crowd plus my own group of swinging hairdressers. I met a lot of guys, and I drank and drank and drank.

"My second husband, Greg, insisted we get married, and I knew it was illegal cause my divorce wasn't final, but we did anyway. That marriage lasted six months, and he got into heavy-duty drugs and started stealing money.

"Then I got married *again,* all the while drinking, drinking, drinking. He was a tall, skinny criminally insane man named Jethro, who wound up going to Patuxent State Hospital for the Criminally Insane. I only lived with him a few months, but I stayed married to him eleven years as insurance against future marriages. I knew that I was crazy enough to marry anybody!

"I got a terrific job at Harry's Bar, a famous saloon near the Baltimore Harbor, where the seamen came to drink. Those people became lifelong friends and they loved me cause I was funny and dressed sexy—and I would drink *anything* with any of the customers. I made lots of money for them.

"Then one night my first husband, Ramsey, came in and we got bombed out of our gourds and ran away together. He was out of prison and back into crime—a fugitive. We moved all over the country, from Ohio to Texas to California, having a ball, drinking up a storm. He got me all the booze I wanted, and he bought me a dog, a big poodle which I named 'Walter.'

"I lived three years with Ramsey, until I finally came back to Baltimore, where I continued to drink and get involved with men.

"The last guy I got involved with was a thin, little jerk called Sonny, who followed me around like a dog and begged me to marry him. Sonny was crazier than a bedbug—had been to the nuthouse several times for heroin addiction—but I was crazier to marry him. He beat me up every day, and he's the one who knocked out my front teeth. I despise him for it!

"Liz told me to put him on my Mad List and pray for him, and I'm trying, but it's hard. Anyway, I guess I hit my bottom with Sonny, and that's when Liz and I met. I kept on drinking for four years off and on, but last week I almost died.

"I was so weak and skinny, just a doormat for Sonny's abuse. I never realized that alcohol and people had manipulated me all my life. My guilt and remorse were so bad, I always felt like the worst person in the world. I hated everybody and everything all the time. Even *love* was just plain old lust. I believe I was demon-possessed, because I did things that I didn't understand. It's going to be hard to forgive myself, but I know I have to do it.

"I had an addiction to being hurt—being made to feel bad all the time. I was so used to feeling bad, that if I wasn't, I didn't think it was normal.

"Anyway, a month ago I stopped eating and started drinking round the clock, trying to kill myself. I went down to ninety-two pounds, and I didn't wash myself or my clothes for three weeks. The whole apartment smelled rotten. I didn't care.

"Then the D.T.s set in and I heard crazy party sounds, people chopping wood, dogs growling, demons throwing up green vomit, hideous laughter, and screaming, 'It's just a matter of time—we'll soon have you.'

"Then right in the middle of the voices a razor-sharp buzz came in my inner ear, and Liz's voice said, 'Praise the Lord!'

"Her voice said, 'Laura, this is your own hotline to heaven. Do what I tell you!' and at the same time, I heard a satanic giggle, which would envelope the whole room. And I was totally alone at the time.

"Finally, I promised God I would go to the hospital, and that's when the miracle occurred! Jesus came and told me how to pack; told me to take *The Living Bible* Liz gave me; what nightgown to take; to leave my makeup at home—everything. When Liz and Bob came, I was still wild, but they got me to the hospital. I was so weak and ill, I couldn't stand up, could hardly breathe, couldn't go to the bathroom, but Jesus continued to tell me what to do, step-by-step. I know today that it was Jesus' voice speaking through the one I trusted.

"Anyway I knew I was dying. I had four ulcers and cirrhosis of the liver, and I was bleeding from every opening of my body except my ears. My heart started hurting, and Jesus said, 'Lie still and open your mouth to breathe.'

"Then the pain started coming real bad, and again I heard Liz's voice saying, 'You must praise the Lord, Laura!' I knew I had to beg Jesus for forgiveness, I had been so bad.

"I said, 'Oh, Jesus, forgive me of my sins! Oh, God save me!' There was a big battle going on over me! It was the devil and Jesus, and I kept saying, 'Jesus is Lord! Jesus is Lord!' Over and over I said this, for what seemed like hours.

"Suddenly I felt big, long arms under my body, the arms of Jesus Christ. He said, 'Just come and rest, it's okay now.'

"Then He said, 'Laura, you will never have to suffer again!' and He was gone! I took a big, deep breath and sat up.

"I was a brand-new person in Jesus!

"That day I started reading my Bible, and I asked Jesus, 'Where do I begin?' And it came to me to begin at the beginning, Genesis. I read the Bible to all the other patients, told them all about Noah and Jabal, who was the first herdsman. They thought I was cute, and that the Bible was hip. I asked someone what day it was, and she said, 'The Fourth of July!'

"So I claimed my independence from alcohol, and I haven't had a drink since— don't even want one! That's a miracle!

"Well, those are my first three A.A. steps. 1. *I admit I am powerless over alcohol*—that my life was unmanageable—boy! was it unmanageable! 2. *I came to believe in a Power greater than myself*—Jesus is my Power, and He came to me! and, 3. *I made a decision to turn my will and life over to Him*—and I did.

"The next thing I have to do is to write out my inventory. I'll probably be doing that next month or so. Anyway that's my story, and I thank you for listening."

Everyone was very quiet as Laura spoke. A roomful of miracles themselves, they knew that they had heard a remarkable tale of direct and divine intervention by God who saved the life of a hopeless, dying drunk.

What a wonderful God I found as a result of being an alcoholic, I thought, as we drove home.

Laura was quiet, too, her strength depleted by the emotional experience. She needed to rest and regain her health, so she could begin her new sober life with Jesus.

When I got home that night, I found that my husband had moved his furniture and clothes out of the house, leaving no note. After six years of sobriety, trying every way I knew to salvage my marriage, I was alone without a job or a mate.

Jesus had performed a great miracle for Laura, but what was He going to do for me?

31

Mary Lynn, Marijuana, and Medication

Columbia, Maryland, July 1982

The chairman banged his gavel and said, "This is the Columbia meeting of Narcotics Anonymous, and tonight we're celebrating the first anniversary of our own Mary Lynn."

Applause and whistles filled the smoky, church basement, as the small, pretty, brown-haired honoree smiled nervously.

"Here's your anniversary chip," he said, kissing her and handing her a little token.

Mary Lynn held it for her husband, Bart, Hal, and me to see. My eyes filled with tears, as I remembered how we had met.

It was a hot, July Sunday. After church, the congregation had broken up into small groups, visiting under the trees behind the YMCA, where church services had been held, because of the heat. Bart, the young man who played guitar, pulled me over to the side.

"I want to ask a big favor," he said seriously.

"What is it?" I asked.

"I know you work with alcoholic women, but would you consider taking on my wife? She's a drug addict, just getting out of rehab tomorrow," he pleaded.

"Which drug? The only kinds I ever took were Valium and Librium, prescribed by my doctor."

"Fiorinol—also prescribed by a doctor! But Mary Lynn needs a Christian sponsor in Narcotics Anonymous. Please consider, Liz!"

"We'll work something out," I said, giving him my number.

Shortly, Mary Lynn called my office at the King's Kid Korner.

Harold Hill and I had gone into business in 1979, writing and selling books and teaching tapes. The young man who used to help him resigned, so Liz, the volunteer secretary, became Liz, the office manager, Public Relations person, chauffeur, speaking companion, and friend. Just when I needed money, Hal came along with the best job I ever had. I still answered tons of mail, plus managing a business and traveling to speaking engagements.

I didn't know if I had enough time for Mary Lynn, but I agreed to sponsor her when I was in town, advising her to get a second sponsor whom she could call when I was gone. The plan worked out fairly well, although her first year was very rough. But now she was celebrating her first drug-free year. So she began:

"My name is Mary Lynn, and I'm a drug addict.

"There was always drinking at our house. My father is a heavy drinker, and my mother is an alcoholic, but booze always made me sick, so when I got to college, someone said, 'Try marijuana; you can get high without hangovers!' So I did and I *loved* it.

"For the next four years I smoked dope when I was happy, when I was sad, as a cure-all for everything. I thought I'd found the answer to living: instant peace, instant happiness, instant munchies. Really, eating chocolate and smoking dope was wonderful!

"I'm a chocolateholic, too. I didn't know that a love for chocolate accompanies many diseases, making them worse. Today I'm also chocolate-free, as well as drug-free."

I nodded, along with many others in the room, recalling my own chocolate cravings when I was drinking. My good friend Tom had just died from putting too much chocolate in an already-weakened body. He was able to kick the booze, but not the huge chocolate almond bars, which he gobbled every day. The nickname for these cravings is "the munchies," and, after alcohol, it was the next addiction I had to battle. (Luckily, I read a marvelous book on fasting, tried it, and broke the craving for sugar, chocolate, and caffeine. They say fasting breaks nicotine addiction, too.) Mary Lynn continued:

"My habit increased slowly at first, but then in my sophomore year I stopped going to class and stayed in my room smoking dope all day long. Bart and I were living together on the campus, and he was doing drugs, too. It was an incredible waste, because I was a straight *A* student, the youngest person ever asked to join the Honorary English Society. I just threw it away.

"You see, although I made wonderful grades, emotionally I didn't have what it took. I was a real wreck from growing up in an alcoholic home, constantly abused by my mother, who yelled and screamed at me, blaming me for everything. My sisters just shrugged her off, but I took everything personally. When I got to college, I just wanted not to hurt anymore. The emotional pain I was feeling interfered with everything I did. Everything was a struggle.

"So that was the major reason I did drugs—I didn't want to hurt anymore. I wanted to be happy and loved, and I thought Bart would fill the bill. He was a real hippie with long hair, faded blue jeans, and no shoes on his feet, but he drove an absolutely wonderful car—a red Mach 1. We started dating because I was impressed with his car, and we partied, smoked dope, and had sex.

"We started hanging around the 'druggies'—we called them 'freaks' in those days—and we became like a family. I never had a family sense, so I really liked that. Later it turned out to be a farce, but at the time it filled a need.

"Then I turned to hash, and popped Black Beauties, a potent form of speed, since taken off the market. I was awake five days with no sleep, but Bart took one and went to sleep an hour later. Dope always worked differently in each of us.

"The thing that saved my life was that I never never mixed alcohol with the dope, because alcohol had always made me sick. I didn't like it, also, because of my mother. But the drug of my choice was marijuana.

"Let me say this about marijuana: it is a form of speed. I didn't know that although I smoked a boatload of it! With marijuana you get an initial high, which is the speed part, sometimes overcome by fits of uncontrollable laughter. This stage is followed by the 'munchies' where food tastes *so much* better and you can't get enough of it. Then eventually you crash, which is falling asleep with a thud, almost like passing out.

"Marijuana killed my feelings, and I could sleep my life away, so this was perfect for me. It took care of all my emotional pain and insecurity. When I got high, I felt accepted and loved, real cool, and just wonderful. Then Bart and I decided to get married, and within a month I got pregnant!

"I was completely ignorant about drugs, addiction, and withdrawal, so I just cold-turkeyed all drugs—marijuana, cigarettes, hash, speed, alcohol, everything—I just didn't do any of them, and I had a very severe withdrawal. Looking back on it, I thought I was having a nervous breakdown. I cried for nine solid months, because I knew I was in no shape to become a mother.

"When my daughter, Cheryl, was born, I wanted to die, because I had no feeling at all. I had nothing to give her, so I just left her alone for fear I would abuse her. Her crying drove me mad and made my head hurt. You know, when you take all the alcohol and drugs out of your system, you're left with the same person you were before—and I was one, huge emotionally fried wreck.

"Bart continued to do drugs and my life became completely unmanageable. I suffered from paranoia, a result of marijuana use, and I'd check doors eight times before I went to sleep. I just knew someone would break in and murder me. It kept getting worse and worse, and I blamed Bart for everything. One night I even asked him for a divorce.

"Well, I knew I was nuts! So I went outside and prayed: 'Lord, I can't take it anymore. I don't know if You're even out there. I don't know if You even care—but do something! Jesus, take my life and do something with it.'

"And I left it. I just walked away. I really didn't have any hope that things would change. If I died, I died.

"Two weeks later Jesus baptized me in the Holy Spirit and entirely removed the desire for drugs. It was a tremendous spiritual experience, better than I ever got from drugs. It was the new wine instead of the old.

"Bart smoked dope for another year, and then he cried out to the Lord, who took it away from him, too.

"During this period of my spiritual awakening my son, Kent, was born, and I loved him dearly from the start. I was on a pink cloud and nothing fazed me. I didn't have a problem in the world, and I thought God was a Candy Man who would float me through life on beds of ease. So when the problems began to come, I started to panic again. I developed tension headaches, very severe migraines. And that's when my troubles really began!

"In 1979 I went to a doctor. He gave me Fiorinol, a barbiturate made up of butalbital, aspirin, phenacetin, and caffeine, and I began taking it regularly.

"About that time Bart got hooked in with a church, and he was gone six to seven nights a week. He was really churched out! I got terribly resentful—mad at Bart and mad at God. *Now neither God nor Bart loves me,* I thought, and my headaches increased. The more Bart churched it up, the more I popped Fiorinols. I felt like I was a 'bad' Christian, while Bart was a 'good' Christian. I lost all my spiritual experience, and dove deeper into my 'medication.'

"To me the Fiorinols were *not* drugs! The doctor prescribed them! They were good for me! I was just following the doctor's orders! I was being a good little wife! They were my *medication!* I wonder how many women are hooked on their *medication?*

"Today I know that when I picked up my first Fiorinol, I was in the third stage of addiction, because of all the drugs I did in college and early married life.

"I remember thinking one night, after I had taken eleven Fiorinols, trying to kill a headache, *Mary Lynn, you have overdosed on barbiturates and will die in your sleep!* And I *did not care!*

"The next day I called my doctor and said, 'I'm ill and I think it's the Fiorinols!'

" 'No, it can't be!' he said. 'It's all in your head!' and he sent me to a psychiatrist.

"The first thing I told the shrink was, 'I'm ill and I don't think it's emotional. I think it's these Fiorinols.' I told her how many I was taking, and she gave me a schedule to taper off of them. But by that time I couldn't do it.

"For five months I tried to quit, and in the meanwhile, the pharmacist, who was keeping tabs on how many the doc was prescribing, reported him to the state. So the state forbade my doctor to treat me anymore.

"He called up and said, 'I can't prescribe for you anymore. You'll have to find another doctor to do it. I'm bowing out.' He wasn't even concerned about the danger of my withdrawing from them abruptly. He never even told me I was addicted.

"I've met a lot of women in N.A. who have been treated by this doctor, and who are now addicts. You see, the drug companies push their products on the doctor and give him free samples, telling him it's a miracle drug. Then when you come in with a problem, he hands you a prescription, and he's off the hook.

"I have a feeling that this doctor was taking drugs himself. If you talked to him, he didn't answer, and he walked around with a perpetual smile on his face. He was a real air head.

"Anyway I was in a real spot—addicted to a barbiturate and the doctor had cut me off. People die from abrupt barbiturate withdrawal, and I was sinking fast. I went to another doctor who told me that I was a *drug addict!* Oh, I was so indignant, but he put me in a detox unit, where they proceeded to beat into my head for the next ten days the fact that I *was a drug addict!*

"I refused to believe them! It was my medication! The *doctor,* my earth god, prescribed it! I called Bart to come get me.

"As we were driving home, I said to him, 'All I want to do is to go home and take a Fiorinol and forget everything!'

"When I heard myself saying that, I *knew in my heart that I was a drug addict.* Bart turned the car around and took me back to the rehab, where at the next meeting I admitted that I was a drug addict, that my life was unmanageable.

"My first year was a nightmare. Just total paranoia. Very, very insane thinking. Complete emotional upheaval. All from prescription addiction. I think we don't catch it until it is very, very late, because there is no education.

"In the future I hope to work with drug addicts, but for now, I am working the steps and principles of the program.

"I've made a Mad List and prayed for the people on it, especially my mother, for whom I pray daily.

"I've tried to practice *live and let live* and mind my own business, but I'm so dependent on Bart that I don't do too well with leaving him alone.

"I practice keeping my mouth shut, except for positive comments, and I don't tell everything that comes into my head.

"And I try to *let go and let God.* Every day I turn my life and affairs over to Jesus and let Him run the show. This has been the hardest step of all to practice because it is so simple—just letting go."

"But Liz says that we seek progress, not perfection. And she says she is proud of me, so for that I am grateful!"

The room burst into applause when she sat down, and tears were in all our eyes.

Mary Lynn had almost died from prescription drugs, but the Lord Jesus Christ, working through another marvelous program, brought her through.

32

How to Grow Up
Before You Go Up

Linthicum, Maryland, 1984

Opening the door to the King's Kid Korner, we saw the flashing light on our telephone answering machine. After two weeks in Canada, sharing our answers to booze and pill problems, and talking about our Higher Power, Jesus, we could expect numerous frantic recorded telephone messages. We were right.

1. Sharon, Des Moines, can't stop drinking, needs help.
2. Jim, Spokane, Washington, deeply in debt.
3. Betty in Salt Lake City wants prayer for her marriage.
4. The Washburns in Maine have a dying daughter.

The list seemed endless. People in trouble, reaching out for help, at the end of their rope, asking Hal and me to pray for them.

"Liz, how about taking over the phone ministry, while I sort the mail," Hal suggested. So I began with my usual prayer for guidance.

"Dear Lord, please show me what You have for Sharon," I prayed, as I dialed the first number. The conversation that followed was typical. Fifty-eight-year-old Sharon sulked, cried, and raged when I suggested that she attend an alcohol Recovery program. She wasn't that bad, she claimed.

Besides, it was all her parents' fault because they didn't love her enough when she was a child. Her husband was a bore, and her employer was a monster. The world had conspired to make her miserable. She *had* to drink.

I told her that when she was ready for help to call back, and I hung up. Alcoholism had claimed another victim in Iowa.

Twelve years of sobriety and working with others had proved to me that what a number of eminent psychologists and doctors claimed was true. We didn't want to admit it, but these distinguished men said that most active alcoholics were still childish, emotionally sensitive, and grandiose.

In other words, we had failed to grow up.

At first, I greatly resented that verdict. I didn't want to believe that my adult dreams were truly childish. Considering the rough deal life had given me, I felt perfectly justified in being supersensitive. My delusions of grandeur had been a legitimate ambition to win the battle of life. I had to be Number 1 to cover up my deep-lying inferiority.

But twelve years and many sessions of "judging myself lest I be judged" restored my distorted drives to something like their true direction. I no longer attempted to control those near me in order to gain self-importance. I tried not to seek fame and honor in order to be praised. I came to realize that I did not have to be especially distinguished among my fellows in order to be useful and happy. I learned that God is no respecter of persons, loving all people alike. Even me.

By helping others, the mature person develops positive attitudes which lift him above childishness in thought and behavior and free him from introversion. When he goes into action for someone else's benefit, he progressively achieves the following characteristics:

1. He accepts criticism gratefully, being honestly glad for an opportunity to improve.
2. He doesn't indulge in self-pity.
3. He doesn't expect special consideration from anyone.
4. He controls his temper.
5. He meets emergencies with poise.
6. His feelings are not easily hurt.
7. He accepts the responsibility of his own acts, without trying to alibi or to scapegoat.
8. He has outgrown the "all or nothing" stage. He recognizes that no person or situation is wholly good or wholly bad.

9. He is not impatient at reasonable delays. He has learned that he isn't the arbiter of the universe, and that he must often adjust himself to other people and their convenience.
10. He is a good loser. He can endure defeat and disappointment without whining or complaining.
11. He doesn't worry unduly about things he cannot help.
12. He is not given to boasting or "showing off."
13. He is honestly glad when others enjoy success or good fortune. He has outgrown envy and jealousy.
14. He is open-minded enough to listen thoughtfully to the opinions of others.
15. He is not a chronic faultfinder.
16. He plans things in advance, rather than trusting to the inspiration of the moment.

And best of all, he begins to think in terms of spiritual maturity.

17. He has faith in God.
18. He realizes that he is a child of God, a member of His family, and contributes his part of God's work.
19. He wraps everything in praise, turns it over to Jesus Christ as the New Manager of his life, and trusts Him for results.
20. He obeys the Golden Rule:"Thou shalt love thy neighbor as thy self."

(Some of the above twenty points are taken from the "Moral and Spiritual Values in Education," used by the Los Angeles City Schools as part of their educational program.)

So there you have it folks, how things are with us since we learned how to live without alcohol and other drugs—**the impossible takes a little longer.**

Are we experts? You know it! We're specialists in living sober, drug-free lives.

Do we have all the answers? We certainly do—all we need to live sober, happy lives, without alcohol or other drugs.

Are there other ways of doing it? We can't answer that question from personal experience. We're only able to tell you about what works for us. Anything else is pure guesswork. We're impressed with results, not theory.

So you don't believe alcoholism is a disease? Neither do scores of others, but please keep this in mind: since we began treating it like one, it hasn't been around to bother us!

Results are better than arguments, aren't they?

To sum it up, here's how we former alcohol and drug abusers do it. Try it on your own problem.

Just *one day at a time* we avoid (stay away from—fast from—run from—or hide from) the first drink, puff, snort, sip, bite, nibble, or fix.

We do this by depending on Jesus Christ, our Higher Power, to make it work.

That's how we live happily *one day at a time* without alcohol or other drugs.

Here's a prayer we find helpful. We call it the Serenity Prayer. It's a powerful tool in sorting things out when the going gets sticky, yukky, or just plain revolting.

> *God grant me the serenity to accept the things I cannot change, courage to change the things I can, and the wisdom to know the difference.* Amen.
> REINHOLD NIEBUHR

And while we're at it, here's another goodie to keep in mind. Should you be inclined to criticize, put down, or feel superior to any of us "poor souls" you have just read about, remember:

God places *overeaters* and *drunkards* in the same category!

Where did we get such a crazy idea? From Proverbs, which says it like this:

> *The glutton and the drunkard will end in poverty.*
> *See* Proverbs 23:21

Revolting, isn't it?

That's why God gives us a better way than judging one another. It's stated in First Corinthians 11:31 (NKJV).

> *For if we would judge ourselves, we would not be judged.*

Here's the good part. We've saved it for last. It's in Second Corinthians 5:17,18 (NKJV):

> *Therefore, if anyone is in Christ, he is a new creation; old things have passed away; behold all things have become new. Now all things are of God, who has reconciled us to Himself through Christ Jesus, and has given us the ministry of reconciliation.*

And that's what we're doing—sharing the Good News that successful living without alcohol or other drugs *is* "Christ in you, the hope of glory" (Colossians 1:27).

Another important truth to remember: God's blessings must be *shared with others*, in order for them to be permanent in our lives. We give them away in order to keep them and make room for more.

When you have been set free from your own brand of bondage, tell someone about it right away. That's the backbone principle of our Recovery program—sharing with others the marvelous works of God in our own lives. That way we fulfill our destiny as King's Kids.

Someone has summed it up in six words:

FIND GOD—CLEAN HOUSE—HELP OTHERS

How does it work?

Real good!

God bless you and thanks for listening.

For quick help, call Alcoholics Anonymous. They're generally listed on the first page in your local phone directory.

And if you don't have a personal Higher Power of your own, you can borrow ours right now. Just pray this simple prayer:

> *"Lord Jesus, I'm not sure You're the real, living God. I've been told that other gods were just as real. I just don't know. I'm confused. I'm at the end of my rope. I need help. If You* are *a real, live God, and can make Yourself real to me* right now, *will You please so do? Thank You. Amen.*

Try it and report back. We'll send you some free goodies to help your life get started under New Management.

And our thanks to all you other King's Kids who shared your experience, strength, and hope, so that others may find help in time of need.